REDESIGN THE WORLD

AUTHOR

SAM PITRODA is an internationally respected development thinker, policymaker, inventor and entrepreneur who has spent over fifty-five years in telecom development.

Credited with having laid the foundation of India's technology and telecommunications revolution in the 1980s, during Rajiv Gandhi's government, Pitroda has been a leading campaigner in helping to bridge the global digital divide. In the mid-1990s, he founded Worldtel in London to help privatize telecom in developing countries. He invented the electronic diary in 1974, the mobile wallet in 1996, and set up C-SAM Inc., acquired by MasterCard in 2013. From 2005 to 2014, Pitroda was chairman of the National Knowledge Commission and adviser to the Indian prime minister with a cabinet minister's rank.

He was also chairman of the National Innovation Council and Smart Grid Task Force, and a key part of efforts in railway modernization, and the development of public broadcast reforms. He is the founder, investor and chairman of six start-ups and five non-profit foundations. Pitroda holds over 100 patents and 20 honorary PhDs and has published and lectured extensively around the world. He is a member of the American Academy of Engineers. His autobiography, Dreaming Big, was published in 2015.

contact - info@sampitroda.com

Author photograph by Rakesh Patel
Cover photograph by Getty Images
Cover design by Akangksha Sarmah

REDESIGN THE WORLD

A GLOBAL CALL TO ACTION

SAM PITRODA

@sampitroda @samgpitroda @sampitroda

/sampitrodaa www.linkedin.com/in/sampitroda

www.sampitroda.com

PITRODA GROUP

USA | Portugal | France | India

Published by The Pitroda Group LLC
1, Tower Lane, Suite 1825,
Oakbrook Terrace, IL - 60181. USA

The views and opinions expressed in this book are the author's own and the facts
are as reported by him which have been verified to the extent possible, and the
publishers are not in any way liable for the same.

ISBN 978-1-7325804-5-9

For sale in other than Indian Subcontinent only
(Rest of the World)

Typeset in Bembo Std by Manipal Technologies Limited, Manipal

www.redesigntheworld.co
www.sampitroda.com

To
my grandchildren,
Aria, Ishaan, Nylah,
and all the children of the world . . .
Hope you experience and enjoy peace, prosperity, health, happiness and
fulfilment in a redesigned world

Gandhiji's Talisman

'I will give you a talisman. Whenever you are in doubt, or when the self becomes too much with you, apply the following test: Recall the face of the poorest and the weakest person whom you may have seen and ask yourself if the step you contemplate is going to be of any use to him. Will he gain anything by it? Will it restore him to a control over his own life and destiny?
In other words, will it lead to Swaraj for the hungry and spiritually starving millions?
Then you will find your doubts and yourself melting away.'

(*Collected Works of Mahatma Gandhi, Volume 89,* https://archive.org/details/HindSwaraj-CWMG-089/page/125)

Speech by Robert F. Kennedy
(University of Kansas, 18 March 1968)

'Even if we act to erase material poverty, there is another greater task,
it is to confront the poverty of satisfaction—purpose and dignity—that
afflicts us all. Too much and for too long, we seemed to have surrendered
personal excellence and community values in the mere accumulation of
material things. Our Gross National Product, now, is over $800 billion
dollars a year, but that Gross National Product—if we judge the United
States of America by that—that Gross National Product counts air
pollution and cigarette advertising, and ambulances to clear our highways
of carnage.
It counts special locks for our doors and the jails for the people who break
them. It counts the destruction of the redwood and the loss of our natural
wonder in chaotic sprawl.
It counts napalm and counts nuclear warheads and armoured cars for the
police to fight the riots in our cities. It counts Whitman's rifle and Speck's
knife, and the television programs which glorify violence in order to sell
toys to our children.
Yet the gross national product does not allow for the health of our
children, the quality of their education or the joy of their play. It does
not include the beauty of our poetry or the strength of our marriages, the
intelligence of our public debate or the integrity of our public officials.
It measures neither our wit nor our courage, neither our wisdom nor
our learning, neither our compassion nor our devotion to our country, it
measures everything in short, except that which makes life worthwhile.
And it can tell us everything about America except why we are proud
that we are Americans. If this is true here at home, so it is true
elsewhere in world.'

THE BOOK

The world was last designed seventy-five years ago, about the same time that Sam Pitroda was born. That design, which gave birth to organizations like the UN, World Bank, IMF, NATO and WTO, among others, has now outlived its utility. Hyperconnectivity and the COVID-19 pandemic offer a unique opportunity to redesign the world and take humanity to the next level.

Redesigning the world is not about looking at it from the point of view of liberal or conservative; left or right; capitalism or socialism; public or private; democracy, dictatorship or monarchy; open or closed systems; rich or poor; urban or rural; east or west; white, brown, black or yellow. This proposed redesign of the world has the planet and its people at the centre; it is built on the foundations of sustainability, inclusion, equality, equity and justice so that everyone on earth can enjoy peace and prosperity. It is not an idealist or a utopian vision, but one with humanity at its core.

Contents

Introduction[*]

'The earth does not belong to man; man belongs to earth. All things are connected like the blood that unites one family.'

—Chief of Seattle's Duwamish tribe

As I sit down to pen this book, I look out of my eighteenth-floor window at Oak Brook Terrace Tower and see the skyscrapers on Chicago's skyline. It is a sight that I have witnessed grow over the last fifty-five years, reaching up to the white clouds, telling the story of technological marvels and human achievements the world over. Our world has changed in many ways in the last seventy-five years. Democracy has taken root, the population has quadrupled, economies have developed, and peace has mostly prevailed. In this period, infrastructure has increased, poverty has reduced, education has spread, and technology has become pervasive. We are all connected now.

For the last five years, I have been pondering the meaning of these changes and how they have affected the millions of people at

---

[*] There is no reference section in the book because the Internet is more efficient and effective.

the bottom of the economic pyramid. How do we use innovations and technology to make a significant difference in their lives and our environment? What tide will lift every boat? While thinking about this transformation, I realized that our world order was last designed around the time I was born. This design has served us well for over seven decades, but it has undoubtedly outlived its utility. Now is the time to create a new design for the world and to face a new reality. COVID-19 is a wake-up call from nature to prod humanity into rethinking the path we have chosen and to make course corrections that shall enable us to take proper care of our planet and its people.

The current world order was designed during World War II and was led by a small group of nations under the USA's leadership. This design created the United Nations (UN), World Bank, International Monetary Fund (IMF), North Atlantic Treaty Organization (NATO), World Trade Organization (WTO) and other institutions to manage international affairs. It also established essential parameters for measuring gross domestic product (GDP), gross national product (GNP), per capita incomes, balance of payments, trade deficits and foreign exchange reserves. All nations, institutions, businesses, trade and individuals essentially operate on the World War II paradigm.

It has served us well, especially after the destruction left behind by the War, and played a key role in establishing peace, growth and prosperity. Over the last seventy-five years, the current rule-based liberal order introduced by the US has indeed been a generous contribution to the world. It has helped rebuild Europe and Japan, and expand global business and trade. Our world has gone through substantial mega changes in demography, technology and connectivity in this process. In 1940, the world's population was around 2 billion. Now it is close to 8 billion. This population growth has generated substantial pressure on our environment, resulting in global warming and endangering our planet's future. Technology has improved the quality of life while at the same time it has increased inequality. Hyperconnectivity is essentially turning everything upside down: it has finally made our planet a global village where distance has disappeared, and time is instant. All this has enormous implications for our future and the future of our world.

The old world design does not, and cannot, work in the hyperconnected world. Surprisingly, in the last seventy-five years, we have not created any new major global institution to help us deal with these mega challenges. In the 1940s, our world was bipolar, with the USA and the Soviet Union being the two major superpowers. After the Soviet Union's break-up and the fall of the Berlin Wall in 1991, the USA became the only superpower in a unipolar world. With the expansion of the Internet, mobile telecom and social media triggered unprecedented connectivity, content and context. People's aspirations have changed globally. Nineteenth-century mindsets and twentieth-century politics and processes do not work for the twenty-first-century ambitions and expectations of a globally connected and youthful population. They want more, and they want it now.

The rise of China and India, both countries with a population of around 1.5 billion each, is changing the global power equation. With its thriving democracy and well-established norms of freedom, rule of law, diversity, capitalist economy, large market, growing consumption, leading universities, broad scientific community, state-of-the-art technology and entrepreneurial drive, the United States of America enjoys leadership and respect globally. However, the US global leadership is seen to be declining. In several countries, democracies are being hijacked by populist and nationalist governments, and in the process undermining institutions, creating a social divide, and generating fear. Across the globe, capitalism has concentrated wealth in the hands of a few, and inequality has increased. Yet, in this hyperconnected world, where information and knowledge are democratized, there is a potential opportunity to redesign the world.

At present, there are two competing visions of the world: an American vision—fundamentally based on the current world order, with a focus on democracy, freedom and capitalism; and a Chinese vision—based on its emerging military prowess and manufacturing strength and bolstered with the Belt and Road Initiative. Unfortunately, both visions are based on narrow national interests with the traditional command-and-control architecture. The American vision is 'open', with an opportunity to empower people, while the China vision is 'closed' for the people and empowers the central communist party. Both visions do not meet the real needs of our planet and our people at large. The world needs a 'third vision' based on nations' networking, ideas, interests, resources and talent, all designed to save our planet and uplift all our people. This vision will be based on a novel organizational architecture focused on global consultations, collaboration, cooperation and enhanced communication. Now is a unique opportunity to 'Redesign the World', not merely to manage the tensions between 'open' and 'closed', but to save our planet and promote human potential as we prepare for the next seventy-five years.

The Planet and the People

In 1854, the chief of Seattle's Duwamish tribe sent a letter to US President Franklin Pierce. The letter, an iconic and influential epistle in human history, stated the following:

> The earth does not belong to man, man belongs to the earth. All things are connected like the blood that unites one family. The man did not weave the web of life; he is merely a strand in it. Whatever he does to the web, he does to himself. The earth is sacred and men and animals are but one part of it. Treat the earth with respect so that it lasts for centuries to come and is a place of wonder and beauty for our children.

The chief knew that everything is interconnected—land, sea, soil, seeds, flowers, plants, trees, birds, fish, farms, animals, mammals and everything else. For one to survive and flourish, everyone and everything has to survive and prosper. Everything on our planet is interconnected, interdependent, interwoven and interrelated. The earth does not belong to man; man belongs to the earth. The planet belongs to everyone. If man takes care of the planet, the planet will take care of man.

What the chief said about 170 years ago is now more real and relevant in this age of new global connectivity, where people from all over the planet are instantly connected in time and engaged in transforming talk, travel, trade, tourism, transaction and technology as never before imagined. At the same time, nature's connectivity is equally apparent and alarming during the present COVID-19 pandemic, which has literally shut down large parts of our planet all together for the first time in human history. It is an excellent time to review and reflect on what 'man has done to man'—what we have done to our planet and our people.

In the last 170 years, the earth's human population has increased from 1.2 billion to 7.8 billion, which has exerted substantial pressure on the resources of water, land, energy and minerals. Only one-fifth of the planet's original forest cover remains undisturbed. Half of the forests and woods that had once covered the land surface are already gone. Many of our drinking water sources have run dry and, with water tables going down consistently, there is a looming global water crisis in many countries of the world. Seventy per cent of the world's coral reefs, which nourish a large part of all marine life, could disappear in the next twenty-five years. Thousands of marine mammals are disappearing from our waters.

More than 20 per cent of non-freshwater species have already become almost extinct. A large number of birds, insects and wildlife are also disappearing rapidly. Some estimates suggest that 30,000 plant species and 5000 animal species, including birds, will face extinction soon. Almost a quarter of the world's mammal species will be facing death and extinction in the next twenty-five years. Over 50 per cent of the world's plant life is also at risk of extinction. Our large metro cities, jammed with traffic, pollution and garbage mountains, add to this environmental crisis. We have created floating islands of plastic waste in the middle of the ocean, thereby threatening our precious marine life.

Global warming, which has been active on the international agenda for over two decades, poses a great danger to our planet and our people's survival. As our planet's temperature is expected to increase by a couple of degrees in the coming years, it is bound to have severe consequences for the survival of many species, including our own. Despite much global debate, discussions and dialogue regarding carbon emission and its impact on our environment, we have not developed a consensus on taking global warming seriously and securing our future. It is a well-known fact that burning coal, increasing pollution, global warming, melting icebergs, etc., will change rainfall and weather patterns, increase tornados, disturb agriculture, and raise sea levels: all this will lead to a devastating impact on our planet and our people. In a sense, our planet is crying for help.

In the last 170 years, we have made much progress in improving infrastructure and quality of life. The invention of electricity, railways, automobiles, highways, civil aviation, the radio, television, telecommunication, etc., has transformed our education, economy and overall development. Besides, we now produce enough food to feed almost 8 billion people. Technology has substantially improved and enhanced the standard of living for billions. Longevity has increased, infant mortality has declined, education has expanded, health has improved, and energy, transportation and telecom are widely available and accessible worldwide.

Unfortunately, at the same time, 3 billion people still live in poverty. A billion people do not have enough food to eat. A billion lack access to primary health care and have no access to clean drinking water. Two billion people have no access to adequate sanitation. Over a billion live in slums with no real homes to go to. Even in the world's wealthiest countries, hundreds of thousands of poor homeless people live on the street. Millions are forced to migrate, seeking work and hoping for a better tomorrow. Millions are on drugs. Global violence and terror have increased, and prisons are full and overcrowded in many countries. Homicides killed more people in the twentieth century than all wars combined.

It is a fact that the rich have become more affluent and more prosperous. The number of millionaires and billionaires have skyrocketed recently. The wealthiest 1 per cent of the people earn more income than 50 per cent of the people on this planet. The top 10 per cent earn as much as the bottom 90 per cent. Income inequality has substantially increased in the last seventy years. Many people also face discrimination based on race, religion, colour, culture, language and geography. There are untouchables in countries like India who are discriminated against because of their caste, or their birth in a particular social milieu, and denied access to essential services. Inequality between the rich and the poor, the educated and the uneducated, rural and urban, etc., has substantially increased in the last few decades.

One-third of the people live in political systems where individual freedom is curbed. Their voices are suppressed. Their movement is restricted and monitored. They have practically no freedom to decide their destiny or that of their children. Millions live in bonded labour like slaves. Women are the victims of rape and human trafficking. Child labour is practised routinely in many countries. Many poor people are lost, frustrated and depressed and see no hope for the future.

Despite all the comforts, wealth, luxury and technological development, people, communities and nations fight like cats and dogs. After World War II, the last major war, seventy-five years ago, we have had over 200 battles and confrontations, in which over 20 million people have been killed, and a similar number displaced and rendered homeless. Over the past seventy-five years, there have been wars in Korea, Vietnam, Cambodia, the Middle East,

Afghanistan, Iraq, Libya, Syria, Serbia, Ukraine, India, Pakistan—
to name a few. In many regions, children are deployed to fight
wars with lethal weapons. Even after wars are over, landmines kill
a large number of innocent civilians.

While we live in peacetime, military machines continue to build
deadly weapons of mass destruction for the world market. Millions
of jobs are created in armament factories. Military manufacturers
are well respected, and world leaders openly and proudly indulge
in arms trade and technology with great publicity and passion.
Many nations display their missile warheads in parades and flex
their military muscle in the name of nationalism and security. The
nuclear arms race is always in the news: tens of thousands of atomic
warheads are stationed everywhere, with thousands of personnel
on high alert. Unfortunately, some are in the hands of trigger-
happy leaders. More than half a billion arms circulate all over the
planet in the name of security and safety. Over $1 trillion a year is
spent globally on the military.

What is going on with our planet and our people? With all the
available global technology and talent, why can we not mobilize public
opinion and the necessary resources to resolve our environmental
issues? Why can't we heal our planet and lift millions of the poor
from the bottom of the economic pyramid to a decent standard of
living? The answer lies in the present design of the world and the lack
of global leadership. We sadly lack compassion, character, concern,
commitment, moral high ground, humility and wisdom to develop
a consensus for creating a new vision for the world.

The agricultural revolution has taught us to productively
organize and exploit soil, seeds, plants, fruits, vegetables and
animals. We now know how to improve food supplies and ensure
and enhance survival and sustainability through farming. The
industrial revolution has taught us to mobilize and convert our
planet's natural resources into goods and services. We have the
means to increase our quality of life and assure people of their
social, political and economic future. The Information Revolution

is based on the new hyperconnectivity that is under way. It has the potential to unite our people and create a new economy and a unique opportunity so that we can live with each other in peace and harmony. It also has the potential to heal our planet. Every major revolution—agricultural, industrial and information—brings hope for a better future. The key is to understand this opportunity and provide the best possible strategy, platform and leadership to execute this vision. Are we prepared to harness the ultimate potential of the new hyperconnectivity and the Information Revolution? Can the existing world design and the present narrow-minded global leaders deliver the solutions our planet and people need? Is it time to 'redesign the world' and help build the next generation of global leaders with higher values and character?

Values and Character

Chicago, situated on the shores of freshwater Lake Michigan, was once inhabited by the Potawatomi tribe. What the Potawatomi elders taught their children in the eighteenth century is still used as guidance by millions across the globe. The Potawatomi taught their children the seven teachings that my father and grandfather taught me in India, which I, too, now teach my grandchildren in San Francisco.

The Potawatomi taught their children to live a life based on seven golden rules—truth, trust, love, humility, bravery, wisdom and respect towards each other. They taught them the essential rule: to live life like a single tribe—remembering that we are all nature's creation. The Potawatomi elders knew that human values matter. These values are fundamental for survival, peace and prosperity, and are preached by all religions in all countries.

In the last seventy-five years, after World War II, people have primarily focused their attention on material prosperity and financial success, with a widespread emphasis on consumption and capitalism. In the process, we seem to have lost human values. In the present system, we are judged by the money we make, and the material comforts we accumulate—not by the values we practise or the character we possess. As people in America say, 'If you're smart, how come you're not rich?' In other words, if you are rich, you are bound to be smart. Too much attention to money, material comforts, power, prestige, and name and fame has created a world of competition, jealousy and conflicts, filled with stress, tensions, fear and chaos. We regularly publish, promote and preach about the wealthiest people's achievements to encourage and motivate our youth to follow them. We equate success with money and power. Our global and national media pay too much attention to financial markets, wealth creation and affluent personalities. We never publish a list of the best teachers, doctors, scientists, public servants, social workers, etc., because we do not seem to consider them potential role models. How one acquires money and power is rarely questioned. Highly educated experts cheat, lie and get involved in fraud to make extra money. Businesses in highly competitive markets do not hesitate to cut corners, steal secrets and sell unreliable products. They ignore regulations, avoid taxes, over-invoice, poach talent and do many wicked things to succeed. Even the big banks resort to illegal methods to make money and do not mind paying millions of dollars in financial penalties when exposed by the government.

Our business schools teach more about how to extract value and less about how to create value. After a good education, people get busy chasing their dreams to get rich quickly. In the process, people ignore themselves, family and friends and forget about joy, happiness and fulfilment. In this materialistic world, people spend their lives trying to make sure that the pot of gold they have accumulated keeps growing, even as they lose sight of the precious nature of life, relationships, community and culture. Unfortunately, we spend billions on building six sigma quality products and services but are not concerned about creating six sigma quality people. Formal education is solely concerned with preparing people for the workforce. Despite a highly educated population and leading universities, the USA has the largest number of people in prison. Why? Because good education does not assure good values and good character. What the Potawatomi taught their children in the eighteenth century needs to be taught repeatedly at a very early age in families and schools to create better people. We need to focus on teaching values and character to build better communities and better lives on the planet.

After World War II, America was seen as a world leader, a role model, and the envy of many countries. People respect the American Constitution, democracy and freedom, capitalism and financial markets, technology, education, science and openness. People believe that anything is possible in America. Suppose people are willing to work hard, achieving the American dream of success, money, name, fame and fulfilment. People worldwide wish to migrate to America for a better future, safety and security; and to grasp the American dream. This is now changing due to the rise of China. China has a different political, social and economic system from America. America is open. China is closed. The world still looks to America and Americans for leadership, values and character.

During the agriculture age, we worked hard in farms and fields to feed ourselves. In the Industrial Age, we worked for long hours in factories and offices to increase our comforts and improve the quality of our life. In the Information Age, we have an opportunity to live life differently and to the fullest, with more time to enjoy with our families, to seek knowledge and experience human potential. We can discover ourselves, collaborate, cooperate, communicate and help take humanity to the next level. At present, we are using the new connectivity, the latest knowledge and information technology, with the sole objective of improving productivity and efficiency of the very same things that we had been doing earlier. Perhaps we do it a little differently, but our efforts are primarily geared towards creating products and accessing markets. We are not geared to do new things to improve our people and planet that have never been done before, primarily because the mindset, ecosystem and boundaries created around us by the existing world order do not permit us to do so.

In the Information Age, we shall need a whole new environment regulated by new rules of the game; only then can we innovate and bring generational changes to commerce, finance, manufacturing and governance. We need to give a new direction to humanity. Unfortunately, the current world order and its design do not allow us room to think outside the box and break the barriers necessary to leapfrog into a new trajectory. It is time to 'redesign the world' and lead with those values and character that the Potawatomi elders taught us in the eighteenth century. In this Information Age, it is time to take human civilization to the next level to achieve sustainable peace and prosperity for all our people.

Hyperconnectivity

Connectivity is at the core of our civilization. Without connectivity, there is no community, and without community, there is hardly any life worth living. Connectivity is at the heart of all social, political and economic activities. For the first time in human history, we are all incredibly connected in a unique way. Now we have around 10 billion mobile phones for 7.8 billion people on this planet. Multiple innovative devices connect them through a massive network of cables, radios, fibre optics and millions of creative and practical applications. There are simple and straightforward user interfaces, satellite systems, software and service centres, with many new tools and technologies that had never existed before. Now almost everyone in any part of the world can be connected in an instant. Indeed, for the first time, distance has disappeared, and time is instant.

The first similar breakthrough came when fire was first discovered. Fire is now worshipped by all races and religions the world over. Similarly, harvest and crop cultivation are also celebrated with festivals and feasts in all countries. Most cultures have their annual rituals, which are observed with much joy and excitement. However, one of the most critical accomplishments in human history of connecting every human being on the planet instantly has gone unnoticed. There was no global celebration for achieving global connectivity. It has happened suddenly and swiftly in the last decade.

There are essentially three aspects of connectivity: the first was assigned to us by nature through our evolution and ecosystem. We are just a small part of our planet, which abounds in many other species. We are one among many—all connected because of our shared evolution, our chemical composition and cell structure, our water, air and land. We all have red blood. We have DNA typical to many of our species, which reminds us that we humans are connected with the animal kingdom. We also know that all of us initially came from Africa. As our early ancestors started moving out of Africa to different parts of the planet, people were separated geographically. That gave birth to the second aspect of connectivity: connectivity over large distances, starting with travel, by walking long distances to connect. Then people used animals such as donkeys, camels, elephants and horses to travel and connect. Ships came later, followed by railroads, automobiles and airplanes to effectively bridge geographical distances. The journey to connect in time across distances was the third aspect of connectivity, which started with the invention of the telegraph and the telephone, instantly connected in time, separated by geography. Alexander Graham Bell was issued the first patent for the phone in 1876, and soon began its commercialization. That was the beginning of the new connectivity that ultimately brought us to the Information Age of today.

It took us over 125 years to get to 1 billion landline telephones for the entire world. For a long time, the phone was considered a luxury only for the rich and famous. Most of the phones were in wealthy, developed countries. Phones improved productivity and efficiency and made rich countries richer. It was believed that telephone density (number of phones per 100 people) was directly proportional to GDP and prosperity. It used to cost about $1000 to install one telephone line. All of that changed with the introduction of mobile phones, which did not require the digging of streets to lay copper cables. We learnt to talk through radio waves. Its increased facilities, features and convenience improved access and reduced cost. All of a sudden, we added 9 billion more phones in the world.

While mobile phone development was under way, a series of breakthrough innovations related to microchips, microprocessors, memories and displays burst into the new world. Along with smaller desktop computers, laptops, tablets, software and smartphones, the Internet revolution exploded into our collective consciousness to change the way we communicated with each other forever. It enabled us to connect and communicate with computers and machines worldwide in real time. Together, Internet and mobile connectivity opened up a world of new possibilities never imagined before. The telecom story is the story of connectivity, and the Internet is the story of sharing content. Together they have become the foundations for tomorrow's Information Age and a catalyst to help create a new world order with opportunities to develop a new, modern civilization.

Three Dimensions of the Information Age

- Connectivity—to enable people-to-people, machine-to-people and machine-to-machine exchange of voice, text, data, files, pictures and videos.
- Content—to create documents, books, music, movies, art, entertainment, etc. Content, in multiple languages customized to meet local needs, is the key to a network economy for education, health, business, finance, governance, security, trade, training and so much more.

• Context—to offer personalization with preferences, intimacy, informal space, behaviour and empowerment suited for individual needs with interactivity and specific tastes.

These three dimensions of the information economy offer a lifetime opportunity to dream and develop new products, services, markets, and distribution and delivery systems that have never been conceived before. They also empower people from the bottom up, instead of being thrust on them from the top.

The rise of social media has been a boon for consumers to connect globally at no additional cost. Well-known social media platforms in the US like Facebook, Twitter, Instagram and WhatsApp, to name a few, have a vast customer base with implications on almost everything that matters. Social media has the power to mobilize markets, media, masses and movements. Social media makes local events global and global events local. Telecom, the Internet and social media are now coupled with new technologies related to big data, analytics, image recognition, machine learning, artificial intelligence, etc. They are also associated with open-source software, cloud computing, Internet of Things (IoT), quantum computing and mind-boggling possibilities to change the world order. Information brings about a new perspective based on openness, accessibility, accountability, transparency, networking, democratization and decentralization. As a result, social, economic and political transformation is enabled to empower the people. This improves communication, cooperation and collaboration with meaningful compassion, leading us to a new non-hierarchical organizational architecture. This will be very different from the traditional hierarchical structure of command and control. Information has now become the fourth pillar of democracy along with the judiciary, legislative and executive. The legislation for Right to Information has also made democracy more open and transparent.

Three unique dimensions of information technology, namely, democratization, decentralization and demonetization, have allowed us to change the world order. The Internet democratizes information and gives immediate open access to everyone to access global resources on education, health, entertainment, news, politics, etc. Earlier, knowledge was controlled by a few elite universities and libraries, mainly in the West. Now it is only a click away.

Democratization

In 1963, when I wanted to learn about courses being offered by the University of Illinois, I had to travel by train from Baroda, where I was studying at the university, to Mumbai to visit the American embassy's US information service and obtain limited access to the catalogue. After an all-night journey, I had to wait in line one early morning in Mumbai to enter the building. After the proper formalities, I was given the catalogue for just fifteen minutes because others were waiting in line. In a few moments, I had to find the required information, take notes and leave for the all-night train back to Baroda. To get information from a simple two-page document, I had to spend one day and two nights. I also had to pay for train and bus rides. What a waste of time and resources!

Today, it is possible for a poor kid in a small, remote village in Africa to get any catalogue online, for as long as he wants, without spending any money or extra time. In the process, he can also visit the Guggenheim Museum in New York and the Tate Modern art gallery in London. If desired, he can also take online courses from the best universities in the world. The democratization of information permits every individual on this planet to acquire education and knowledge at no cost. To learn, you essentially need three things: motivation, time and content. If you are motivated and willing to devote the necessary time, ample content is available on the Internet for you to explore and learn about everything and anything. There are no limits to the education and knowledge you can access on the World Wide Web. The democratization of information, knowledge and understanding leads to more informed citizens and societies. However, to explore our curiosity and to travel to new frontiers, we require a change in our mindset and in our ideas of learning as a lifelong process. The democratization of information is a compelling concept to educate and empower every person on the planet and help change the world.

Decentralization

Mobile telecom technology is based on cellular architecture. Every area is broken down into small cells for, say, 1000 phones, to operate independently with freedom, flexibility and the ability to connect to nearby cells, which links to the global network. This decentralized architecture has allowed cell phone technology to be affordable, scalable and sustainable. The first set of cell phones were brick-sized and cost almost $2000 each. As volume increased, cost decreased, and ultimately when the price came down to below $100 a line, demand grew exponentially. The decentralization architecture works from bottom to top as opposed to centralized architecture, which operates from the top down. Earlier, telecom networks were based on vast and extensive systems with over 1,00,000 lines per switching centre. It was an expensive top-down approach.

There are many lessons to learn from this decentralized architecture of the Information Age in power, transport, health, education and governance. For example, power is generated centrally and distributed to various communities through massive networks of big power grid cables and towers. In the future, we need to develop distributed power with microgrids. Similarly, our health system needs to be decentralized to improve outcomes. All governments have lessons to learn on decentralization from information technology architecture. Vertical silos do not work any more. Horizontal, flat, independent structures with a network of resources deliver results.

Demonetization

Information technology has reduced the price of calls and communication substantially, and at the same time, created innovative business models for retail, financial services, delivery, distribution and many other areas. Compared to twenty years ago, telecommunication services are essentially free now. You can make an international call on WhatsApp or FaceTime at no extra cost. You can watch a movie on your phone for free. This model of demonetization of products and services changes the financial services' price along with mobile wallets and mobile payments. Big banks are closing their brick-and-mortar infrastructure and offering new digital platforms at substantially lower costs. Soon banking and money transfer will be free. This model will also apply to transportation, power, education and health services with enormous employment and job implications. The concept of forty hours of work per week, permanent jobs, pensions and benefits will be things of the past. Future work will be based on the power of information technology to demonetize various sectors of the economy.

Besides, we live in an era of surplus, as opposed to the earlier generations of scarcity—we still think in terms of the economy of scarcity instead of the economy of abundance. Now, we can produce anything. The critical question is, what do we want to make and for whom? We always produce only for those who can afford to buy, instead of those who need it. Unfortunately, we still think in terms of the economy of scarcity instead of the economy of surplus. We need a whole new mindset to think differently and produce things for people who need them. Hyperconnectivity has the power to organize the global supply chain and produce large quantities of what we need. This approach offers a unique opportunity to manufacture products and services for the people at the bottom of the economic pyramid and find ways to pay for them.

These three fundamental concepts related to democratization, decentralization and demonetization will profoundly impact the future of our society and civilization. New hyperconnectivity is changing almost every aspect of our lives at home and work. It is changing every part of human activity all over the world. It is slowly changing our family, home, work, education, health and governance, while at the same time seriously impacting our personal lives, relationships, our understanding and activities. Hyperconnectivity forces our political, economic and social systems to be open and transparent; that is why democracy and freedom become essential to empower people. In the long run, closed systems cannot survive in a hyperconnected environment.

The critical question that I have been asking for several years is not about how new hyperconnectivity will affect everything we do, but what we can do to take advantage of connectivity to raise our civilization to the next level. How can we convince people in leadership and governments worldwide to respond to the reality of the new Information Age and to take the lead to redesign the world? How can we identify, enrol and mobilize large numbers of change agents to help in this endeavour? The answer to these questions is found in another question: Why would anyone of any importance want to change the world's design? It is working very well for the rich and the powerful. It works equally well for rich nations. A club that benefits from the current order will defend and preserve the status quo. Minor tweaks and small changes may be acceptable, but not a wholesale redesign.

Those who have the power to change have no incentive to change. Those who want a change have no voice in the system. They are not equipped or sophisticated enough to raise their voices and articulate their demands. The main message was that unless there is World War III, no one of any significance will pay attention to the call for action to redesign the world.

COVID-19 Crisis

In March 2020, COVID-19 was declared a pandemic by the World Health Organization. It originated in Wuhan, a city of 11 million people in China, and started spreading across the world due to connectivity—people travelling to various countries. This virus apparently resided in bats, and probably jumped to animals and then to humans. It started spreading in Wuhan, perhaps at meat and fish markets, infecting people who came into contact with it. It was soon spreading like wildfire. Within a few weeks, COVID-19 moved to other cities in China and then to almost all other parts of the planet.

The virus is similar to the flu but more contagious and deadly because it attacks the lungs in the respiratory system and makes breathing very difficult, with the possibility of death looming large. It can cause complications and be more severe for older people and those with comorbidities. The virus is more like a seed. It has no life of its own. However, when it finds a suitable host, it enters the cells and rapidly starts multiplying. It also spreads through droplets from the mouth. It resides on material surfaces and spreads through simple human touch. The recommendation is to wash hands often, not touch new surfaces, not meet people socially, and stay locked within your homes, complying with government instructions. There is no known medicine, treatment or cure for it, and we do not understand enough about the real nature of COVID-19 to predict the path it will take. By mid-November 2020, it had reached about 200 countries and infected about 50 million people, causing the death of about 1.25 million.

COVID-19 created total panic the world over because of the fear of its uncontrolled spread and the potential loss of lives. Most governments declared a national health emergency and locked down their countries with orders to stay inside, wear masks and maintain social distance in public. This led to the complete closure and breakdown of the global economy. Travel was banned, and all airlines, trains and other modes of public transport were shut down. Stores, retail shops and restaurants, movie theatres and sports stadiums, offices, factories, banks, government services, schools, colleges, etc., were all ordered closed. Only provision outlets, drugstores and hospitals were allowed to operate to meet daily requirements. Nothing like this had happened in recent history. This enemy is a part of our natural environment. It has exploded like a neutron bomb to kill people without causing damage to buildings and other assets.

After China, COVID-19 created havoc in Italy, Spain, India, the UK and the US. Some countries handled it well by imposing early lockdowns, implementing extensive testing and ensuring well-managed health infrastructure. Some could not arrange enough test kits, masks, supplies and ventilators, which were needed in large numbers for people with breathing difficulties caused by the virus. Italy and New York became examples of centres with massive traffic at overcrowded hospitals, leaving tens of thousands of people dead. Doctors, nurses, scientists and healthcare workers the world over gave their best and risked their own lives to save others.

The entire world came together to save lives. It was like World War III, a global epidemic that was affecting people everywhere, uniting them in times of immense difficulty. Doctors, healthcare workers and volunteers rushed to the aid of others, providing medicines, attempting to develop new vaccines, purchasing hospital supplies and managing the rush of patients in hospitals. Data was collected from all over the world, and modelling and analytical studies and experiments were carried out. The rich took good care and protected themselves and their loved ones. Poorer countries received aid in the form of medical supplies, food and funds. The effect was devastating for billions, mostly the poor and migrant labourers who depend on daily wages and have no other savings. The halt in normal life also had a similar impact on all small businesses and employment the world over—with the poor paying a hefty price. Millions lost jobs and faced severe problems getting food and paying rents. In India's metros, hundreds of thousands of migrant labourers lined up to go back to their villages. With no transportation facilities, some even walked for over 100 km. Many governments announced large financial packages for low-income families and small businesses to help them get back on their feet. The real impact of the COVID-19 crisis is not known yet. Recovery plans are also not clear. However, it has caused many people worldwide to think about the real meaning of life, and analyse their performance, priorities and purpose.

I have been at home in Chicago in self-quarantine for over twelve months. I am working comfortably online, holding Zoom conferences, writing, reading, cooking, painting and chatting with my grandkids on video calls. I have also been staring at all that I have accumulated for the last fifty-five years in my house. Did I need all this—suits, shirts, ties, shoes, watches, pens, books, furniture, art, craft, carpets, cars, etc.? Would I simplify my life after the world gets back to normal? Would world leaders come to their senses to develop a vision for the planet?

Life after COVID-19 will not be the same as before. What will change and what will remain the same will determine the path going forward for the planet and the people. Is this nature's wake-up call to wage World War III? Is it enough to bring all of us together to seriously review and reflect personally, nationally and globally, and take measures to set things right?

Hyperconnectivity has provided the most incredible opportunity ever to humanity to put in place a new paradigm— one that will strengthen democracies, democratize knowledge, empower individuals, decentralize execution, demonetize education and health, and bring about a generational change. There are essential opportunities never dreamt of before, resulting from China's rise, India's rise and the emergence of the new economy, new knowledge and new technological innovations. To take advantage of these unique opportunities, it is essential to redesign the world once again after the COVID-19 crisis is behind us.

REDESIGN THE WORLD

1

World Design @ World War II

'The future depends on what you do today.'

—*M.K. Gandhi*

The world was last designed during the 1940s when World War II came to a close—many nations were in ruins, and they desperately needed peace and prosperity to rebuild their countries. A small group of enlightened intellectuals from a select group of nations led by the United States of America conceived the design. It ultimately created a series of global institutions—the UN, IMF, WTO, General Agreement on Tariffs and Trade (GATT), etc. Economic measurement standards were developed and adopted by most countries, such as GDP, GNP, per capita income, balance of payments, trade deficit, etc. Knowingly or unknowingly, at personal, institutional and national levels, we all still follow and abide by this rule-based system created seventy-five years ago.

The great American secretary of state Dean Acheson, in his memoirs entitled *Present at the Creation: My Years in the State Department*, refers to his being a witness to creating a post–World War II world. The image he portrayed was of a new world that came into being after the mind-numbing destruction of the war, which was altogether different from the world that had preceded it.

Amongst all wars, World War II, the global conflict that stretched from 1939–45, was the fiercest and most destructive war in human history. The earlier World War had killed 20 million and wounded another 20 million. In the course of World War II, there were gigantic struggles in Europe, Asia, Africa and the Pacific's far-flung islands. The war lasted nearly six years and came to an end in Europe with Germany's unconditional surrender on 8 May 1945. In Asia, it ended with the surrender of Japan on 14 August 1945. While this war's total losses were simply incalculable, the casualties have been estimated to be around 25 million dead and 35 million wounded. The major participants were Germany, Italy and Japan on the defeated side, and the United States, Great Britain and the Commonwealth, the USSR, France and China, which emerged victorious. War efforts engulfed all aspects of national life in almost all of America, Europe, Asia and Africa. For nearly six years, it was an enormous drain on resources. Besides being emotionally involved, many people had been engaged directly or indirectly in wartime hardware production.

The war impacted every major player's economy, from the US, UK, France and the Soviet Union to Germany and Japan. Hundreds of thousands had been killed and millions of dollars spent on unnecessary bloodbaths everywhere. No one was the victor after six long years. Everyone was exhausted and searching for some way for it to end. Finally, on 6 August 1945, the US dropped the first atomic bomb on Hiroshima. Three days later, the second was dropped on Nagasaki. The war finally ended a week later, on 14 August 1945, when Japan's emperor announced surrender on the terms laid down by the Allies. World War II thus ended after the use of the first high-technology atomic weapons.

The implications of World War II were many, including the world's new design, which has shaped our modern world. With the end of the war, we had to move ahead with the task of rebuilding the lives of hundreds of millions of people. Someone had to take the lead to build confidence, provide hope and show the path forward. The challenge was to get farms and factories running, provide jobs, open schools, assure safety and security, and build back the economy to restore life to normality as soon as possible.

The US took the lead with a group of nations to provide a design for a better future for all. This design had the perspective of the West with an emphasis on democracy and development. However, the world was divided into two opposed subsystems, each dominated by one of the two world powers, the United States and the Soviet Union; Europe remained a passive body divided between them. On both sides of the Iron Curtain, political leaders welcomed and fuelled the clash of the two opposing ideological camps. In the West, the Cold War and the resulting arms race were ascribed to a sinister communist master plan deployed through political, military and psychological warfare and increasingly directed against the free world with the aim of world domination.

In the East, conflicts and problems throughout the world were attributed to the class struggle. Since war is rooted in the capitalistic system, the counter-revolution centre was identified as Washington DC. With greater polarization, the Western bourgeoisie and the Eastern socialist ideologies condemned each other as a 'totalitarian police state' and 'rotten capitalism' respectively. Each side predicted that the other system was destined to disintegrate or collapse. Each side had created a complicated and expensive global intelligence network, such as the CIA and the KGB, both practising espionage and counter-espionage.

Significant developments in both blocs, however, ran parallel despite the differing internal socio-economic structures. The United States and the Soviet Union held similar positions of undisputed authority with the exclusive power to formulate policy and maintain control. Since World War II, the struggle between Communism and Western democratic political ideas, each representing a powerful coalitions of states, had been casting its shadow over all world politics. For many years, world affairs were dominated by a so-called Cold War. It was marked by extreme hostility between the two factions, including psychological warfare and uninterrupted mutual vilification.

The Five Pillars

Like a pentagon, the world's US-led design was based on five main pillars—democracy, human rights, capitalism, consumption and the military. These concepts were fundamental to the value system of the West, especially in the US. The US vision was to build a world order and provide world leadership based on this rule-based system and these five core concepts to achieve peace and prosperity for all. The rule-based liberal order has been a significant contribution by America in the last seventy-five years.

Democracy and human rights are essential elements of governance, the judiciary and people's freedom. Capitalism was necessary to conduct global business and trade. Consumption was the key to increasing demand, which would, in turn, strengthen the economy, create new jobs and keep the factories humming for growth. The military was the main machine that fuelled the war economy by producing weapons and technology needed to fight the enemy and maintain peace and resolve conflicts. These core concepts had a counterpart in the Soviet system—dictatorship, socialism, controlled and limited human rights, controlled and limited consumption, and the military apparatus.

Focus on the military was essential to both superpowers to keep industry, employment and the economy going and respond to a future war's eventuality. These core concepts were designed to encourage other nations to follow the US model of development, and to some extent, to maintain US leadership, dominance and control over world affairs. The real power play was visible between western Europe and eastern Europe. The rest of the countries were poor or had been colonized for too long to have an independent voice in the global system during World War II. Like most other countries globally, China did not matter much, and India was a British colony. The UK was still the dominant global colonial power ruling over Africa, the Middle East and its crown jewel, India.

The new design was well-accepted by the worldwide community that mattered because the US promised to rebuild Europe and Japan, both destroyed by the war. The plan required the UN, World Bank and IMF to be situated in the US. The US gave itself the right to appoint the president of the World Bank, while the Europeans could appoint the IMF's managing director. The world's design resulted from this carefully crafted and strategically constructed organizational architecture—with a vision to maintain peace and prosperity and dominate the world. This vision to build a democratic world, enhance global trade, open new markets and use military power when necessary was the real long-term objective.

Democracy

Democracy is defined as the 'government of the people, by the people, for the people'. It is considered an 'open' system. A more in-depth discussion on democracy must appreciate the world's present design and examine the new design's contours.

Humanity is a plurality of many different peoples forming complex, connected and interconnected communities, even as they exercise power as individuals. Democracy is designed to balance interests through discussions amongst the members of various communities and organizations. In 2020, more than half of the world's countries practise democracy; out of 192 countries in the world, 123 define themselves as democracies. But where did democracy start, and why has it become so popular in the last decades of the twentieth century? The origins of democracy can be traced to various ancient civilizations. Between 594 and 593 BCE, Solon, a lawmaker and statesman of Athens, played a critical role in establishing what may be seen today as the foundation of democracy. He helped write the Athenian Constitution, which maintained the right of all citizens to participate in the Athenian assembly.

In the nineteenth century, democracy was regarded as the grand prize of civilization, a system reserved for the elite with advanced wisdom, and the most superior race. This justification was used to determine limits on the right to vote and participate in politics. Large masses of people, whose lack of property or education, race or gender had become a reason for their exclusion from these political rights, clamoured and struggled to gain equality. Similarly, another critical rationale of European empires was that their colonial subjects were incapable of governing themselves. Popular movements in the colonies were agitating for independence, though at first they had reluctantly accepted the mother country's definitions of economic development and just political order. With time, they proclaimed their right to self-determination and self-government, vehemently decrying the denial of democratic rule and the continuing poverty of their peasant masses.

Over the years, democratization gradually began, which helped restrain tyrants from the arbitrary exercise of power, and instituted measures to protect ordinary citizens. Over the centuries, revolution—though often interrupted with regression to tyranny—slowly strengthened the slow process towards safeguarding sovereign citizens' rights and obligations in a state governed by the people. Many brave men and women fought for and thought about the idea of a just and democratic society. Aristotle, a student of Plato, who lived from 384–322 BCE, is well known for his writings on political theory, comparing democracy to other forms of governance. For him, it was clear that the benefit of democracy, to be free and not to be ruled like a slave, was a necessary part of a government. Another significant development was the Magna Carta of 1215 CE in England. The charter, put forward by barons in England to limit the power of the reigning King John of England, was able, at least in theory, to determine the absolute authority of the king. While this was far from being a democracy, it is often seen as the first cornerstone in the West's long process to establish freedom and citizen rights and pave the way for a parliamentarian government.

Centuries later, John Locke, born in 1632, came up with an important idea. He emphasized and used for the first time, the term 'social contract'. His famous book *The Two Treatises of Government* outlines how the government's right to rule must be based on the consent and legitimacy of the people governed. For his time, when the dominant modus operandi of nations was monarchical rule, this idea was radical and visionary. He can be regarded as a forefather of liberal democracy, mainly since he argued that all men are equal. Another critical thinker whose ideas influenced the French Revolution was Jean-Jacques Rousseau. He proposed that public representatives should be voted in by the people through direct election. This ideal is at the heart of the modern French Constitution and governance system. Today, when we think about democracy, we often take many things for granted; we forget the struggles that countless people undertook with their hearts and minds and the high price they paid with their blood and their lives.

Mahatma Gandhi spent a significant part of his life fighting against injustice perpetrated by a colonial power against innocent citizens on their soil. His extraordinary selfless struggle and ability to 'be the change he wanted to see in the world' was crucial to ending British domination over India and to achieve independence through a peaceful and non-violent struggle. While he was not alone, and millions of brave women and men responded to his call, it was his just cause, his character, values, wisdom, determination and methods that inspired the establishment of the world's largest democracy. Gandhiji's concept of democracy to uplift the rural poor in India was rooted in decentralization and the principle of bottom-up development.

Still, all of this does not explain what democracy means, how to define it, or even how to measure it. It is essential to understand that democracy is an ongoing process, and there are many forms and variations of it. Today, in the age of democracy, we have many different models of governance. A simple definition of democracy can be found in the Merriam-Webster dictionary: 'a government in which the supreme power is vested in the people and exercised by them directly or indirectly, through a system of representation, usually involving periodically held free elections'. The particular system of government can vary. Today we have many forms of practice and theory: parliamentary democracies, liberal and direct democracies, socialist democracies, and supranational and non-governmental democracies.

Democracy should incorporate at least four basic principles. First of all, there needs to be some rule of law applied equally to all citizens regardless of age, gender, ethnicity, status and position. Second, citizens should actively participate in civic life and politics: without citizens' active participation, there is no democracy. Third, the basic needs and human rights of all citizens should be protected by the state and not be violated. Finally, in every real democracy, fair and free elections are a necessary prerequisite. Often, we tend to focus on the rights we enjoy within our societies and tend to forget that with democracy come responsibilities, and with responsibilities come obligations and duties.

The rule of law is the key to democracy. In Greece, the councillors' ancient oath was 'to advise according to the laws' and 'do what was best for the people'. To a great extent, this indicated the importance of the rule of law. Particularly today, our role as citizens is not only to take part in elections and enjoy our rights; we also have to respect our laws and practise non-violence. Political disagreement can often be highly emotional in today's polarized world, but nothing justifies the use of violence against political opponents. Governments that have been legitimately voted to power need to be questioned, controlled and held accountable by us as citizens, and even if they do not reflect our opinion, we should accept their authority as they are in power legitimately.

The basic principle of democracy is to respect the laws and follow the rules of the game. When one party wins a fair election, the political process does not stop—we need to continue to listen and to work along with political enemies. As we live in a diverse and pluralistic society, we need to negotiate many things, knowing that compromises and trade-offs are a part of democracy. At the same time, our core values, as outlined in the Constitution, are non-negotiable. Without them, we lose the essence and legitimacy of democracy; we break our social contract. Lastly, the rule of law is fundamentally about inclusion—if we start to exclude people because of their skin colour, beliefs, gender or sexual orientation, they will feel betrayed and eventually turn against democracy.

The second requirement for any democracy is the participation of individuals in the public sphere. If citizens from all walks of life are not engaged in the democratic project, it is ultimately doomed to fail. Everybody must be informed about public issues and current political debates; only if citizens are alert and accountable can democracy function. It requires each of us to raise our voices and articulate our opinions and interests. At the same time, since we have two ears, we should make sure to listen twice as much, especially to the arguments of political opponents, to engage in a meaningful dialogue for the democratic principle as a whole. We should not take our right to vote lightly; it has been won after a hard fight.

The numbers of people not voting are, unfortunately, rising in many Western countries. Today, we are in danger of losing our moral stance due to the lack of discussion about and formulation of our standpoint. The Internet too often supports the echo chamber, the world view and ideas we are most drawn to, without critically questioning our assumptions, blind spots and limitations. Therefore, civil society is vital to the health and survival of democratic governance. While we should not be forced to participate in civic groups, we should ask ourselves what we can contribute as active citizens. Joining an association representing our interests as workers, doctors, entrepreneurs, farmers or religious believers is an example of how we can organize and become active in society.

Another example would be to join a political party that represents our view of life the most. Internal motivation should play a key role as well: What am I drawn to? How do I participate in society? What are the core values I need to stand up for? These are questions that many people do not even dare to ask in authoritarian regimes around the world. Nevertheless, in a free, democratic society, they are prerequisites to secure the conditions that guarantee freedom, prosperity and equality.

While democracies demand responsibilities and obligations such as active participation and the rule of law, an equally important principle is the state's rights guaranteed to its citizens. The Dalai Lama, the former political leader and spiritual head of the Tibetan exiled community, argues that there is an intimate connection between democratic values and fundamental values of human goodness. 'Where there is a democracy, there is a greater possibility for the citizens of the country to express their basic human qualities; and where these basic human qualities prevail, there is also a greater scope for strengthening democracy.' While he continues to be a spiritual leader, he chose to give away his political power, supporting a transition from authoritarian rule towards democratic governance. In his view, 'democracy is the most useful basis for ensuring world peace'. While history will judge if this is true or not, the role of basic rights and their protection is fundamental to the idea of democracy. Basic rights and basic needs are and should be internationally protected. The freedom to choose your religion, to enjoy free speech, and the right to protest against government actions are fundamental to any free society. Also, we should focus more and more on making sure that basic needs are met.

Many of us have never lived in dictatorships under authoritarian rule. Particularly today, in an age of information, where the

Internet is challenging individual privacy and security arguments to counter personal freedom, we must remind ourselves that these rights are non-negotiable and must be protected. In the US and Europe as well, the erosion of these rights can be perceived. The rise of populist movements demonstrates that 'the end of history' and the final victory of liberal democracy has not yet arrived. We will need to reinvent our domestic and international institutions to continue this great adventure of democracy.

In the end, every democratic system is defined by the principles of free and fair elections. Without them, we do not have a democracy. While this is easily understood, it is harder to put it into practice. The allegation of election fraud in the US in 2016 is only one minor example. Still, it shows how vulnerable our information systems are against virtual attacks and the unregulated spread of misinformation. While trust arrives on foot, it often leaves by horse, and it is hard to build it up again. This could also be said for our democracy. We choose our leaders by the vote today, and they represent us. While elections are times of political debate and verbal fighting, in the end, it is the president or the prime minister who is the head of the country for all of us.

Democracy very often does not lead to the outcome most favoured by us. Churchill once famously observed that it 'is the worst form of government, except for all the others'. And George Bernard Shaw argued that 'democracy is a device that ensures we shall be governed no better than we deserve'. Nevertheless, the beauty of democracy and the purpose of its achievements are overall to ensure peace and to guarantee that the majority opinion is taken into account. This requires that votes are cast in secret, that voting is free and without intimidation and violence. Elections are the critical cornerstone for democracies, and they need much preparation and training of social organizations, including citizens, election officials and political parties. Civil society has to play an active role in monitoring this fair and corruption-free process.

Dictatorship

While dictatorships are defined as the absolute rule over a nation and its people, there are many different forms of related governance systems. Tyranny is probably the oldest and most brutal form, common in ancient history when warriors ruled over their clans with lethal force. Monarchies can be understood as forms of absolute rule, usually justified through blood and family ties. Centuries ago, the aristocratic elite in Europe exercised power by creating a web of complicated relationships and power dynamics through marriage and war. Totalitarianism, racism and authoritarianism in Nazi Germany and the Soviet Republic and other countries brought suffering and pain to many people. A dictatorship can be defined as the rule of one over many, and therefore it is the opposite of democracy. Dictators who run their governments are usually surrounded by a small elite group of powerful allies who control society's critical elements of culture, including the media, ministries, courts and influential economic organizations.

By definition, dictatorships rely on force, often with the military's help and police brutality. It is considered a 'closed' system. Political power is used to intimidate, terrorize and even eliminate the opposition that threatens the dictatorship. Mass media and social media is used to spread propaganda and false beliefs, often creating an 'Us vs Them' narrative. Minorities and nonconformists within society are often used as scapegoats to channel frustration and distract people from the status quo. Colonial rule can be perceived as a form of dictatorship and was established mainly by European empires, particularly in Africa, Asia and Latin America.

In the nineteenth century and at the beginning of the twentieth, after the decline of colonialism, authoritarian governments started to rise out of former colonies' ruins. Military forces and certain privileged classes took control of various arms of the government and established regimes to remain in power. Some scholars would argue that today, after political colonization, financial or economic colonization has taken over. But these forms of dictatorship are different in size and method, without the brutality of earlier totalitarian regimes such as that of the Third Reich and the Soviet Republic. Communist and racist dictatorships, while very different in their ideology, were based on similar patterns. Charismatic and almost godlike leaders exercised terror and total control, not hesitating to abuse modern technology to serve their particular doctrine and expansion. Millions on both sides perished, and some of the most horrible crimes against humanity were committed by such dictators and their willing aides and followers. Such regimes created the concentration camps, the Holocaust, the Gulag and the Soviet purges.

Modern totalitarian dictatorships did not leave any room for freedom of the individual; they even ignored the idea of individual will. They argued that, like a cell in the body, one needs to submit to the collective will. Brutal force and mass surveillance justified the means to ensure absolute control.

In authoritarian regimes, power is centralized, and only minimal political freedom is guaranteed. Juan Linz, the Spanish sociologist and political scientist, argued that four characteristics define an authoritarian rule. First, limited political plurality; sometimes there is minor opposition, but restrictions are enforced on political institutions such as political parties, courts, legislation and civil society.

The second indicator is the legitimization of this rule through emotions and the narrative of 'good vs bad'. Control of power is justified because it is necessary to protect the people and represent the people's will, though without taking them into confidence. Poverty, chaos and security issues, such as after the Arab Spring in Egypt, often drain people's energy and make it easier for influential leaders or the military to seduce them to support authoritarian rule under the pretext of providing governance and solving problems. While the authoritarian regime can stabilize the country in the short term, unfortunately, it tends to ignore the root causes of the issue, resulting in people's exploitation.

Third, the right of free assembly for political opponents and critics of the regime is forbidden or suppressed; social mobilization, necessary and vital for any democracy, is considered dangerous by authoritarian regimes. The fourth and last characteristic is the absence of a genuine rule of law, where power is exercised through non-transparent and informal channels. The government's executive branch becomes biased and enforces power solely based on regime support; it is no longer capable of taking independent legal decisions.

There are five factors that support the establishment and survival of authoritarian rule. The first is the level of economic development—most wealthier countries are democratic and, as often seen in history, democracy has followed successful economic development. Another problematic factor is the concentration of national wealth. If oil and minerals are in the control of a few, the commercial revenue gained from it can solidify and strengthen the status quo. Besides, many non-democratic countries have to face identity-based divisions—whether on lines of ethnicity, religion or tribal conflict. It is also essential to understand that where governments have had historical experience with political pluralism, the shift towards evolving democracy is easier. If this were not the case in the past, the transition is likely to be more difficult—there are no supporting and unifying narratives from which to draw strength. The fifth factor is the neighbourhood—if surrounding countries are also totalitarian or authoritarian regimes, the struggle to become a democracy is harder.

In the 1970s and 1980s, the world suddenly became a lot more challenging to understand. Several Third World countries underwent a seemingly endless series of coups and revolutions. The problems and demands of nations in Asia, Africa, Latin America and the Middle East increasingly became the focus of international issues and crises. Third World dictators, whose personalities and motives were mysterious to Westerners, dominated the headlines.

Cambodia's new communist rulers massacred millions of their countrymen. Ugandan dictator Idi Amin played the tyrant at home and a clown abroad. Iran's Ayatollah Khomeini held US diplomats as hostages and challenged America to intervene. Libyan leader Muammar al-Qaddafi threatened to cut off President Reagan's nose. Americans, accustomed to thinking of dictators as necessarily unpopular, found it unfathomable why tyrants dominating the Third World could often inspire fanatical loyalty among their people. They found it incomprehensible that the number of strong political men sponsoring anti-Americanism, terrorism and aggression against neighbours was increasing. Seemingly popular and democratic revolutions against dictatorships in Iran, Nicaragua and elsewhere created new kinds of repression and despotism.

Some Third World countries seemed incapable of achieving stability. In others, rulers clung to power despite frequent defeats, failures and broken promises. And many of these leaders were so colourful, their policies so strange and contradictory, that insanity seemed the only logical explanation for their behaviour. The Third World dictators' rhetoric was challenging to decipher. They called their aggressive wars 'liberation'. Their brand of freedom resembled servitude, their state-run media were mouthpieces, and their systems of 'true' democracy seemed to be despotism. And yet, the more the West backed their domestic rivals, the more such 'moderates' were discredited as puppets and traitors.

As of now, democracy is considered the preferred form of government all over the world. It can empower people, and challenge them to cooperate to create wealth and build a better future for the people and the community. It also has the potential to offer freedom, flexibility, opportunities, options, autonomy and independence. Democracy is designed to encourage diversity and, as a result, bring about innovation and creativity. However, it comes at the cost of a built-in complexity, including delays, inefficiency, imperfections and a particular risk. Democracy works best when it is decentralized and power is distributed. At present, democracy is yet to deliver the fruits of development to many at the bottom of the economic pyramid. In any future redesign of the world, democracy will have to be perfected, expanded, extended and enhanced.

Democracy is still a work in progress. The concept is noble, but its implementation remains a challenge due to vested interests, greed, power-hungry politicians, corruption, competition, money power, the clique between business, bureaucracy and politicians, and many other issues. In the process, the real fruits of democracy do not reach people at the bottom of the economic pyramid. Hyperconnectivity offers a historic opportunity and hope to refine democracy and redesign democratic institutions and infrastructures.

Human Rights

Human rights are rights inherent to all human beings regardless of race, religion, gender, nationality, belief, ethnicity or any other parameter. Human rights relate to the right to life, liberty, opinion, expression, voice, values, education, food, etc. Human rights are universal, egalitarian and fundamental to modern societies. Human rights are much more than a mere component of democracy. They represent the sine qua non requirements for the necessary performance of a democratic system. Development and evolution of human rights are only possible when humans live in a democracy. It is so, given the fact that within this system it is the people themselves who can draw up the legislation to publicly control the three powers: the legislative power (ability to propose and vote for laws), the executive power (power to enforce rules) and the judiciary (power to interpret laws and to decide on them). Moreover, human rights are efficient only when state power is linked to autonomy and independence, and when, in the eyes of the law, all individuals are treated on equal terms. In the same way, it is essential, in any democracy, to establish a clear separation of powers so that the judiciary can remain autonomous and independent.

The Universal Declaration of Human Rights is a historic document adopted by the UN General Assembly in 1948. It consists of thirty articles, serving as guidelines to be adhered to regarding an individual's rights. Based on this document, an International Bill of Human Rights was proposed in 1966 and came into force in 1976. A great deal of work has been done in the last seventy years on human rights at the UN and by global domain experts and various national and international agencies. However, in practice, we have a long way to go to implement many acceptable practices and laws. In 2021, we have to contend with child abuse, bonded labour, human trafficking, injustice, discrimination, violence, terror and many other issues that do not follow the Bill of Human Rights spirit. People at the bottom of the economic pyramid are usually the victims of human rights violations. Any new design of the world will have to focus on taking human rights to the next level.

Capitalism

Capitalism was born and not made. It grew merely as a way of conducting the business of buying and selling, which ultimately became an economic principle as well as a way of life. It is about ownership of land, natural resources, labour and production and distribution. It is also about ideas and inventions that are entrusted to private control rather than the public. Capitalism has been extant for a very long time. What started as a simple concept evolved over centuries, has become a very complex superstructure, encompassing various disciplines to generate enormous new opportunities for employment, production and wealth creation.

Capitalism is well-accepted and practised all over the world. The concept started as 'trading' capitalism, where people took to trading goods and services nationally and globally to make private profits. Later, with the invention of the steam engine and electricity, a whole new version of modern capitalism began to integrate multiple disciplines to deliver more products and profits.

Capitalism has been the most potent engine of unmatched human progress and prosperity. It has lifted billions from poverty, provided much-needed energy, and made available employment, education, home and health services. It is connected with the economy, financial markets, technology, innovation, entrepreneurship, management and much more.

Capitalism has also created a great divide between the rich and the poor, with wealth being concentrated in the hands of a few super-rich individuals. At times, these super-rich factions influence government programmes and policies to further enhance their wealth and power. Capitalism has taken undue advantage of our planet, destroyed our forests, endangered wildlife and damaged our soils; it has polluted air and water and adversely affected our overall climate. Capitalism has also encouraged the corrupt to get rich quickly; it has also led to greed, crime and violence.

Worldwide, the new capitalism is based on globalization, privatization and liberalization with an unpredictable impact on the local population and their priorities. There are many forms of capitalism, including what is known as 'crony capitalism', where the state gives out-of-the-way support to their favoured elite persons, including licences for business, for promotion, preferences, pricing, etc., in exchange for personal favours. Capitalism is about a free-market economy where market forces related to the buyer and the seller decide the value of the goods, ultimately impacting the economy. The general belief is that democracy, freedom and capitalism go hand in hand, unlike the state-owned enterprises predominantly found in communist countries where the state owns all property and wealth, and the right to produce and profit.

As opposed to the capitalist system in a democracy, the Soviet Union and other communist countries practised a state-owned form of economy where governments owned and operated production and distribution. They followed a different set of rules of the game and, through central planning, decided on what, when, how much and for whom to produce. They controlled supply, demand and production.

When I first went to the Soviet Union in 1987, I was surprised to learn that you could not walk into any restaurant and expect to be served. Similarly, you could not go to any market and wish to get what you want—the state controlled all products and services. Supply was controlled by the state, which decided what should be produced for the consumer. The state also dictated the price. I saw long lines of people on the streets to get whatever was available. On my electronic factory tour, I learnt that the state also dictated the supply chain. Top executives did not know the difference between cost and price.

Having lived in the US for a long time, this was an extraordinary experience for me. Once, I requested a telephone operator at my hotel to find me a number and connect me to a person who lived in the area. She asked me, 'Do you have his number?'

I said, 'No.'

Strangely, her reply was, 'If you do not have his number, why do you want to call him?'

I was puzzled. The message was that there was no telephone directory, and information was not shared. In a capitalist system, this would be seen as an opportunity to build a business and make money.

Capitalism in China has flourished under communist party rule in the last few decades. It has been built on the back of cheap labour, Western markets and substantial government subsidies and support. How this will affect local politics is still an important question. The hope is that as China develops, it will move towards democracy. Chinese capitalism is a work in progress. The world is closely monitoring this experiment, and the jury is still out on it.

Consumption

Consumption was a crucial part of the grand world design to generate demand after World War II to run factories and provide jobs. The aim of it was first to meet basic human needs and get post-war life back to normal quickly, and it began growing in leaps and bounds in all areas that helped improve the quality of life. This soon provided an increased supply of comforts, white goods, transport, entertainment, travel, tourism and fashion. Coupled with creative advertising, marketing and promotion in a capitalist system, demand and growth kept growing over these last seven decades. Along with the rising world population, the need for monetizing mines and minerals also increased. This exploitation of natural resources generated pressure from environmental activists and tribal communities which felt left out as outsiders derived benefits from their land.

Factories produce goods and services only for those who can afford to pay, not those who need them. This has kept the poor where they are and made the rich richer. For example, the global market for luxury goods is estimated to be around $400 billion a year—twice that of what it would take to eliminate global hunger. The rich like to display their purchasing power, because of the ultimate social rank in the hierarchy that it bestows. They go on conspicuous consumption binges to flaunt their social superiority. In the process, productive systems suffer and social inequality increases. These are some of the contradictions of the capitalist economy and its emphasis on consumption.

What was essential seventy-five years ago to kick-start growth after World War II has become a challenge in terms of exclusion and inequality. Too much of a focus on capitalism and consumption has caused damage to our environment and ecosystem. The quantity of garbage we create in every major metro city in the world is unmanageable. We buy 1 million plastic water bottles every minute. Where do all these empty bottles go? What do our consumption patterns tell us about ourselves and our concern for the environment? An emphasis on conspicuous consumption and vulgar display of wealth is visible in every significant rich community. What are we trying to convey? Is consumption more important than conservation?

Military

History can tell many tales of war, revolution and restructuring of the world order to achieve the diverse objectives of individuals, communities and nations. Conflicting aspirations and expectations give rise to tensions, leading to fights, revolutions and wars. Family feuds, religious differences, the ideological divide, economic disparity, social inequality, injustice and territorial imbalances have been some of the causes of war throughout human history.

In the past, wars were fought with hardware such as stones, bows and arrows; later came guns, machine guns, battle tanks, bombs, missiles and other sophisticated technological equipment. World War II was concluded only by the destructive power of atomic bombs. This, in turn, gave birth to an arms race and started the era of the Cold War between two superpowers. Both superpowers spent trillions building mighty military complexes to protect themselves against each other and their allies. In the process, the military establishment became a way of life for national leaders. They took and continue to take great pride in acquiring the most sophisticated weapons. The military has been a significant part of the design of the world after World War II.

The military is the largest industry globally, with investments of $2 trillion a year. This works out to an expenditure of $250 per person per year. For one-tenth of $2 trillion, we can eliminate hunger and poverty from this planet. However, no one pays attention to this truth. The military employs many people and spends vast amounts on research, development, technology, innovations and the eternal competition to build new mass destruction weapons. All countries in the world spend a substantial part of their GDP to wage wars for land, oil, conflicts, power and control. It is mainly the young, the poor and the innocent who lose their lives in wars to protect assets that enable the rich to become more prosperous. War heroes are celebrated. Military parades are a part of national pride.

It is estimated that in 3500 years of recorded history, we have had less than 300 years of peace. Violence and war arise from the choices we make. Similarly, non-violence and forgiveness are also choices that we can make. After World War II, we have preferred violence and war as a way of resolving conflicts. War has essentially been a weapon to rob others. Perhaps this arises from the old mindset of scarcity and insecurity. We live now in a world of opportunities and surplus. Does it make sense to fight wars now?

International Institutions

To implement the world's US-led design, it was critical to establish new international institutions to guide, execute, manage and monitor global developments. To focus on democracy and human rights and to maintain peace, the UN was conceived. To facilitate financial markets to fuel funding for reconstruction and development, the World Bank and the IMF were created. To promote and facilitate global commerce, the WTO was established. The military was never mentioned as a part of the design of the future world order. However, for both the US and the Soviet Union, the military was critical to flex their muscles and build arms export business with their allies and developing countries to protect borders and maintain peace. Later, in 1949, NATO was conceived. Similarly, to facilitate cooperation and collaboration, G8 and G20 were set up, which provided a forum for global leaders to interact regularly and focus on the economy.

Measurements

Along with global institutions like the UN, World Bank and IMF, the following major international measurement standards were introduced to manage and monitor global and national economies.

- Gross domestic product (GDP): A monetary measure of the market value of all the final goods and services produced in a specified period.
- Gross national product (GNP): The total value of goods produced and services provided by a country for one year, equal to the GDP and net income from foreign investments.
- Per capita income: The average income earned by a person in a given country or area in a specified year. It is the national income divided by the population.
- Balance of payments: The record of all economic transactions between a country's residents and the rest of the world in a particular period.
- Trade deficit: The amount by which the cost of a country's imports exceeds its export value.
- Foreign exchange reserve: Cash and other reserve assets held by a central bank or any other monetary authority that are primarily available to balance the country's payments. It usually influences the foreign exchange rate of its currency.

All international institutions use these standard measurements to rate a country's performance and determine parameters to enter into business and trade with it. However, these measurements do not necessarily represent the health of the economy of a nation. They are simply a way to make a judgement in favour of the hard currencies.

In the late 1980s, a US trade representative visited my office in Delhi with a World Bank officer to discuss indigenous design, development and telecom equipment production in India. In their view, I was instrumental in blocking the import of foreign technology in India. During our conversation, the US trade representative said that India is practically broke and has minimal foreign exchange reserves to pay for more imports abroad. He added that I should use this opportunity to borrow money from the World Bank to buy telecom equipment. I could not understand how India, with 700 million people, could be considered broke. I was taken aback at his logic. My off-the-cuff response was, 'What happens if we sell one of our temples or the Taj Mahal for several billion dollars?' I said, 'We have a lot of gold in our temples. How do you say India is broke?'

He said, 'That does not count.'

'Why not? Why do you not consider Indian assets in art, craft, gold, culture, and human resource? Why just hard cash in foreign currency?'

Later, in 2004, it came to light that in one of the 108 centres of worship in Vaishnavism, the authorities of the Shree Padmanabhaswamy medieval temple in Thiruvananthapuram discovered approximately $22 billion of treasure at a depth of 20 feet underground, including gold idols with 20-foot-long diamond bracelets, golden elephants, countless bags of gold coins, 66 pounds of concrete gold coconut shells studded with emeralds, rubies and sapphires and much more. It was believed that the value of hidden treasure in these underground chambers at the temple was perhaps $1 trillion. How did you judge a country like India based on foreign exchange reserves?

The world design after World War II was focused on an 'open system' with democracy, human rights, capitalism, consumption and military to oppose the 'closed system' of dictatorship, robust controls, limited human rights and limited consumption. Military strength was necessary on both sides to wage wars. Unfortunately, democracy is not universal. Nor is it for all the people all the time. Human rights are well-understood but not delivered. Capitalism has distorted opportunities. Socialism has suffocated human potential. Consumption has been carried too far and has choked conservation and sustainability. The military has become war-centric and not peace-centric. Development today is wealth-centric and not health, well-being, education, culture or human-centric. In pure economic and human terms, the present design has many fault lines. This gives us an opportunity to redesign the world seventy-five years after World War II.

2

Tipping Points

'*Look at the world around you. It may seem like an immovable, implacable place. It is not. With the slightest push—in just the right place—it can be tipped.*'

—Malcolm Gladwell

The world design conceived seventy-five years ago has done well in maintaining peace, avoiding a possible World War III, rebuilding Europe and Japan, creating a new economy with new technology and high growth, lifting billions from poverty, and providing prosperity. Many things that happen in the sphere of geopolitics today are difficult to grasp unless we understand what happened during World War II and its aftermath, resulting in this world's design and the creation of new institutions to get us going again. However, a lot has changed since then in all areas of our lives— politics, economy, demography, technology, civil society, business and governance have matured to the point where this old design is not working well and cannot meet the aspirations of the majority of the people and their hope for a better future.

There have been seven tipping points in the last seven decades that have had a profound, transformational and ubiquitous impact on nearly every individual and the world. Each of the mega events has had a say in the historical development of the world, the influence of which may not be evident at the outset. However, it is evident that after seventy-five years, these events, and especially the recent COVID-19 crisis, demand that we begin a new conversation.

Decolonization

The process of decolonization had erupted at the beginning of the twentieth century. After hundreds of years of European control and domination of many countries in Asia, Africa and the Middle East, a new era of freedom and self-determination began emerging in the twentieth century. Even as early as 1936, the Arab population rose against Palestine's British rule, leading to violent clashes and conflicts. One of the most popular and extraordinary uprisings, mainly due to its non-violent nature, was the Indian freedom movement. Mahatma Gandhi, who headed the Salt March and raised the clarion call of 'Quit India', led India into state sovereignty, and thus began the decline of the British Empire. By the year 1947, India was partitioned, and two countries, India and Pakistan, had declared their independence from Britain, thereby ending 200 years of formal occupation and colonization.

India was the jewel in the crown of the British Empire, which ruled over many countries. It was said that the sun never set on the British Raj. When the British landed on the Indian subcontinent at Surat's port on 24 August 1608, India was the world's largest economy and the most important manufacturing and international trade centre. India then possessed 25 per cent of the global economy and had most of its industrial and commercial power. However, at the time of its independence in 1947, India was left with only 3 per cent of the global economy. Like many other colonies, India, too, had been robbed and ruined by the British Empire.

The battle to gain India's independence, led by Gandhi, essentially started a domino effect. Within a decade or so, the entire world was decolonized. The Indian freedom movement turned out to be the movement that began the process to decolonize the world. During World War II, no one would have thought it would happen so rapidly. In fact, within a few years after that, millions joined the free world and were empowered to pursue their dreams and destiny. This flood of freedom was to change the world forever. My father, who was educated only up to the fourth grade during the British Raj, could never have imagined that all his eight children would go to college and study English. After Independence, like millions of others, he felt empowered and confident and knew that he could dream big, like any free man. In the mid-twentieth century, the impact of decolonization was uplifting and empowering for millions.

~

In 1952, the king of Egypt, who was regarded as a puppet of the colonial powers, was overthrown. The United Arab Republic was formed in 1958. It was the first independent nation in Africa that gained freedom through a political process. In 1960, three years after Ghana, Congo separated from its colonial master, Belgium. Due to her rich mineral resources, Congo did not have a chance to become politically stable; many ethnic conflicts and wars followed which continue even today. After the nationalist uprising, the Mouvement National Congolais (MNC) party, led by Patrice Lumumba, won the elections and declared independence. Most of the 1,00,000 Europeans had fled the country by then, giving the people of Congo a chance to fill the positions of the former colonial elite and rebuild their country. However, internal power struggles started almost immediately. With support from external forces such as the US, the political battle was influenced later towards a pro-Western government. Algeria achieved independence only after a long and brutal guerrilla war against France. Their fight for freedom was mainly achieved through blood and suffering.

In 1963, the Organization of African Unity (OAU) was founded. Many argued that the need to free oneself from the White mask worn by many Blacks was an integral element in the struggle for independence. Forced learning of White people's languages labelled as 'good' French or English, and biased education and socialization experiences created an internal psyche of colonization amongst the oppressed people. It was widely thought that along with the brutal force and violence at the core of colonization, class-constructed colonial societies had been created which distorted race and national culture. Many people in Africa believed that an armed revolution or violent struggle for national liberation was legitimate.

Frantz Fanon was one of the most influential anti-colonial thinkers of the century, and he influenced leaders like Ali Shariati in Iran, Steve Biko in South Africa, Malcolm X in the United States and Ernesto Che Guevara in Cuba. Many revolutionary liberation movements were drawn to him primarily because he justified violence against the colonial power. Fanon himself later became a part of the Algerian Liberation Front and was actively engaged in the war against French-occupied Algeria. For him, nationalism and imperialism, in the form of colonial powers dominating Black people for centuries, contaminated the Black psyche and established inferior identities in collective and individual minds.

Simultaneously, the apartheid regime had a firm grip on South Africa from 1948 until 1994. The successful transition towards the Rainbow Nation was possible due to the extraordinary effort of Nelson Mandela, who first fought violently, and later, after twenty-seven years in prison, led the country towards a peaceful transformation. Gandhi, Martin Luther King, Mandela and others have demonstrated that though the path is difficult, painful and prolonged, progress towards a world free of colonial rule and injustice is possible.

While the struggle for decolonization has been successful, the deeper economic and cultural footprints left behind by colonial countries are still quite substantial in many postcolonial countries.

In recent decades a new form defined as neocolonialism has surfaced. It is defined as the practice of financial and economic power exercised over weaker nations. Investments serving neocolonialism, often disguised as developmental support, prevent the expansion of real financial strength in developing countries. Ultimately, this widens disparities and makes the rich more affluent while also draining human and material resources from the former colonies through capitalistic processes. Instead of military force, foreign capital and economic power become the modus operandi for control. In international relations, this practice is studied and analysed through the dependency theory, and it describes how wealthy countries stay in the centre while developing countries remain at the periphery. Today's discourse about inequality and the fact that 1 per cent of the people own 99 per cent of the world capital indicates how neocolonialism is apparent everywhere.

Large multinational companies, earning revenues far higher than many developed countries, play a significant role in such a global system. As non-democratic actors with work and influence worldwide, they can use and abuse national legislation to secure and expand their power all over the world. As business organizations, they often achieve high growth and monetary profit, regardless of the long-term effect. Interest rates on debts can be used to pressure governments and influence them in negotiations. While an inflow of investments often leads to a short-term increase in developing countries' economies, they stay dependent on these large multinational companies in the long term. The companies exploit cheap labour and appropriate goods, and through privatization often take control of services that were formerly under public management. Developing countries have no capacity or opportunity to take independent investment decisions or build the industries required for national growth. Power stays in the hands of a few. Most of the capital generated benefits only the ruling elite; and multinationals form a club in partnership with wealthy locals to exploit it. Multilateral agencies and banks support this model and corner natural resources.

For instance, Africa's overall debt is over $200 billion. Most countries there will never be able to repay the loans they have received. American economist Jeffrey Sachs recommended cancelling the entire indebtedness of Africa so that its economy can develop and it can free itself of the burden of high interest rates. International financial institutions such as the IMF and the World Bank are sometimes seen supporting one-sided neoliberal politics and developmental visions—this only helps strengthen the status quo. They do not implement their avowed intentions, nor do they even wish to change, for it would imply that the US and the West share a substantial part of their global power.

In the 1970s, many practitioners and activists in academic circles became aware of the tenor and contents of Western textbooks and how they influenced public life through a pro-colonial or one-sided perspective of history. Colonization was and is still justified through the labelling of colonized peoples and cultures as inferior, uneducated or mediocre. In many subtle and non-subtle ways, this narrative is given widespread coverage through written and published works. Through novels and textbooks in schools and universities, this form of thinking plays a vital role in justifying and legitimizing colonialism. Influencing the current discourse for colonial supremacy has been a critical strategy of European empires.

Colonialism took many institutional and economic forms. However, one characteristic common to all European empires, with varying intensity, was the importance of trade. Soon after a conquest, colonies were forced or encouraged to produce tradable goods consumed in the mother country or sold in international markets. In some cases, these products were being made by the colonies for a long time; in others, a brand new production line was implanted by the colonizers, both under public and private initiatives. Even though sections of the colonial population were forced to participate in such production, the colonial groups benefited from these operations. Thus, this form of production resulted in trade for the colony, generating exports (mainly agricultural commodities and raw materials) exchanged in Europe for imports into the colonized countries (primarily manufactured goods). The result of this process was that by the time the country attained independence, essential segments of the erstwhile colonial populations were dependent on international trade for their well-being.

Despite its long and complicated history, two aspects of European colonialism's modus operandi, both essentially economic, remained remarkably constant over time. The first was trade between colonies, their colonizers and the rest of the world. In many territories, right from the very beginning, trade was the cause of military action. For example, England first deployed troops in the Indian Ocean to protect the East India Company's monopoly and trading. When administrative control over the Indian states was established in the mid-eighteenth century, its officers executed this. A significant restructuring of colonial economies usually followed colonization.

The second aspect was the exploitation of capacity of the subjugated colonies to produce goods consumable in Europe. Sometimes, this simply required the boosting of pre-existing industries. For example, in the late sixteenth century, the Spaniards organized the Latin American economy around the production of Peruvian and Mexican silver, which the Incas and Aztecs had been producing long before their arrival. In India, in the first part of the eighteenth century, the export of calicoes to Europe was strongly encouraged. In other cases, brand new productions were imported and established: the sugar plantations introduced by the Portuguese in the Azores and Brazil in the sixteenth century, or the merino sheep that the British settlers of Australia grazed after 1810. Throughout the history of colonialism, Europeans became accustomed to consuming or processing many commodities produced in the colonies.

They were exchanged for manufactured goods made in Europe: coffee, tobacco, indigo, cotton, wool and timber.

European colonialism began in the fifteenth century with the Portuguese exploitation of African coasts and the sea route's opening to the East Indies. This was enormously accelerated with the Spanish discovery of the Americas. In the seventeenth century, the early colonizer's power was eclipsed by France's rise and, a little later, by the Netherlands and England. A long series of wars (1652–1763) saw the latter emerge as the most powerful colonial power, particularly after India's control was established in the mid-1700s.

In many countries, after colonial occupation, there was a period that could be defined as anti-imperialism. It was spurred by local populations wishing to be free from their colonial masters. This period had the American Revolution of 1776, the independence wars of Latin America (1810–30), and the concessions of self-government granted to several British settler colonies by the mother country in the second half of the nineteenth century. Yet, the imperialist momentum slowly built up again to eventually accelerate into the 'scramble for Africa' and the division of China and the Middle East into areas of influence. By the 1930s, European colonialism had reached the point of its most massive expansion ever.

One of the striking political and economic changes of the twentieth century was the near-complete elimination of colonial power. However, decolonization is not a linear process. The real need is to liberate the hearts, minds and souls of the oppressed and the oppressors. Many countries are still struggling in a postcolonial world; their quest to redefine, reconstruct and redesign their community's narrative remains and is ongoing. Storytelling, as ancient as history itself, plays a significant role. Today, stories are told only through the Western media, the Internet and movies. After seventy-five years, it is a challenge to understand and blend the stories of all people.

The Rise of China

After taking over the leadership of China from Chairman Mao Zedong in 1976, Deng Xiaoping helped change the image of the nation by encouraging capitalist economic reforms in the communist country. It was generally believed that capitalism goes hand in hand only with democracy. Xiaoping proved this wrong. Within three decades, China was the second largest economy in the world. It became a global manufacturing powerhouse by using the communist construct to mobilize millions of workers from rural areas to live in bunkers in urban production centres and meet the low-cost labour needs of the West.

A close friend of mine once asked a youth leader of the Chinese Communist Party, 'What is your main job?' The answer was straightforward: 'My job is to recruit people from rural areas to come to live in bunkers in cities and work for the multinational factories.' It is not possible in any democratic country to force people to do what China has done. At the same time, China used its power to force Western companies to transfer technology so that local companies could gain exclusive access to extensive local markets. China also prevented some large foreign companies' entry into economic activities related to the Internet, telecom, power, agriculture and other vital sectors, thus enabling Chinese multinationals to compete globally.

In the process, China robbed every country of its local manufacturing base and, at the same time, acquired all the significant technologies and related capabilities to become a new global player. With the emphasis on expanding export and limiting imports, China built the largest foreign exchange reserve ever. Today, the Chinese presence is prominent in all countries and all markets. China deserves credit for this. And all other countries need to pay attention to what it means for the rest of the world.

Asia looks and feels very different now, compared with the Cold War period. Back then, American pre-eminence was a given, even though the US presence in the region was far from ubiquitous or overwhelming. Washington shaped events in Asia with comparatively loose reins. The sense that Asia now works differently and is marching to a different drumbeat can be traced to a single source: China's re-emergence. During the past thirty years, China has set new benchmarks for fast and—above all—sustained economic growth.

The pace and scale of China's economic transformation have no historical precedent. In 1978, China was one of the poorest countries in the world. Its real per capita GDP was only one-fortieth of the US level and one-tenth of the Brazilian level. Since then, China's total per capita GDP has grown at an average rate exceeding 8 per cent per annum. As a result, China's real per capita GDP is now almost one-fifth the US level and at par with Brazil's. This rapid and sustained improvement in average living standards has occurred in a country with more than 20 per cent of the world's population; China is now the second largest economy in the world. In the process, China has lifted over 700 million people from poverty—a remarkable accomplishment in human history.

In the 'premodern' era, too, China was a world economic and technological leader. Many historians think that China's pre-modern financial performance reached a peak in the Song Dynasty when it was believed to have the most advanced technologies, the highest iron output, the highest urbanization rate and the largest national economy in the world. However, sometime between 1500 and 1800, China lost its leadership position to Western Europe. According to estimates, its per capita GDP stagnated between 1500 and 1800, while Western Europe's increased steadily during the same period. Some historians and economists attribute China's lagging behind during this period to the more centralized and inward-looking political systems of the Ming (1368–1644) and Qing (1644–1911) dynasties that stifled innovation and commercial activities in China. During this period, the country's economic failure was due to an imperial political-institutional system that protected elite groups' vested interests, such as imperial households, members of the bureaucracy and the local gentry, who were resistant to new technologies.

This imperial system was significantly weakened and eventually collapsed after two Opium Wars between China and Great Britain in the 1840s and 1850s, and the Sino-Japanese War of 1894–95. In effect, the series of Chinese defeats led to a forced opening of China's borders, and its territories and treaty ports being conceded to the West and Japan. These changes brought industrial technologies and factories to China. However, continuous civil wars and World War II prevented the industrialization process from gaining momentum until the 1950s. Indeed, industrialization had so little effect during this time that China's per capita GDP declined between 1800 and 1950.

After the People's Republic of China was established in 1949, the Chinese Communist Party government, like governments of many other countries at the time, thought that the most effective way to speed up industrialization was by increasing investment in heavy industries such as steel, concrete and heavy machinery. China's government mobilized the required investment resources by limiting household consumption and setting low agricultural goods prices. The forced savings and surpluses extracted from the farm sector could be used for investment in such industries. This comprehensive growth strategy based on capital accumulation was not sustainable and had grave consequences for people's welfare. The big push towards industrialization during the years of the Great Leap Forward (1958–60) not only failed to raise the GDP growth rate, but also had disruptive effects on agricultural production, resulting in a severe famine when adverse weather shocks hit China in 1959. The Great Leap Forward became the Great Leap to Famine of 1959–61, with even official statistics admitting to 15 million deaths, though unofficial estimates suggest double that number or more.

In the late 1970s, the agricultural sector included more than 70 per cent of China's labour force. Still, it could not provide

China's population with 2300 calories per capita per day (the UN-established minimum). Emergency grain imports were frequently needed to meet food deficits. China's non-agricultural sector was a little better. It was dominated by the state-owned enterprises in which resource allocation and production activities were carried out according to the government plan, rather than being calibrated by market signals. At that time, most state-owned enterprises were inefficient, overstaffed with redundant workers, and often produced no market demand. Simultaneously, very few firms were in the light industries sector, such as home appliances, furniture and clothing. There were constant shortages of consumer products. The industrialization policies pursued by the Chinese government during this period from 1952 to 1978 created adverse incentives and gross misallocation of resources, resulting in declining aggregate productivity, recurring food crises and relatively little improvement in living standards.

When the Cultural Revolution ended after the death of the Communist Party chairman, Mao Zedong in 1976, the Chinese government, under the leadership of Xiaoping, sought to increase its legitimacy by improving aggregate economic performance and raising living standards. In December 1978, it decided on a general policy of *gaige kaifang* or 'reform and opening up'. Since China had experienced recurring food crises before 1978, it is not surprising that its economic reform started in the agricultural sector. There were two critical reforms. First, the government increased the prices of agricultural goods. Second, the previous 'collective farming system' was shifted to the 'household responsibility system'. Under the new system, each farm household was assigned a fixed quota of grains to sell to the government at official prices. However, any extra grain the family produced could be sold at market prices.

The reforms were implemented gradually and completed in 1984. Between 1978 and 1984, total factor productivity in the agricultural sector grew 5.62 per cent per year. As a result of productivity growth, China's agricultural output increased by

47 per cent during this period. The increase in food availability alleviated its earlier constraints on subsistence food and started a structural transformation that reallocated a large amount of labour from agriculture to industry. From 1978 to 1984, agriculture's share of total employment fell from 69 per cent to 50 per cent. In just six years, 19 per cent of China's labour force—more than 49 million workers—was reallocated out of the agricultural sector. Most of the reallocated workers did not move to urban centres. Instead, they went to work in the rural industrial enterprises set up by township- and village-level governments, known as township and village enterprises (TVEs).

The 15th Congress of the Chinese Communist Party held in 1997 was a milestone in China's economic policies. Congress formally sanctioned ownership reforms of state-owned firms and also legalized the development of private enterprises. With the reduction of legal barriers, private enterprises proliferated. As part of China's run-up to joining the WTO in 2001, the government also started to cut tariffs, broaden trade rights and liberalize its foreign direct investment regime. In the last three and a half decades, China's leaders have chosen to carry out economic reform without political reform or establishing the rule of law. Instead, they have implemented institutional changes and policy reforms in a piecemeal fashion that usually benefits crucial interest groups within the state sector. Giving monopoly rights to state-controlled or politically connected firms is one example.

While this approach has helped to reduce political resistance to economic reform, it has also resulted in corruption and income inequality, in addition to economic distortions. While decreasing the state sector's monopoly rights in various industries may be necessary to reduce distortions and resolve associated sociopolitical problems of corruption and income inequality, it remains to be seen whether China's leadership will be flexible enough and strong enough to do so. China's rapid rise and the COVID-19 crisis that emanated from China will have far-reaching consequences on the world's future.

Fall of the Soviet Union

After the rapid changes in the leadership of the Soviet Union, Mikhail Gorbachev became the general secretary of the Communist Party in 1985. He decided to do precisely the opposite of what China did—he focused on political reforms before economic reforms. His plans failed, leading to the disintegration of the Soviet Union. The world became unipolar, with the US as the only superpower.

In a speech in May 1985, Gorbachev, younger and far more liberal than any previous Soviet leader, advocated reforms and a campaign against alcohol consumption. He planned to strengthen the Soviet Union while pushing progressive reforms to address the widespread apathy and moral decline, which had resulted in high levels of alcoholism. Gorbachev was not the first to push for sanctions on alcohol; Tsar Nicholas II had used a similar programme during World War I to boost troop morality and enhance readiness for war and use of grain, thus rescuing food production. In 1985, there was no need for additional food production; nevertheless, a similar idea was behind Gorbachev's reasoning. However, as had happened during World War I, Gorbachev was confronted with massive economic decline. According to Alexander Yakovlev, a senior member of the Politburo, it was estimated that the Soviet Union lost 100 billion roubles of tax collection annually due to the anti-alcohol policy. Alcohol production itself did not disappear but became part of the black market.

Another significant and symbolic blow to the Soviet Union came with the explosion of the atomic power plant in Chernobyl in Ukraine, leading to massive environmental and human losses through radioactivity. For the first time in human history, the terrible effects of a nuclear meltdown were experienced. Once built as a symbol of Communist progress, the image of the destroyed reactor symbolized, in retrospect, the early signs of Soviet decline. Gorbachev pressed for more political liberalization in 1986. The most prominent Soviet dissident, Andrei Sakharov, was allowed to return to Moscow.

In the Baltic republics, which had once been forced to join the Soviet Union, considerable opposition started to form. In July 1986, in the port town of Liepāja in Latvia, three workers from the Latvian Human Rights Defense Group known as Helsinki-86, Linards Grantiņš, Raimonds Bitenieks and Mārtiņš Bariss, made speeches referring to the human rights statements of the Helsinki Accords. It became the first pro-independence movement openly critiquing the USSR. In the same year, on 26 December 1986, after a rock concert, 300 Latvian youngsters marched towards the Freedom Monument shouting 'Soviet Russia out! Free Latvia!' and clashed with the police.

Gorbachev stuck to his course during this time and even introduced a policy called 'Demokratizatsiya'. His idea was to let people vote for candidates in future Communist Party elections; however, most of the party members did not welcome his thoughts. Further, he started to implement the Glasnost process, opening up public space for discussion and free media. While the press and the intelligentsia stayed cautious and did not trust the regime, Gorbachev won ground against the Party's conservatism, which had been facing increasing pressure.

While Gorbachev's idea was to reform and support the survival of the Soviet regime, his policies became the virus in the system that ultimately led to its destruction. Nevertheless, even before it reached that point, it was still a rocky and turbulent road. One milestone was the forty-eighth anniversary of the secret pact between Adolf Hitler and Joseph Stalin (the Molotov–Ribbentrop Pact), which had paved the way for Soviet annexation of the Baltic states. On 23 August 1987, thousands of demonstrators in the capitals of Latvia, Estonia and Lithuania sang songs of independence and demanded justice for the victims of Stalin's regime.

Various demonstrations broke out in the Baltic states, mostly peaceful, but some leading to clashes with the military and police forces. Popular fronts began emerging a year later in 1988, with Estonia leading the challenge to Soviet supremacy. They gained a significant victory and were able to legalize the flying of the old blue-white-black flag of Estonia, and they declared Estonian the official language of the republic. In the same year, a declaration was adopted by the chairman of the sixth Supreme Soviet of the Estonian SSR, Vaino Väljas, maintaining national sovereignty and legal superiority of Estonian laws over Soviet laws.

In addition, local natural resources were nationalized and not considered the Soviet Union's shared resources any longer. The same treatment was given to industrial facilities, state-run banks, transportation networks and municipal services. Estonia had stood up to the Soviet regime and won a legal, non-violent revolution. Latvia and Lithuania followed the same strategy. In other regions, too, Soviet leadership was losing control: Armenia and Azerbaijan caused turmoil over the Nagorno-Karabakh Autonomous Oblast, rebelling against Soviet direction and fighting among themselves as ethical tensions rose. In the West, Ukraine as well as Moldova demanded more independence. In 1989, the Soviet Union gave in and promised limited democratic control for the first time since 1917.

Not even the finest experts and scholars could have imagined what would follow after the Soviet Union allowed a democratic experiment in Poland. On 23 August 1989, the people of the Baltic states formed the longest human chain ever in the history of Europe. The Baltic Chain or Chain of Freedom consisted of 2 million citizens of Latvia, Estonia and Lithuania. The length of the chain was 370 miles (600 km). The Chain of Freedom was formed on the date of the fiftieth anniversary of the secret pact between Hitler and Stalin, which had led to the occupation of the Baltic states in 1940. After 1 million people marched on the streets in East Germany chanting 'We are the people', the impossible became possible with the fall of the Berlin Wall. The Berlin Wall was one outcome of the Cold War, which had divided East and West Germany. The Wall was now torn apart, and East and West Germany moved a step closer to unification.

The history of the Berlin Wall is worth recounting. At the Potsdam meeting of July–August 1945, Germany had been divided into four zones controlled by the US, Britain, France and the Soviet Union. Berlin fell in the Soviet zone. With France's increasing cooperation, Great Britain and the United States concentrated their efforts on Germany's western zones' economic and political integration. In August 1961, the Soviets sealed off their Berlin sector from the western sectors with barricades erected overnight. The city was simply partitioned down the middle and reinforced by the construction of a 15-metre-high wall designed to prevent any further illegal mass migration from east to west.

Tensions continued till 1964, when the Soviet Union signed a treaty of friendship that, excluding the Berlin issue, offered mutual assistance and cooperation with the German Democratic Republic (GDR). The treaty brought to an end the Berlin crisis, but it resulted in a concrete division of Berlin that mirrored the division of Germany. However, the universal German desire for unity and independence found expression in late 1989. A mass uprising in East Germany rejected the post-war arrangements and brought down the Berlin Wall. The process of unifying the two Germanys began once again.

The fall of the Berlin Wall on 9 November 1989, was the most dramatic event in an extraordinary sequence of incidents that led to the collapse of communism in central and East Europe, finally leading to Germany's unification and the dissolution of the Soviet Union. In the early 1960s, the Wall had been a monument to the brutality of the communist system and diplomacy's failure to resolve Berlin's crisis. The peaceful revolution that led to its collapse was a testament to a few remarkable, courageous people and the thirst for freedom of millions behind the Iron Curtain.

It took only eleven months between the Wall's destruction and the 'day of German unity' when the two Germanys came together formally—West Germany absorbed the GDR into its fold in a historic unification that transformed Germany and Europe. The dynamics and politics of the European Union were changed and soon led to the disintegration of the Soviet Union.

In 1990, an additional six republics left the Soviet Union after popular public elections. Even as Gorbachev's idea of modernized communism failed, the former Soviet states were deciding to eliminate communism once and for all. But old hardliner communists, including Vice President Gennady Yanayev, Prime Minister Valentin Pavlov, Defence Minister Dmitry Yazov, KGB chief Vladimir Kryuchkov and other senior officials, staged a coup during Gorbachev's holiday in Crimea on 19 August 1991. Tanks were aimed at the White House in Moscow. Nevertheless, the Soviet leaders involved in the coup could not gain public support from the people as had been expected.

Thousands of Moscow's citizens came out on to the streets to protect Yeltsin and the White House, the Russian Federation's Parliament and Yeltsin's office. Special forces were deployed, but they did not engage with the public; the revolution was thus defeated. Gorbachev won at the end but lost his political power. Yeltsin took over with a public speech after Gorbachev resigned on 25 December 1991. The official end of the Soviet Union is recorded at 7.32 p.m. Moscow time, with Gorbachev leaving and the Soviet flag lowered for the last time. The flag now raised was the Russian tricolour with its red, blue and white colours. The world was shaken and a new power vacuum allowed the rise of neoliberal ideology and hypercapitalist globalization. As Francis Fukuyama, the American political scientist and writer, said, with the dissolution of the Soviet Union, the last alternative to liberalism had fallen. It was the end of history.

9/11: The Terror

It was on a bright, sunny September day in New York in the late summer of 2001 that the world's profile changed. The implications of 9/11 were immense, and its impact profound. Highly coordinated missions of Islamic terrorists attacked the US and the financial centres of New York, including the defence establishment at the Pentagon, killing almost 3000 people. There were also failed attempts on the White House and Congress. How could such a massive terror attack take place on US soil?

~

At 7.59 a.m., American Airlines Flight 11 took off from Boston's Logan International Airport towards Los Angeles, with ninety-two people on board. Fifteen minutes later, another Boeing 747, United Airlines flight 175, took off with sixty-five people on board, heading from Boston to Los Angeles. Flight 11 was hijacked at 8.19 a.m., as notified by the FBI, through flight attendants who reported to ground services. Nobody expected that there were more airplanes that would soon fall under the control of terrorists. From Dulles International Airport outside of Washington DC, American Airlines flight 77 took off at 8.20 a.m. towards Los Angeles with sixty-four people on board. Four minutes later, on Flight 11, the leader of the terrorists, Mohamed Atta, accidentally contacted ground control while trying to communicate with the people on board. Meanwhile, United Airlines flight 93, delayed by forty minutes, started towards San Francisco.

At 8.40 a.m., the North American Aerospace Defense Command (NORAD) and Northeast Air Defense Sector (NEADS) went on high alert on being notified through the Federal Aviation Administration (FAA) about the possible hijacking of Flight 11. NEADS ordered fighter planes located at Cape Cod's Otis Air National Guard Base to find and follow Flight 11, but they were too late. Before the fighter jets could take off, Mohamed Atta and three other terrorists on Flight 11 crashed the Boeing with full tanks of lethal fuel into the North Tower of the World Trade Center, hitting floors ninety-three to ninety-nine like a bomb. All passengers, the terrorists, the flight crew, and hundreds inside the building, were killed instantly, burnt alive or struck by brutal burns and injuries. It only took seconds for the New York Police Department and Fire Department of New York (FDNY) forces to send in units towards the World Trade Center, around 8.47 a.m. The Port Authority's police officers started evacuating the North Tower. In Sarasota, President Bush, who was visiting an elementary school, was informed that a plane had crashed into the World Trade Center.

It is confirmed that at 9.02 a.m., after initially telling people to stay in the South Tower of the World Trade Center, the Port Authority started evacuating it as well. Around 10,000 to 14,000 people were in the process of leaving the buildings. Unfortunately, just a minute later, United Airlines flight 175 took aim at the World Trade Center's South Tower and crashed into floors seventy-five to eighty-five, killing and burning hundreds of people as the airplane's fuel exploded in a massive fireball over New York. As a result, at 9.08 a.m., all flights to New York City, or moving through the airspace around the city, were banned from taking off. Shortly after, all bridges and tunnels leading to the New York City area were closed by the Port Authority.

On board Flight 77, a new tragedy began to unfold as passengers began reaching out to relatives on mobile phones and alerted them that terrorists had taken control of the aircraft. In his first speech, at 9.31 a.m., President Bush spoke about Florida's events as an 'apparent terrorist attack on our country'. Six minutes later, Flight 77 crashed into the Pentagon in Washington DC, killing fifty-nine people on the plane and around 125 military personnel and civilians inside the Pentagon. The heart of US military strategy and intelligence had been targeted; yet the attack was not over.

Realizing the scope of the assault and the possibility of more attacks, for the first time in US history, all flights going to the US, or flying in US airspace, were redirected or grounded. In all, 3300 commercial flights and 1200 private planes were taken out of air traffic in only 2.5 hours. They landed in other parts of the US as well as in Canada. The tension was running high, and with the unimaginable scale of the attack, rumours spread like wildfire. Authorities took drastic measures, including evacuating the White House, the US Capitol Building and other high-profile structures, public spaces and landmarks.

The drama continued to unfold when at 9.59 a.m., the South Tower of the World Trade Center collapsed, killing and wounding more people and causing chaos in the streets surrounding the area. One can only imagine the tragedy that took place on Flight 93 just eight minutes later. In a brave, selfless and heroic act, crew members and passengers, who had become aware of events in New York, rebelled against the terrorists in a desperate attempt to take back control of the plane and prevent more casualties. They succeeded but the aircraft crashed into a field in Somerset County, Pennsylvania, killing all forty passengers and crew aboard.

At 10.28 a.m., the second tower of the World Trade Center also collapsed. Three hours after the flight took off, Mayor Rudolph Giuliani ordered the evacuation of Lower Manhattan, south of Canal Street. The massive operation included 1 million workers, residents and tourists. On the tragic site, rescue efforts continued through the afternoon in a desperate search for survivors. At 1 p.m., President Bush addressed the US people from the US Air Force base in Louisiana. He made it clear that all US military forces were on high alert throughout the world. By 2.15 p.m. missile destroyers from the US Navy were stationed in New York and Washington DC. Another smaller building, 7 World Trade Center, burning all day and evacuated, collapsed at 5.20 p.m. With the fall of the forty-seven-storey building, rescue forces had to run for their lives.

At 6.58 p.m., President Bush was back in the White House, and at 8.30 p.m. he addressed the nation and spoke for the first time about a war against terrorism. He termed the attacks as 'evil, despicable acts of terror' and argued that America, its allies and friends would stand together to win this new war.

~

With 9/11, the US suffered a collective trauma that will be imprinted in the fabric of American culture for decades if not centuries. The changes since then, now twenty years after the attack, are breathtaking. Today, the US is safer than ever and paradoxically more afraid than ever about terror.

Not only did the aftermath of 9/11 affect millions of people in Afghanistan, Iraq and beyond, it also called into question the fundamental values America was built upon. It buried the dream of the 'end of history' and neoliberal globalization as the only choice, and gave rise to radical Islam on a global scale. The mighty US was shaken to its core. Over the next decade, Muslim minorities in the US, amounting to only 1 per cent of the US population, would suffer from discrimination against their beliefs and way of life. Individual freedom, the core of US culture, was sacrificed for highly sophisticated security measures, culminating in the National Security Agency's (NSA) surveillance scandal that infringed on millions of individuals' privacy. The Department of Homeland Security was set up, wars were fought, and polarization became more and more pronounced in the US and abroad. Secret torture camps, drone attacks on innocent people, war crimes in Afghanistan and Iraq, etc., began eroding the US's core values of freedom and diversity.

The 9/11 terror attack fundamentally changed the United States' approach to the geopolitical landscape. As global terrorism emerged on a new scale and the US was shown to be vulnerable on its soil, President George W. Bush made it clear that it would not differentiate between terrorist groups and nations which harboured or armed them. An axis of evil was identified even before the process of collective mourning could start—the War on Terror had begun. Terror was, perhaps, a response to the US-led unipolar world. Without the Soviet Union, there were no perceived checks and balances. The US became the envy and fear of a few who perhaps felt left out. In the process, Islamic fundamentalists were encouraged and empowered to fight on multiple soils. The battle continues and will define the kind of world we will build.

Rise of Technology

While historical, political and economic realignments merged and the new world order took shape, another event occurred in Murray Hill, New Jersey, that changed human civilization in an even more profound and thorough manner. In 1947, at Bell Laboratories, William Shockley, John Bardeen and Walter Brattain created the first working transistor or semiconductor.

Before long, the transistor impacted various commercial products: first radios, then tape recorders and televisions. Over time, and especially after the development of the microprocessor in the early 1970s, the technology generated by transistors would begin to impact almost every aspect of human life and become pervasive. Over time, transistor-based large-scale integrated circuits and innovative software made satellites possible. TV and telecom were upgraded; smartphones, tablets and laptops were introduced. The Internet, the World Wide Web, data centres, cloud computing, big data, machine learning, image processing, drones and robotics—all these stunning developments began to bring people together in a way the world had not considered possible before.

~

For more than half a century, the United States has been a global economic leader and the seedbed and cradle of innovation and technological progress. For fifty years, it has been unchallenged as the world's creative engine. It can be said that significant innovations and all great inventions have come from there, and little from anywhere else. Path-breaking technologies such as semiconductors, microchips, open-source software, Internet, DNA, genetics, biotech, nanotech, laser, smartphones—practically everything has its origins in the US. This is so because the US has invested hugely in defence, from where technological advances ripple out continuously into the civilian sphere. Besides, the US is blessed with a world-leading research-based education infrastructure: MIT, Stanford, Caltech, Chicago, Harvard, Yale, Princeton, Cornell, Columbia, Berkeley, Michigan and many other prominent private, public and state universities with diversified global talent and creativity.

We are experiencing the most significant period in human history since the invention of language 15,000 years ago. Language connects small communities. New hyperconnectivity is bringing the entire global humanity together. New technologies are bringing comfort, diversity, opportunity and prosperity to the masses. The Internet and the web democratize problem-solving, empower individuals and offer new business models with a unique reach and richness.

The last seven decades have shown that without science and scientists, there can be no progress. The future cannot be predicted without understanding science and technology. Science exists in a framework of truth, trust, reason, rationality, repeatability, reliability and open debate. Science is at the core of our unending curiosity to discover nature and improve human existence. It is not about blind belief in stories and glories of the past, nor about superstition, race, religion, caste, cult, charisma, personality or autocracy. We have seen that science has the power to revolutionize societies, change mindsets and human habits, and transform work and behaviour. I know because science education erased my caste and empowered me to think beyond narrow national boundaries to explore connectivity and its human potential. In the process, I have learnt that the free flow of information and ideas cultivates respect and relationships, leading to prosperity for all.

There is a difference between science and technology. Science is the fundamental knowledge in terms of which the US has been leading for several decades. Technology is about applying science, from which many countries have benefited and delivered the products and services that people want. Technology, like human beings, has a life cycle. It is conceived with an idea in a person's mind which then takes birth as a product or service. As people use it, the technology reaches adolescence. As demand and production increase, technology matures, ages and then enters decay, finally dying a natural death. Each technology goes through this life cycle and has a selfish system with its urges and aspirations. Technology, like nature, is also a tremendous unpredictable force.

Technology is an entry point and not the end point to bring about generational change. Besides technology, what is also required is time, energy, material, money and a skilled workforce for economic and social development. Technology solves many problems and also creates some of its own. It is yet to solve hunger, poverty, violence, health, environmental blunders, etc. But this is partly because the world's best brains are busy solving the problems of the rich, who do not have problems to solve. As a result, the issues of the poor do not get the attention they deserve.

Increasing Inequality

Income inequality has increased substantially in the last seven decades and become a primary global concern. Capitalism has made billionaires, but it has not distributed wealth fairly and equitably. In most countries, a handful of wealthy people control politics and policies. The fifty wealthiest people in the world have more wealth than 50 per cent of the total number of underprivileged people. Many people cannot meet their basic needs to lead respectable and dignified lives. They work long hours and have little to show for savings at retirement. Despite the growth, progress and prosperity worldwide, poverty and hunger remain a global challenge. In India, small farmers can barely feed their families. Youth from rural areas leave their homes to seek jobs in crowded urban cities. Migrant labourers live in slums and hardly make enough to send back savings to their families back home.

Most people around the world feel frustrated and discouraged. They observe the rich and the famous on TV and feel unhappy about their own situation. They also think that working for others in manufacturing or services can never give them the financial security they deserve. People believe that the way to obtain financial comfort is to start a business. Once it is thriving, they become part of a club that focuses on perquisites, privilege and patronage to help create more wealth and grow businesses. Then they hobnob with leaders, politicians and government officers to protect their interests and increase their empires. This cycle continues: the rich become more affluent, and the poor remain poor.

From a global perspective, the situation looks even more tragic now. Today, 2.7 billion people earn less than $2 per day. Eight hundred and ninety million people risk their health drinking dirty water. Two and a half billion people still do not have access to a toilet. Even though we have made some progress, we still have 870 million people going to bed hungry each day, and 2 billion people without electricity. These numbers give a glimpse of how many people are excluded and marginalized in society. Every year, 11 million people die because they do not have enough to eat—this includes newborns, small children, women and senior citizens.

The most important question is how to achieve equality in a world where emerging countries have to repay debt to rich countries, an amount that is estimated to be nine times more than what they have received in aid. Inequality does not depend on financial assets.

We still live in a world where women do not earn the same kind of salaries as men. They are abused, raped and discriminated against. Income inequality is connected to other inequalities related to race, religion, caste, colour, country, etc. The scars of slavery are still seen in many communities. Bonded labour is still practised. Child labour is common in factories in developing countries, as is human trafficking for cheap labour and prostitution.

These practices are a part of the inequality resulting from poverty, hunger and ignorance. In the US, Blacks and Hispanics are victims of discrimination and hate crimes. The US also has the largest percentage of people incarcerated in prisons, of which large numbers are Black and Hispanic. If you grow up in a slum, you are excluded from certain other places and privileges in society. Two hundred and seventy-five million children never attend or complete primary school education. Over 100 million live in slums in dire circumstances. For people growing up in such circumstances, it is almost impossible to climb the social ladder, because they are deprived of even the most basic fundamental needs.

Income inequality is a significant challenge in developed as well as developing countries. For the first time, people feel that their children will not have the same opportunities or lifestyle they have themselves enjoyed in the developed world. The benefits of top-down development have not percolated to the poor. Income inequality is starkly visible in the corporate world, where top management earns 100 times more than shop–floor factory workers. It is even more prominent in the financial services industry, where investment bankers routinely have seven-figure salary packages. Income levels depend on education and college degrees, which are expensive, and only the well-to-do youth can afford to go to good colleges. This further increases the income gap. The cycle of income, education, health and other inequalities continues to favour the rich. If we are to benefit the masses, this cycle must be broken. We have reached a tipping point. Government and society must address inequality as this will be integral to achieve further development, growth, wealth and wellness.

COVID-19: Another Tipping Point

Earlier in this book, I have described the nature and impact of the virus on our planet. Here, I wish to examine the tragedy of this pandemic as a tipping point in the context of our search for a redesign of the world. The need to redesign our world has, in recent times, indeed been recognized by a few individuals and interest groups due to their concerns for the environment, global warming, inequality, poverty, hunger and other pressing issues. However, it has never received adequate attention to initiate a serious public discourse. This suddenly changed from the first quarter of 2020 due to COVID-19, which has affected every country and essentially put our world on a long pause. It has exposed inequality and injustice to the poor and marginalized, and migrant workers across the globe. It has forced people to look inward and ask fundamental questions about life, the meaning of living, our livelihood, relationships, community, work, business, globalization, health, education, governance and politics.

The pandemic has forced us to seek alternatives never imagined before. It feels as if the time to rewrite our history has been forced upon us by nature. It is a crisis that could perhaps bring about the generational change that the world has been waiting for. We have gone too far in ignoring the real needs of our planet and our people. This is the time to put new ideas on the table and initiate new conversations to guide our destiny. Identifying the problem is not good enough. We need ideas with concrete solutions and a road map to redesign our future.

This pandemic has had severe implications on health institutions and infrastructure in every country. Most countries have not been able to keep up with the increasing demand for beds in hospitals and the associated requirements for ICUs, equipment, supplies, health workers, doctors, data science, etc. Destruction and damage of this magnitude have not occurred even during World War II. It was essentially World War III caused by nature against humanity. Instantly, it has become the mega event of the century.

Lessons Worth Reflecting Upon

- COVID-19 is a message from nature that we are all interconnected and interrelated in this world. What affects one of us affects all of us in one way or the other, directly or indirectly.
- In this incredibly complex world, one small invisible, innocuous virus generated at random can spread like wildfire and travel worldwide without a passport or visa to create fear and havoc amongst the entire global population.
- A tiny virus like this has the power to shut down the entire world completely, disrupt the global supply chain, keep everyone at home for long periods and kill many innocent people, very similar to a missile or high-tech weapon.
- The virus and nature in general do not differentiate between people based on nationality, race, religion, colour, caste, profession, sex or age. They also do not distinguish between rich and poor, young and old, rural and urban. The pandemic has suddenly changed the lives of millions.
- COVID-19 has proved the need for governments and communities to work together to save lives. When people see that their lives are in danger due to an external attack, they cooperate and collaborate. The success of the vaccine development around the world, its availability and application has shown how global experts can collaborate in human crises.
- Governments are using technologies for contact tracing, big data, analytics, facial recognition, etc. This has privacy implications. In our efforts to preserve our health, are we going to lose our freedom?
- Will a travel ban, closing national borders and tracking people entering the country, harden our national borders, increase nationalism and restrict people's free movement in the world?

- Medical professionals, doctors and scientists who save lives are heroes and are better role models to follow than millionaires and billionaires.
- People spend their lifetimes chasing material wealth, financial dreams, corporate success, market valuations, power, prestige, etc., without realizing that unprecedented events we have no control over can wipe all that out instantly. No one has a way to retaliate.
- Those of us who had been ignoring close family and friends while working hard to make more money have been forced to spend all our time in quarantine at home. The destructive power of the virus has compelled us to think about our purpose and our priorities on this planet.

Opportunity to Redesign

COVID-19 and its impact on the world have raised many questions about the future world order and its implications on geopolitics, including China's relationship with the world, alternate supply chains, and the need to move production out of China. Interconnected issues have also arisen, such as economics, low-interest rates and debt restructuring. The more comprehensive issues of globalization and localization, the new normal of working from home, the growth of online commerce with supply chain alternatives, the use of the Internet for telemedicine, online education, virtual social groups, etc., are significant issues that have come to the fore. There is a need to re-examine our food habits, health systems, livelihood issues and rights, wet markets, the state of migrant labourers and much more.

The critical questions in the minds of many are: What will the post-COVID-19 world look like? What will change and what will not? What does it mean to be back to normal? What is the new normal? Are we prepared to change? Have we learnt our lessons from this crisis? Is it a turning point in human civilization? What is next? Is it nature's way of showing us we must stop invading and exploiting the environment? A message that we must focus on equality and inclusion? Is it time to value life and livelihood more than material and money?

We must have a collective rethink about what it means to live in these times. What is the new design that will define humanity going forward? What is the global pact that the world must forge? How can a new design be developed and accepted among nations for the planet's collective good and that of the people? Can these goals be accomplished by espousing a parochial outlook centred on national boundaries, narrow self-interests, personal propaganda and greed? If we were to redesign the world now, what should we focus on? Are chasing money, the market, manufacturing and the military as important as human life and our environment? Should we spend more on health infrastructure than defence? Does it make sense to spend more resources on killing people than healing them? Are family and community the key to well-being? What do we do to eliminate poverty, hunger, violence, terror and inequality? What do we do to ensure basic human needs for all? Can we focus on a change for the people's well-being at the bottom of the economic pyramid, rather than on business and trade that only make the rich and powerful even richer at the top? How do we change people's mindsets to be fairer, just, honest, respectful and helpful to fellow human beings? How can we stop competing and start collaborating? How do we address global warming? Is bottom-up development better than top-down? Is more decentralization better for efficient implementation? Should we consume or conserve more? Do we need a new network-based organizational architecture for better governance?

Do we need to restructure the UN, World Bank and IMF? Are these institutions relevant? How do we help Africa? How do we ensure our environment's protection, safety, security, peace, delivery of basic needs, and prosperity for all people?

World War II forced us to redesign our world to bring order and promote peace and prosperity. After seventy-five years, we have another historic opportunity to reset the world and begin the discourse on another redesign. This redesign should consider all the seven mega-events and their associated implications described above to propose a plan to take humanity to the next level. Can we capitalize on the COVID-19 crisis to bring global change agents to initiate new conversations on what is working, what is not working, and what needs to be fixed in our world? Can we also use this crisis to energize and empower our youth to help design this new world to meet their aspirations?

This kind of opportunity comes but once in a century, and forces us to bring global attention to global challenges. The critical question is, what ideas are lying around the table? Unfortunately, most of the time, views and opinions are based on narrow national interests or business, trade, investment, employment and financial benefits. These ideas are based on old power equations with a command-and-control-based mindset that keeps an eye on wealth and resources. Most of these ideas are selfish and have no sense of sacrifice or service for humanity. They also float around with obsolete labels of conservative, liberal, unrealistic, unreasonable, revolutionary, socialist, communist, radical, etc.

These ideas are conceived by our understanding of the Western media–driven narratives and social media–driven sound and video bytes. There is little sympathy or empathy for inequality, injustice, discrimination and diversity. Indeed, the poor have been left behind for decades. It is time to seize this moment of soul-searching and silence forced upon us so that we can begin the new narrative for humanity.

The seven tipping points in the last seventy years have significantly impacted the world design. Decolonization changed the identity, aspirations, dependency and attainments of hundreds of millions of people worldwide. China's rise created a new superpower— it lifted millions from poverty and increased corruption and inequality. The fall of the Soviet Union, while declaring victory for democracy and capitalism over communism and the command economy, eliminated one of the two superpowers and created a unipolar world. The 9/11 attack on the US brought terror, fear and insecurities. Meanwhile, technology has delivered great successes over the seven decades, significantly improving communication, energy, health, education, infrastructure and human comforts. But at the same time, it made the rich richer, while the poor remained poor. Technology has increased inequality the world over.

COVID-19 has given a stern warning to the world that we are all interconnected and interdependent. It forced us to take a long global pause, while it went about destroying our economies, employment, income, institutions and well-being. While in self-quarantine at home, we were forced to think of needs, wants, our purpose in life, mindset, values, wealth, health, roles and relationships. As we think of life after Covid-19, hyperconnectivity offers us a whole new meaning and a new hope for human development, well-being, health, wealth and a novel sociopolitical and economic architecture to help us redesign the world for a better future for the next generation.

3

Redesign the World

'Imagination is more powerful than knowledge. Knowledge is limited. Imagination encircles the world.'

—Albert Einstein

What does it mean to redesign the world now? Is it about a new world order where the powerful and wealthy nations' geopolitical aspirations are propagated and promoted for dominance, trade, finance and minerals, one where the military is at the core? Or is it about a design to ensure a better world for all, with access to opportunities and assured safety, security, peace and justice, along with the potential to democratize education, health and prosperity? Is it about climate change and the better health of our planet and all its species? Or is it about something utopian, romantic, aspirational and ideal but unrealizable? Or again, is it about a more real and just world that can be created in a few decades? The answers to these questions depend on whom we ask and whose interests are at stake.

The redesign of the world means different things to different people. We all have varied backgrounds, with differing understanding, perceptions, values, wisdom, needs and aspirations. In general, political pandits and elites who discuss international issues will emphasize global geopolitical power, American leadership, China's rise, the military, nuclear non-proliferation, climate change, global conflicts, etc. Economists, academicians and business people will look at the new design from the viewpoint of international trade, growth, GDP, GNP, foreign direct investments, employment, manufacturing, services, etc. There are many people out there with varied expertise and experiences, and differing views on what the world needs. A great deal has been discussed and written by domain experts on our challenges and the solutions. However, most of them have taken a narrow view of the trials facing the world. Redesigning the world is complex and difficult to distil into a simple format or formula that can be easily digested, accepted and executed.

We first need to understand and appreciate the design after World War II, in the context of what worked, what did not and what needed to be resolved. As we have seen, the world's design, conceived after World War II, had five main pillars—democracy, human rights, capitalism, consumption and the military. At that time, the world was bipolar, with US democracy and Soviet communism being the two warring ideologies with conflicting priorities. This era was focused on nuclear proliferation, industrial espionage, counter-intelligence and mistrust between the two superpowers.

Seventy-five years on, it is clear that we enjoy world peace, democracy and freedom. We are making tremendous progress mainly because of technology, infrastructure, energy and communication. Democracy has won. Unfortunately, because of populism and divisive politics, narrow interests and exclusion of people from the mainstream, large-scale distortion of facts and erosion of institutions, democracy is under high stress in many countries and they face an uncertain future. Democracy is still a work in progress and needs much more reform to take it to the next level.

Human rights are well-accepted but not delivered, policed or practised in many countries. There are persisting issues affecting inclusion, equality and justice, especially for minorities. Discrimination on the basis of race, religion, caste, colour and economic situation continue to divide communities and create tensions leading to violence. Capitalism has worked well and created substantial growth and prosperity. It has reduced global poverty and created wealth. However, wealth distribution is heavily concentrated in the hands of a very few, thus further dividing people and societies. Consumption has been carried too far and benefits only a few. Overconsumption in some areas has affected our climate, forests and environment to the point where human civilization's survival may be at stake. The military machine diverts too much of our precious resources from the cause of social development, spurred on by false fears of nuclear war and border disputes. Global discussions and dialogues can resolve most of this. Any significant redesign of the world must address all these issues head-on.

The design of the post–World War II world is now obsolete and a fresh approach is needed with a new social, political and economic architecture. We have accomplished a lot, but we could have done much more. We got derailed with our old command-and-control mindset, dominance, military establishments and violence. We continue building warheads and not health systems. We worry about markets and financial systems while we ignore people and poverty. We think top-down and not bottom-up. We do not seek to find sustainable solutions that benefit the poor. We divide people by categorizing and labelling them with our preconceived notions. We build boundaries, not bridges. We design policies to benefit the rich and ignore the hungry and homeless. We promote lies and suppress the truth. We spread hate and hide love. We use religion to separate and not unite.

Now, with hyperconnectivity, we have a global opportunity to change all this quickly. Distance does not matter, nor do time zones, and the opportunities to network and collaborate in the cyber age are limitless. We have new technologies and new tools to work with. We can now deploy innovative models for development and build more inclusive, prosperous and sustainable communities. This is an opportune moment to review and reflect on redesigning our world and taking it forward on a new trajectory. Young people in this world have a lot at stake. They are conscious of climate change and the possibilities of technology. They are progressive with no hang-ups from old-fashioned mindsets. They want peace and prosperity for all. They are willing to share and sacrifice. To redesign the world is to call for action, especially for the youth. It is a call for them to unite and demand a better future for humanity. It is a new vision that they can act upon and use to become empowered.

Today, our most vital requirements are democracy, freedom, dialogues, discussions, collaboration and cooperation. When powered by new technologies, innovations, business, trade, transport and communication, this strategy has an excellent opportunity to become successful. However, what has taken a back seat are the principles of inclusion, equality, justice and trust; the current framework does not ensure income distribution, decentralization, food security, education, health and housing for all. Unfortunately, peace, prosperity, justice and opportunities have not reached many people in this world. Millions live in conflict zones or are discriminated against, trapped and isolated. Similarly, millions are willing to risk their lives to migrate to developed countries for better opportunities.

Like the UN, IMF and World Bank, international institutions have not delivered results to people at the bottom of the economic pyramid. The vices of greed, corruption, lies, ego and violence, along with the complicated procedures set up by the bureaucracy, sometimes under the control of incompetent, selfish and power-hungry leaders, come in the way. Their only focus is on narrow personal interests instead of broad public interest with a commitment to public service. We need policies and policing to address the real concerns of people at the bottom of the economic pyramid. They are required in all countries, developed and developing. Unfortunately, the essence of freedom and empowerment in improving the quality of life in this age of connectivity has not been fully appreciated by the global leadership. This needs to be addressed and resolved. Today, it is possible to address such complex global challenges since we now live in an economy of surplus and not one of scarcity. We can now produce anything, and as much as we need, and we decide what and when to produce. If we develop consensus and political will, we can mobilize global domain experts and resources to resolve complex global problems together. I believe anything is possible if we put our hearts, minds, technology and talent to make it happen. There is enough goodwill in this world to change our present course, provided we collectively agree on what we want to do and where we want to go in 2021.

American Vision

At present, there are two competing and contradictory visions of the world: American and Chinese. The American vision of the world is based on the continuation of the World War II design, emphasizing democracy, freedom, capitalism and balance of power to move towards a new world order with multiple power centres. However, the American model has always been based on identifying the enemy. Earlier it was the Soviet Union. When the Soviet Union dissolved, and after 9/11, a unipolar American vision of the world got blurred. It was diverted towards internal security and financial crises. In the process, America achieved robust economic recovery with vital digital platform companies that influence public opinion and the global information order. Now that America has identified a rising China as the new enemy, it is believed that America will again try to reinforce American global leadership.

This will at first require a focus on strengthening internal democracy and related national and international institutions. America will have to convince the global community to rely on it to promote capitalism and freedom and to fuel global growth. Besides democracy and freedom, the American vision is deeply rooted in military and financial power. It is predominantly based on the command-and-control architecture of various trade groups like the North American Free Trade Alliance (NAFTA) with Canada and Mexico, the Asia–Pacific or APAC, the European Union (EU) and other energy resource alliances. Besides, in its bid to promote broader interests, America continues to depend on aggression and wars to resolve conflicts in strategic locations like Iraq, Libya, Syria and Afghanistan. This will have to be moderated in the future by opening a dialogue with Iran and other inimical countries with a concession to accommodate local power centres.

US influence and its ambitions concerning the EU, Latin America, Asia and the Middle East will remain fundamental to the design of the country in the next phase. To balance a rising China, the US may enhance trade, military and political relations with democratic India, Mexico and others. The American vision is to continue leading the world with its military strength, technology, finance and trade relations. At the core of this vision is the thought: 'What is good for America and American values?' The world has nearly accepted the American vision as an aspirational goal. American culture and lifestyle are now well-received and desired by many.

Unfortunately, it is unrealistic to expect that the American way of life and its income, institutions and infrastructure will benefit the rest of the world. It is not geared to address climate change or poverty and hunger issues, and will generate considerable pressure on our planet. It has not yet moved in the direction of ensuring education and health for the people at large. America is also not designed to address the challenges facing Africa. It is essentially focused on trade, technology, security, cyberwar and the rise of China.

The US design is based on preserving and promoting its own interests while aiming at international leadership and maintaining global peace and order along with its value systems. Unfortunately, governments in the developing world resent America because even while pursuing democracy and freedom, the American administration treats them as unequal partners. It is a part of the institutional culture of Washington DC. The US is used to sitting at the head of the table to dictate its terms. This makes it difficult to network or develop a shared vision with other countries—attributes essential in a multipolar world.

For example, during the Obama administration, we worked with several countries on an open government platform that the US and India had jointly developed. In our first meeting in Washington DC, we agreed to share the podium with various governments. The US administration's immediate recommendation was to set up independent committees to monitor progress in each country. India suggested that each participating country's goal should be aspirational and should therefore not be monitored. The US insisted; consequently, India decided not to participate in the task of monitoring other countries. In general, the rich believe that if they fund, they should have the right to monitor. This must change in the future.

The US is perceived to be relinquishing global leadership as it is not actively participating in international institutions. Its withdrawal from the principle of climate control and the World Health Organization (WHO) sent strong signals to the global community, signalling that America is pulling back and others must step in to fill the vacuum and preserve the current world order. With the new Biden administration, this has changed. The world needs leadership on multiple fronts and forums to continue global conversations on peace, conflicts, trade and development. The world also needs leadership to articulate a coherent vision of global connectivity and the Internet to improve governance, public service and the quality of life for people in the developing world. Similarly, institutions and infrastructures in Asia, Africa and Latin America must be assisted in coping with growing populations, changing aspirations and increasing demands.

The world community wants the US to have the required vision to reform the UN, World Bank, IMF, WHO, etc., or create new global institutions to reflect the needs of the twenty-first century. The lack of US leadership on critical global issues is seen as a sign of US weakness and withdrawal, a symptom of its fragmentation, self-centredness, confusion, contradictions, and its tendency to look inward. Yet, people still desire America to lead the world. The free world believes in America and would like it to show the way forward. It has the required talent, technology, framework and resources. However, it will have to accept the new reality of a multipolar world and the associated need to build strong coalitions going forward.

Chinese Vision

China's vision is based on its rising economic prosperity over the last three decades and its standing as the global manufacturing base and substantial foreign exchange reserve. It is a vision driven by the Communist Party and China's leadership to bring back the glory of the past when China was the world's largest economy. The vision is also to build a new silk road to increase trade with various countries. It is all about expanding the Chinese economy and military presence in the world. China's vision of the world order is to replace US dominance in technology, trade and finance with Chinese capabilities and finance.

The Chinese vision is fundamentally based on the doctrine of the central authoritarian Chinese Communist Party. To advance global power, China is focused on six key issues: control of Hong Kong's democracy movement; Taiwan's inclusion as a part of the one–China policy; control of the South China Sea through military presence; trade war with the US; the Belt and Road Initiative (BRI) to fund ports, dams and other major projects in various countries of interest; and the ongoing disputes with its neighbour India on a 3500-km border in the east and the Himalayan front. It should be recognized that China is not rising in a vacuum. There are other countries like India, Australia, South Korea, Vietnam, etc., which are also growing at the same time.

After World War II, the rise of the Asian Tigers, Japan, Korea, Taiwan, Hong Kong and Singapore, attracted US investment and technology for rapid development. These countries were relatively small, were aligned to US interests, and followed global rules to keep the balance of power intact. Later, China motivated and mobilized US companies to move their manufacturing capabilities to China to capitalize on cheap labour, reduce costs and increase profits. Cheap labour came from hundreds of millions of migrant workers from rural areas known as 'nongmingong'; they were controlled by a registration document known as 'hukou' that defined their contracts and benefits. This was possible because China is administered very differently. It is a communist country, run by a strong central party organization and leadership with complete control over 1.5 billion people. China followed policies that limited access to local markets and forced American and Western companies to transfer technology. In the process, over the last three decades, China built world-class universities, research institutions, modern factories, indigenous capabilities and robust local markets. Simultaneously, it also built up strong military power. As a result of China's rise, the Eurasian continent has become a new integrated trade zone and familiar ground for creativity, innovation and recent development models.

The Asian Tigers now depend more on China and less on the US. This critical region has now drifted from the US model to the Chinese trade, finance and development model. Chinese presence and influence are not restricted to the Eurasian region, and are instead extended to Africa, Latin America, South Asia, Europe and almost every corner of the globe.

To expand Chinese presence and power, China announced the BRI in 2013 to fund and implement a series of infrastructure projects in several strategic countries to influence geopolitics and create a Chinese supply chain. This strategy, inspired by the old Silk Route that once used to connect East and West, has nearly enabled them to compete with the US and the West. The Silk Route was central to the extensive interchange of people and products between various tribes in the region between the second century BCE and the eighteenth century. It connected China, India, the Middle East, Africa and Europe for economic and cultural activities.

The plan is to revive that route to fund and build modern infrastructure, including roads, bridges, dams, power plants, ports and mobile facilities. The purpose is apparent: to enhance the economic and military power of the Chinese Communist Party. Among other strategic decisions, it includes building ports in Sri Lanka and Pakistan by providing low interest loans and to export products to the Middle East and Europe. The US, India and other countries have shared their concerns over the BRI.

As a part of the BRI, a controversial dam is being built on the Indus River in the Kashmir region, disputed territory between India and Pakistan. The safety of a 270-metre-high roller-compacted dam in an earthquake-prone zone, and its impact on the environment, is of great concern to experts. If the dam bursts, it will have a hydrogen-bomb-like destructive power to destroy everything in the region. However, China has convinced Pakistan to take a loan in excess of $10 billion to build the dam.

There are several similar large projects that China has conceptualized as part of the BRI to keep Chinese industry dominant and Chinese money circulating. It initiated and launched the Asian Infrastructure Investment Bank in 2016, headquartered in Beijing, as a multilateral development bank to support the building of infrastructure in the Indo-Pacific region. It also became an active participant in all major strategic international organizations by increasing funding and systematically installing its officers in important decision-making positions.

China has been preparing to consolidate political power on multiple fronts for over a decade. It started with land reclamation in the South China Sea to advance its territorial claims, control the waters, and open up optical fibre routes. This has annoyed the US and several other countries in the region which consider Chinese control of the island as a violation of international law.

There was previously hardly any Chinese presence at the International Telecom Union, the oldest UN organization. But in the last twenty-five years, China has been occupying senior positions and enhancing its telecom industry interests in standards, equipment and manufacturing. Companies like Huawei did not exist thirty years ago. Now, Huawei is the largest global telecom equipment manufacturer with an undisputed leadership in 5G mobile wireless systems. Simultaneously, by actively participating in all high-profile international forums, China is attempting to dilute its dubious record on human rights. It is also curbing the Hong Kong democratic movement while promising freedom at the same time. Taiwan is another issue of concern for China; it wants Taiwan to unite with it as per the One China Policy. Meanwhile, China also has an ongoing border dispute with India along their shared 3500-km border. The US is monitoring all these issues with a great deal of strategic interest to maintain undisputed global leadership.

China is equally interested in a viable alternative to the US dollar as the only international currency of choice in global trade. Today, all international financial transactions are carried out in US dollars on a unique financial technology network to securely, safely and swiftly handle trillions of dollars. China wants to increase global trade in yuan and has announced an ambitious programme to launch a digital currency of its own to replace the dollar trade. There are also others like Bitcoin in the digital currency business. However, unless digital currency is backed by a significant government like China, it is difficult to make a dent in the dollar trade.

China is seen as the new enemy and national security threat by many in America. They believe that the Chinese plan to dominate the world markets, military and technology is evident in the Chinese

Communist Party's programmes to fund and systematically back prominent Chinese companies to steal US intellectual property, replicate products and services, and then replace the US in the international markets. There are several notable examples of Chinese industrial espionage in US universities, technology, manufacturing and markets. Many Chinese students come to the US, work in the laboratories, establish contacts and then go back to work for the government or companies owned by the Chinese Communist Party. This is of concern in the US. The real concern is about the Chinese ambition to turn back the clock on democracy, freedom and liberty through a new world order dominated by it.

These two competing visions of the world predominantly focus on their national interests—which is only natural—to expand global markets for their products and services. At the same time, while preserving international peace and order, they also wish to enhance their control, power and prestige. This has been the history, pattern and practice of all global powers: Roman, Egyptian, Ottoman, Chinese, Persian, Mogul, French, German, Dutch, Spanish, Portuguese, British and other empires. They expanded due to their traditional tribal mentality of violence and wars to grab others' resources by force and enjoy victory, wealth, control and privileges. They promoted and practised slavery, loot, crime, conflicts, violence, killing and wars to gain power and build wealth. This mindset has continued for centuries. Even now, countries align, invest and at times even invade to control natural resources. Unfortunately, this perspective, based on dominance, power, trade and control, has no space for humanity.

We may have avoided another major world war for over seventy-five years, but we are also building substantial military complexes and nuclear warheads as deterrents. With the recent rise in hyperconnectivity, satellites, scanning, image processing and other related technologies, all countries' military assets are open, transparent and visible all over the world. We have learnt to develop coalitions and consensus with built-in checks and balances, and to avoid major global conflicts. Besides, we also have the new light weapon technologies of drones, robotics, biowarfare, etc., to fight future battles very differently. The key takeaway is that, finally, we seem to have matured as a civilization to avert major global conflicts and wars that have traditionally destroyed a large part of humanity.

With substantial improvement in the overall quality of life and communications worldwide, we have learnt to respect human life, share knowledge, avoid confrontations, resolve conflicts, share resources and look at broader public interest issues. We are learning ways to advance peace better than ever before. In this new environment, geopolitics could become irrelevant. The need to invade any country to grab precious resources does not make sense today because countries can enter into trade. For cheaper labour, there are multiple options with multiple incentives from many countries. In a sense, all the methods of the past have become obsolete.

This is the time to look at a world redesign beyond the narrow national interests of America or China, one which would serve the best interests of the planet and the people. The future is not only about national pride, business, markets, religion or race, with the bogey of an enemy at the border; it is about climate change and human development. Now is the time to move from violence and military options to non-violence and the imperative of peace. This will require collaboration, as opposed to confrontation and competition. It may be all right to compete in certain areas. Still, it is more important to cooperate on strategic issues related to the planet and the people of the world. Here, political leadership matters. Suppose world leaders do not come together at this crucial moment. In that case, we will indeed be riding a path to permanent destruction.

Global leaders need to recognize that the future belongs to globalists and not nationalists. It is not about an international liberal order, but global peace and prosperity for all. It is about empowering every human being to explore and experience life and nature in their own way, with freedom and flexibility. This will require respect, sharing, caring and teamwork among world leaders. It will demand a functional and friendly relationship between world powers. The redesign of democracy, capitalism, environment and institutions is not going to be simple. It will require a deeper understanding and appreciation of human values and our character, and addressing climate change issues with the spirit of sacrifice and long-term perspectives. It will also need the collaboration of communist leaders from China and Russia, monarchs from the Middle East, and others. I have great faith in humanity, and I believe we have evolved to a point where we can change the course of human history by redesigning the world for the next era of non-violence, peace and prosperity for all.

The Third Vision

We essentially need a 'third vision' of the world that transcends national interests and takes into account global issues, from trade to environmental impacts. We need a vision that values human capital more than financial capital. A vision that works for everyone to attain a multipolar world, where people at the bottom of the economic pyramid benefit the most. We need to ask the world's people: Do they want to live forever with poverty and hunger, with inequality and unemployment, under the shadow of discrimination and fear, with the police at every corner and the military at all borders? Or do they want to live in peace with friendly neighbours, in a clean environment, and with respect, dignity, equality, opportunities and hope for all? The present reality is scary. Don't we want to change it?

We do not want just the 'open' vision of America or the 'closed' vision of China. We want a third vision of the world where America is open to engagement, and China is engaged in openness. We want a reset of the world so that we can redesign it. We want to reset international interests over national interests, human diversity over human differences, globalism over nationalism, inclusion over exclusion, non-violence over violence, rationality over religion, and respect over race. We want international cooperation on climate change, global health, poverty, hunger, violence, security, amity with neighbours and much more.

I firmly believe that it is possible to redesign the world with this third vision because multiple, intricate and timely technologies with incredible innovations in information, genetics, bio, nano and material sciences are now all coming together. They are taking deep roots across the social, political and economic landscape, which will profoundly impact our livelihood and longevity. This will give new meaning to life, work, values, wisdom and progress. It will lead to a new development model based on cooperation, collaboration and communication, which can finally deliver peace, justice and prosperity to all by the middle of this century.

We are so used to thinking and behaving traditionally with our narrow compartmentalization of people and their ideas, values and experiences. We always tend to look at past experiences and our history to find solutions. We find pleasure in the past, comfort in the present, and fear for the future. The future is prosperous with new bold ideas and different toolkits, such as hyperconnectivity, which did not exist earlier. The future demands a new mindset with creativity, innovation and courage. I firmly believe that we are at a crossroads because of hyperconnectivity. We must think very differently to redesign the global organizational architecture. Only with this can we achieve new goals and growth for humanity's sake. Connectivity is the key to break our past, transcend our present, and build bridges to network for the future.

Recently, a bright young friend of mine showed me a new dimension to global power and conflicts with a different perspective to what I had visualized. He opened my eyes to religion's essential role in society's organizational architecture and its associated conflicts and wars. There are basically four significant religions globally which mobilize the masses and organize power: Christianity, Islam, Hinduism and Buddhism. All significant conflicts, wars and invasions have been carried out predominantly by the big powers like the Romans, Ottoman, Moguls, British Empire, etc., to expand power, influence, control and wealth. He argued that the concept of time for Christianity and Islam is absolute: you live, and you die.

On the other hand, the concept of time for Hinduism and Buddhism is infinite: you continue through rebirth for another cycle. He feels this may have something to do with the idea of accumulating wealth and power in one lifetime. He also pointed out that the wars in Pearl Harbor, Korea and Vietnam were rare wars between Christianity and Buddhism. The ongoing conflicts in Syria, Afghanistan, Iraq, Libya and others are wars between Christianity and Islam. 9/11 may be considered a blow by Islam against the only superpower in the world.

Many people feel that global diversity is not represented at the UN Security Council. Why is Islam, which includes in its fold 1.3 billion people, not at the table? Neither is India, with almost 1 billion Hindus. My friend emphasized the fact that power likes to hide behind religion. To me, that made a lot of sense. In my heart, I am Hindu, Muslim, Christian, Jew, Buddhist, Sikh, Jain, atheist and a lot more. To me, all religions inculcate fundamental human values and promote goodness in people. Perhaps it is obvious, but when you put these things in perspective, it is clear that the challenge going forward will be to build bridges with all religious organizations and associated power centres, provided they have genuine respect for each other with a commitment to peace, prosperity and non-violence. Only by doing this can we together take humanity to the next level.

Bold and brave ideas are essential for driving our new world vision now. Unfortunately, we have always looked for solutions in the economy and the market, technology, military or ideology— we have never explored humanism in our quest for solutions. First, we must understand, appreciate and internalize the simple fact that our planet is a unique interconnected and integrated system where soil and sand, birds and insects, animals and people are all interdependent. We live off the same system of air, water, flowers and forests. Peace, the economy, the environment and health issues are also interconnected and interrelated. The key is to strive for unity with respect, equality and equity for all living systems.

We have to ask what belongs to whom on our planet. Who owns the Amazon forests? Do they belong to Brazil or to the world? Should we all not be concerned about what happens to the Amazon? Our rivers? Our oceans? What affects one affects all of us. What happens to Africa in the next twenty-five years will affect America, China, India and the entire world. We need to think from the viewpoint of biology, life and dynamic assets, and not merely markets or material and static assets. We must remember that the concept of modern states and national borders began only recently. We may live within boundaries and borders, but we must think beyond them with an eye out for humanity at large. The best way to understand what is right for society, the world and the future is to ask young people what they want. They will tell you that they wish to have love, a clean environment, home, education, health, family, friends and fun. They do not want violence, war, power or riches. The answers are simple. We make it complicated.

We need to go beyond national interests with a clear focus and commitment to improving the two most important things that matter: our planet and our people. It is not too complicated to understand and appreciate this fact. However, we require a visionary and charismatic leader with a high sense of morality to network with world leaders and mobilize world opinion.

Our planet has a lot more life and complexity than its people. It can survive without people, but people cannot survive without a healthy planet. Our priority during the world's redesign has to be to improve our planet's health and make it more clean, diverse, prosperous and sustainable, a place where each plant and form of life can flourish and live to its fullest potential. This means improving our environment, soil and air, water, sea, rivers, flora and fauna, mines, minerals, genetic pool and much more. It is a massive task because in the last seventy years we have systematically damaged our environment under the pressure of industrialization, urbanization, and unplanned growth. We have overexploited our forests, fish, mines and minerals for quick monetization and made little effort to replenish resources.

Climate change is a global concern that deserves a lot more attention from international and local political leaders. We have been burning too much coal for too long to meet our energy needs, thus increasing temperatures globally. Scientists have studied global warming extensively and made recommendations on what needs to be done. It is time to listen to them carefully and thoughtfully, and mobilize global resources to improve the planet's health. To do this, we also require bottom-up development that respects local climates, talent, designs, customs, food, genetic pool, etc. The key is to put an end to over-exploitation of natural resources by not building huge dams, not damaging our extensive forests, not eliminating wildlife, and not destroying our coral reefs. This will demand close attention to preserving the earth's natural heritage, biodiversity, medicinal plants and the animal kingdom. The key is to focus on our need to conserve and not consume and destroy our environment blindly. This requires a different mindset that looks at the planet as a treasure to preserve it for the next generation, without abusing and overusing it. We need collective leadership and substantial investments to ensure a better environment for our grandchildren.

Humans on earth are unique because we can walk, talk, read, write, think and create things from natural resources. We work to increase comforts and explore new frontiers with curiosity and courage, investigating nature and creating new opportunities. This also places significant responsibilities on us to take care of the planet, environment, other species and each other. Just 150 years ago, life was dull, dark and boring without electricity, TV, cars, jets, smartphones and many other gadgets that we take for granted in 2021. We are indeed living in the best time in human history. Unfortunately, we are still unhappy and have a lot of work ahead of us. Despite all the technologies and tools, we have a long way to go to create the quality we need for a quality planet. We are all different because of our genetic make-up, race, colour, religion, caste, health, education, upbringing, job, experience, location, exposure and a lot more. Each one of us is wired to be unique, diverse and to think differently. We make our communities, cities and societies. We spend billions of dollars on six sigma quality products but do not spend enough on improving the quality of our people. For example, almost 1 per cent of people in the US are in prison. Why? Because a person's character, values and quality dictate the quality of life in their community and country.

Today, people are losing confidence in their governments, justice systems, police and large corporations. The consequences of global warming, multiple economic downturns, lack of job opportunities, the absence of personal financial security, and the void in moral and ethical leadership in politics and business has made many people unhappy. There is a sense that capitalism has made the rich richer, the middle class poor, and the poor helpless. It has not delivered benefits to those at the bottom of the economic pyramid. Corporations have betrayed them by going after profits and not caring for workers and local communities.

Many people are feeling isolated, alienated and helpless, and some have resorted to drugs and violence. Others lie, cheat and steal to survive. To deal with these challenges, we require a more significant commitment to humanity, human values and social virtues. We need substantial improvements in everyone's overall quality of life and also a commitment to truth, trust, love, simplicity, courage and concern for the community. We need more people who respect inclusion, diversity, love, ethics and morals, which will help us help each other. We cannot depend on governments or businesses to solve all our problems. Local issues will have to be solved at the local level. With new technology and tools, human society should restructure, reorganize and decentralize public service, and ultimately eliminate the police, the army and the military to maintain social order, peace and harmony. To redesign the world, we require a laser-like focus on humanism and human development. To promote this idea globally, we need a large number of domain experts, change agents, innovative leaders and champions with the necessary compassion, empathy and courage to change the mindset of people and affirm that 'family and love matters, and that development is not about financial profits, but about the well-being of our people, our communities and our planet'.

George Floyd, an African American from Minneapolis, became an instant change agent of the first order leading towards better inclusion and police reforms in the US. It all started because of a video recorded by a stranger on the street showing 'the white knee on the black neck', as he was begging for help to breathe. The image with Floyd saying 'I cannot breathe' went viral instantly and became the voice of the people. He died on the spot. There are several recent examples of police brutality by White officers against young Black people in the US. However, this event was highlighted because it touched the soul of America. It was evident in the video that the arrogant White policeman had no mercy to allow the man to breathe so he could stay alive. US cities were lit on fire. People were furious because the fact of such treatment being meted out to poor Black people in America is not acceptable in today's times. But it has been going on for too long.

The death of George Floyd made a lot of people worldwide realize it was time to do something. Within days, there were demonstrations in all major cities around the world. At the same time, people realize that we need restraint, reconciliation, and peaceful perseverance to solve the Black–White divide and other racial issues. This type of discrimination is not unique to America. It is everywhere. In India, Dalits and Untouchables are discriminated against to a point where they cannot enter places of worship or access water resources. How can humans in this day and age discriminate and divide people based on their appearance, colour, caste, race and religion?

At about the same time when people in American cities were demonstrating in the Black Lives Matter campaign, 10,000 miles away in many cities in India, 100 million migrant workers were forced to walk back home. They had lost their livelihood in the cities due to the COVID-19 lockdown. With little children, pregnant women and ageing parents in tow, and just a bag of belongings, these labourers had no savings, no transport, no food— only a desire to get back home. Some walked for hundreds of miles in the heat and dust, even without shoes. It was heartbreaking to see their journeys home.

Like the images of George Floyd dying on a road in the US, the pictures of Indian migrant labourers dying a slow death while walking for days were equally dismaying and poignant. It took time for the government to react and respond; migrant workers are too poor to have a voice. Rich and well-to-do people in Indian cities were safe and secure. Most had little interest in helping the poor people who had built homes, roads, bridges, factories and cities for them, or who served them in the capacity of helpers, cooks, drivers and guards. The migrant workers were rendered jobless, useless, homeless and penniless. How can we tolerate the mistreatment of fellow human beings like this? These two images of a Black man's treatment in prosperous America and the millions of poor migrants in India's growing urban cities raised many fundamental questions about democracy, freedom, inclusion, basic human needs, the nature of our economy and consumption.

The third vision of the world must respond to real challenges faced by the people and the planet, not the needs and aspirations of America, China or any other country, or a group of rich and famous countries. It must address global and human issues related to inclusion and the problems of lack of access to basic needs, security and safety, climate change, environment and wars. It must give a voice to those at the bottom of the economic pyramid and ensure their respect and dignity. The redesign of the world has to be based on an in-depth synthesis of global challenges seen from the people's perspective. There needs to be a basic understanding of what needs to be set right and what people want. Simultaneously, it has to be as simple and effective as the final design after World War II. It has to be brave and borderless. It also has to be evolutionary and not revolutionary, while maintaining deep connectivity and continuity with the past. To keep a focus on the planet and the people, we must essentially work on sustainability and inclusion. These two platforms must define the future of humanity going forward.

Five New Pillars

I have been thinking about these issues for over seven years. I have tried to distil my observations, experiences, feelings, values and wisdom into coming up with five new pillars, like that of a pentagon, that we can follow for the world's redesign: inclusion, human needs, new economy, sustainability/conservation and non-violence. These five new pillars augment the previous design of the post–World War II world, and will help us move to the next level systematically and logically, without breaking away from the past. It provides a logical extension of where we are at present and what has been accomplished in the last seventy-five years. However, it is not a linear expansion or extrapolation, but a radical departure from the unipolar to the multipolar, along with networking the world with a clear eye on human development and fulfilment.

The world's new design is not about left or right, capitalism or socialism, democracy or communism, western or eastern, north or south, but essentially about a radically new form of humanism. It is fundamentally about sustainability and inclusion. In this design, the people and the planet are at the core of all ideologies and actions, emphasizing science, technology, a rational approach, logical thinking and a new mindset. This is the only way we can envision a new world order that works for all of humanity.

Inclusion

Democracy must be restored, respected and elevated to include all human beings all over the world. Unfortunately, all democracies are not inclusive. The US must approach with empathy the issue of inclusion in the matter of Blacks, Latin Americans, the poor and the homeless. In India, the same attention must be paid to the situation of Dalits, tribals, minorities, slum dwellers and the poor. In Europe, it is about migrants and minorities. In China, it is about the rural poor and the Uyghurs. Latin America must care for its indigenous people. Every country must provide dignity, respect, equality and access for the poor and minorities to effectively implement an inclusive society.

Human Needs

Human rights are essential. We now live in an economy of surplus. We can produce enough food to feed everyone and create enough facilities to improve living standards, but these are not accessible to everyone. We must strive to provide basic minimum requirements to every human being on the planet, including food, shelter, education and health. We have the technology, investments, logistics and required capabilities to accomplish this. But do we have the political will?

New Economy

We must uplift the present capitalism model to a regenerative and circular economy based on decentralization, localization, indigenous talent, networking and equitable distribution of wealth. This will require rethinking globalization to save labour costs, optimizing financial returns, building human capital, avoiding the formation of substantial multinational corporations, eliminating conspicuous consumption and reformulating global supply chains.

Conservation and Sustainability

The emphasis on consumption has caused some people to abandon their civic responsibilities; this, in turn, has eroded democracy. Capitalism has morphed into an endless demand for the continuous growth-at-all-costs machine, contributing heavily to the environment's destruction. The focus on conservation includes climate change, global warming, the environment and durable rather than disposable products.

Non-violence

We need to move from the current military–industrial complex designed to wage wars that kill people to a structure that maintains peace and provides safety and security. This will require us to slowly defund militaries the world over and divert substantial investments towards security, health and human development. It is time to spend more on saving lives than killing people.

~

We want democracy for all on all matters, which will assure inclusion of all on all issues. We want to convert human rights to actual human needs. We want to redesign capitalism for a new regenerative economy to benefit local communities everywhere. We want a new, meaningful and not meaningless consumption. We need to conserve and manage our global resources, including water, forests and minerals, to improve our planet's health.

We want to focus on decentralization for speedy development with a bottom-up and circular approach instead of top-down. We do not need huge factories with foreign investments to scale and increase our GDP. We want small local plants to network to scale, to benefit local talent and local resources. We want to capitalize on the local genetic pool and organic farming to grow local food. We want to preserve local art, culture, language, food and festivals. At the same time, we also aspire to be global. In a sense, we want to be global and local at the same time. We do not want to produce only for the rich who can afford to buy. Nor do we want to make it only for export. We want to produce for local people who need it. We want local markets to develop global aspirations. We want new thinking and new theories in politics, economy, human rights and human development. We need to develop new markets, and to reform and repurpose manufacturing and management. We need inspiring leadership and new paradigms in business, trade, community development, and more.

This new pentagon to redesign the world would require a new narrative and a distinctive global conversation to network with change agents worldwide. We need to develop a consensus on innovative ideas that can be communicated and socialized at various levels and initiate mega changes. This will also require a new organizational architecture at national and international levels to implement the five new pillars of the redesign of the world and execute them at various levels. These are complex, challenging, complicated and demanding tasks mainly because, in the future, it will change the way the environment is protected and people are empowered. Power and wealth are shared and distributed more equitably. Thus, we can be enabled to take care of our planet and our people at large.

4

Inclusion

'Our ability to reach unity in diversity will be the beauty and the test of our civilization.'

—M.K. Gandhi

Inclusion is at the core of human respect, rights, dignity and development. Inclusion is about welcoming, accepting and encouraging people with diverse backgrounds, preferences and practices to participate as equal partners in progress and prosperity. It is a complex issue connected to personal identity—it is related to age, gender, race, religion, ethnicity, disability, sexual orientation, appearance, skin colour, income, education, nationality, language and so much more. It is also connected to access and opportunities related to education and health, housing, employment and income, along with financial services, safety and security—all these concerns are interwoven with political power, progress and prosperity.

The lack of inclusion is rooted in prejudices resulting from human diversity and differences. Exclusion affects the individual and society in many different ways. It has an effect on the individual's self-esteem, confidence, respect and dignity. It retards collaboration, access and progress. To understand and appreciate the pain caused by exclusion, one has to enter the mind of a person who has been discriminated against and been deprived and denied rightful and deserving opportunities. Exclusion leaves a scar that goes deep through generations of people in the family and the community. Empathy, and not just sympathy, is needed to understand the predicament of people who are suffering the ill effects of exclusion.

Inclusion also includes coexistence with nature and humanity. It is about living in harmony with birds, animals, trees and fellow human beings, and co-creating an environment that celebrates energy, expectations and enthusiasm for life. Inclusion evaporates ego, anger and jealousy, and builds relationships that enable us to collaborate, cooperate, excel and partake in the journey together. It is about sharing and caring for one another. Inclusion is concerned with a better planet and ensuring equal opportunities for all.

Unfortunately, exclusion has often been a reason for significant conflicts, violence and wars. Even today, most of our global conflicts result from the lack of inclusion, equality and equity. Despite all this, the principle of inclusion often gets only lip service and hardly finds a place on the global agenda. When world leaders meet, they never deliberate on questions of inclusion and the creation of an inclusive world. They always draw boundaries and divide people selfishly to benefit from markets and military machines. Today, inclusion is a large part of the unfinished agenda of democracy and justice—it deserves immediate global attention so that we can build a more equitable and just society.

The challenge is to take democracy towards inclusion—the first pillar in the world's redesign—by ensuring that every human being is treated equally and given the chance to advance on a par with all others. Most democratic countries do not even have fundamental gender equality. In the male-dominated political and business world everywhere, women are not given enough seats at the table to participate in leadership and decision-making roles. Ask women in Japan, India and the US, and they will tell you the same. How do we expect these countries to deliver inclusion to women, minorities, immigrants and others? We have a long way to go to build a genuinely inclusive society. When that happens, poverty and violence will disappear, and peace and prosperity will prevail. Today, most countries are faced with significant challenges to bring equity and justice to women, the middle class, the poor and the marginalized.

Caste in India

India is not an inclusive nation, mainly because of the old caste system, which has divided people into over 1000 castes, setting out their life's trajectory on the basis of the profession they inherit. There are four main varnas or caste categories: Brahmins, who are traditionally priests, known for spirituality; Kshatriyas, the warriors; Vaishyas, the tradespeople; and Sudras, who are at the bottom of the caste ladder. Unfortunately, Untouchables and Dalits are considered beneath even the fourth caste. The historical origins of these prejudices give them credibility in present times. This is the reason why Dalits are perceived as inferior. They form that large share of the Indian population formerly known as Untouchables whose presence was considered so polluting that contact with them was to be avoided at all cost. Some categories of Untouchables till today are not allowed to enter temples or drink water from a common source. Dalits have been historically fighting for their identities and rights and demanding a break from the social and cultural nomenclature imposed on them. Lower-caste people are looked down upon and regarded as impure. This social behaviour has led to their isolation in Hindu social life.

Even in 2021, the caste system is practised in most parts of India. Despite some strenuous government efforts, it has not been eradicated from the hearts and minds of the people. It is so deeply ingrained in Indian culture that breaking away from it can only be a gradual process. It will require individual efforts, state intervention and a change in society's collective consciousness.

People deemed to be lower castes have historically held traditional occupations such as butchering, removal of rubbish and human excreta, leatherwork and cleaning of animal carcasses. Dalits work as manual labourers, cleaning streets, latrines and sewers.

Race in America

Similarly, even after 200 years of independence, and with bitter memories of slavery in America, African Americans are still discriminated against, segregated, targeted and harassed. They are poor and lag far behind on all social and economic indicators. Both the US and India are democracies where, by law, 'equality' is included in the list of fundamental rights. Yet, the traditional systems based on caste and colour still prevail.

When I first came to Chicago from India in 1965, I was pleasantly surprised to see a White American doctor in the cafeteria at the Illinois Institute of Technology (IIT) sitting at the same table with a Filipino nurse, an African-American barber, a German professor, a Latino secretary and a Chinese student. They would regularly enjoy lunch together every day at 12.30 p.m. sharp. I would always see them laughing, talking and joking together at lunch. There were no hierarchies or divisions, and everyone was included in all conversations. I was impressed with this inclusion in such a diverse set of people. I used to wonder if this would ever be possible in India—could a professor and a doctor have lunch on the same table with a barber? To me, this was an eye-opening example of inclusion, American democracy, freedom and the pursuit of happiness.

A few weeks after that, I had an opportunity to travel a few blocks south of the IIT campus to the University of Chicago. I was appalled at the poverty in the south side of the city, along with the lack of safety and security, the broken homes, the drug peddlers and the continuous presence of a police patrol. It was a different world altogether. I could not believe that such a contrast existed in the same city. African Americans who lived on the south side of Chicago were excluded from the American dream, from opportunities and affluence. They were segregated, isolated, ignored and excluded.

Unfortunately, even after fifty-five years, the situation in these parts of Chicago has not changed much. Now there are more gangs, more drugs, more violence and more murders. Why? Why is it that a rich, powerful and technologically advanced country like America cannot provide equal opportunities to African Americans? Is it that complex? Is it a resource issue? Unfortunately, Chicago has not focused on building inclusive communities. The answer to violence in these areas has been to arm and militarize police and provide them with cameras on their collars.

Chicago can be considered the archetype of racial segregation. A survey conducted by the *Washington Post* showed that more than 60 per cent of the Black population in the city believed the biggest problems they faced were crime, violence and gangs. On the other hand, only 30 per cent of the White population cited the same reason; their bigger concerns were economic and budget issues. This difference in attitude can be attributed to racial segregation, with the two groups occupying different parts of the city. The differentiation between the needs and wants of the two races in the same town further corroborates that Blacks and Whites have distinct social and cultural experiences, even if they live in the same physical space. Yet, many contemporary analysts believe that the most profound and widespread forms of racism are institutional rather than interpersonal. The phrase 'institutionalized racism' is sometimes used to describe the policies of a deliberately racist organization such as the Gestapo in Nazi Germany or South Africa's police during apartheid. Institutional racism can be defined as 'those established laws, customs, and practices which systematically reflect and produce racial inequities'.

The segregation of human beings on the basis of skin colour is a most effective form of creating divisions. Skin colour is something you are born with and cannot control. You might as well celebrate and be proud of it.

In August 1963 in Washington, Martin Luther King gave a most eloquent and heartfelt speech. 'I have a dream,' King prayed, 'that my four little children will one day live in a nation where they will not be judged by the colour of their skin, but by the content of their character.' King's speech stands as an anthem for the fight against racism. Colour bias has been a bone of contention in America for a long time, even though for many years now the American government has been promoting the idea of colour blindness. Black people can be regarded as victims of generalization. The perception that violence among Blacks is more significant leads to the illogical inference that every Black person is linked to violence and this is a part of Black culture.

Global Inclusion

Even countries with authoritarian governments have some form of democracy within their boundaries, albeit with limited freedom. Yet, even there, the issue of exclusion is clearly seen. Ethnic cleansing has been going on for a long time in many parts of the world. For example, in China, the Uyghur Muslims are isolated and discriminated against. There are reports of them being humiliated, and their places of worship being destroyed. The treatment of Rohingyas in Myanmar is another example of exclusion and expulsion.

As was seen in South Africa, apartheid was one of the most morbid and fundamental examples of the segregation of humans on the basis of colour. Be it relating to the use of natural resources or the location of human settlements, it cut through each and every aspect of human life. Blacks were segregated into a separate area for housing; intermingling with White people was banned. They were not allowed entry into public places such as restaurants. They were directed to carry identification cards all the time, and were denied many social and economic activities. In 1994, apartheid was abolished, but the residual effects can still be seen in the high crime rate, low prevalence of education and high rate of poverty in South Africa—irrelevant differentiations are prevalent even today. What is essential to understand is that social injustice, when implemented on a mass scale, can have implications for future generations as well. Discrimination is a global phenomenon. People are comfortable with the familiar and fear unknown things and those who are not exactly like them. They have deeply built-in biases. In this process, they lose the opportunity to exercise their curiosity and explore diversity.

While some parts of the world are distorted by a considerable colour bias, preferences based on wealth, gender and religion are much more significant in other regions. Inter-religious conflict is a global phenomenon these days. Religious tensions tend to be fuelled by social conflicts, often resulting in violence. For instance, Europe has been witnessing a surge in anti-Muslim prejudice, with terrorism playing a crucial role in the stereotyping of Muslims. India is a diverse country made up of people from all religions; yet it still sees its urban Muslim population living segregated in different parts of a city, separate from where Hindus live.

It can be argued that some societies are more prone to inter-religious conflict than others. And the reason for this is their history and their lack of education and unemployment. At a global level, religious institutions can play a significant role in propagating tolerance and peace, but the history and social tensions in a country may not allow it. Muslims in Europe and Blacks in America are suffering because they believe that their race is more prone to violence. This leads to them being discriminated against, and this discrimination can get so deeply ingrained that it is difficult to eradicate from a conscious mind. The more divided a society is by religion, the more likely it is that religion can be used to fuel social conflict.

When we look around the world, particularly in places where religious and other social identities like class and ethnicity overlap, we find that such societies are among the most strife-ridden. Indeed, there are religiously diverse and educated societies such as the US, where there is more social tolerance and a lower level of societal conflict. Yet, post-9/11, the kind of ideas created in the minds of the public justifying the Iraq war led to a profound bias against Muslims.

As long as such distinctions continue in people's minds, even without them being explicitly stated, not much can be achieved. Like in Israel, which has been called by some a new form of the 'apartheid state' because of its explicit segregation of Jewish and non-Jewish communities, based on the location where they have settled, the quality of education, and other aspects of social life. As long as a segment of the public has a feeling that they are not equal to the others and that for some complicated reasons they are below the rest in the social strata, they will never be able to achieve the kind of self-confidence that encourages people to move up in the social structure.

Our world is full of painful and bloody stories of struggles for inclusion and equality in America, Europe, Asia, the Middle East and Africa. All countries urgently need new programmes and policies to implement inclusion, maintain peace and provide prosperity.

Financial Inclusion

Another most significant factor which has divided humans for centuries into different classes is wealth. At present, wealth is considered equivalent to dominance and authority. Income inequality plays a crucial role in the lack of social development of an individual. Perceptions are formed based on financial assets, skill and profession; these factors decide status. It is the prime duty of every nation's government to promote policies aimed at the equal distribution of wealth. Unfortunately, government policies have done the exact opposite, and this has substantially increased income inequality over the last few decades. Globalization has also increased income inequality, because only a small percentage of the nation's population is privileged enough to reap the global marketplace's benefits. Income inequality should be an essential concern for any government because it eventually results in the exclusion of a large number of adversely affected people.

Inequality will become an even more crucial issue in the days ahead for two reasons. The first is that globalization is leading to higher living standards and comfort levels of people the world over. As a result, public consciousness about inequality is increasing. The second reason is migration. It is unrealistic to assume that the vast income differences between the US and Mexico, or Europe and Africa, or Indonesia and Malaysia can continue without further intensifying the pressure to migrate. Richer countries have moved towards having a 'fortress mentality', which in these modern times is outdated. It is only diversity in the population that will benefit a nation, and by extension the world.

Education is the most critical aspect when it comes to empowering individuals and enabling them to break free of exclusion. The sad truth is that even good education is often seen as a luxury affordable only to the rich. There are large gaps in educational facilities due to high fees, the quality of facilities, family environment and lack of awareness.

Even if the aim is 'inclusive growth', experience shows that growth alone does not automatically 'trickle down' to those on the economy's margins. Nor can it be achieved solely by redistribution. Redistribution through taxes and social transfers is an essential part of an equitable growth strategy, but it cannot be the only component.

Billions of people in this world do not have access to a bank account or financial services. When they need money to put their life in order, they borrow from local sharks at exorbitant interest rates and hence the cycle of poverty continues. Banks consider poor people high-risk and focus only on the rich and wealthy to make them more prosperous. We need more people like Bangladesh's Dr Yunus, who created Grameen Bank to deliver financial services to poor women in the country's rural areas to stimulate business and reduce poverty. In the process, he had to fight many battles with the government and other lobbies.

Inclusion and Democracy

The key to achieving inclusion is to strengthen democracy, freedom and justice. An inclusive world is a natural extension of democracy, with assured freedom and enhanced justice to deliver equality for all. Unfortunately, what we have achieved over the decades in building a solid foundation for democracy is now being challenged in many countries due to the rise of populist movements. Many thinking people feel that democracies are being hijacked by the unleashing of divisive forces who manipulate social media to promote lies, hate and anger. Through such unethical behaviour, political parties get votes and win elections.

I have personally experienced, enjoyed and benefited a lot from the largest and the oldest democracies in the world, in the US and India, for over seventy years. As a child growing up in independent India in the late 1940s and 1950s, we lived together as neighbours, Hindu and Muslim, Sikh and tribal, in peace and harmony in the spirit of an inclusive environment. The idea of India being rooted in democracy, freedom, secularism, truth, trust, love and non-violence was embedded in my consciousness. After coming to America in the 1960s, I built my professional life around the principles of democracy, freedom, secularism, capitalism and technology. I also cultivated character, courage, values, ethics and respect for others in the process. Now, when I see some of these fundamental values being challenged, I worry about the next generation's future. America's 1776 Declaration of Independence taught me that whenever any form of government becomes destructive towards man's inalienable rights to life, liberty and the pursuit of happiness, the people must rise and defend them.

In the last few years, young people worldwide have lost confidence in democracy. For example, all those who fought the long and hard fight in South Africa with Mandela for 'one person, one vote' do not even feel the need to vote any more. Democracies are seen as a drag on decision-making and development. People think governments are not distributing resources more equitably. Inequalities have increased everywhere, rendering democracies meaningless. People believe that politicians have turned politics into a professional business, with their only interest being preserving and promoting their own power and position. Politicians have forgotten that they are in politics to serve the people. The nexus of politicians, business and media control the policy environment, which serves only the business interests of the rich and famous. In the process, the real needs of the middle class and the people at the bottom of the economic pyramid do not get attention. The present democratic system works on perquisites, privilege, patronage and personal preferences. With the rise of populist movements in democratic countries, this has become exacerbated, thus undermining the principles of inclusion, equality and unity.

After the fall of the Berlin Wall and the collapse of the Soviet Union, the victory of democracy, capitalism and globalization took the world by storm, increasing life expectancy and enhancing systems of education, travel, business, communications, energy, trade, etc. Since the beginning of the twentieth century, hundreds of millions have been lifted out of poverty in most democracies. But this march of progress started losing direction after the 9/11 attack. Along with increasing inequality, the loss of manufacturing jobs, local and international financial crises and anti-globalization movements spread increased frustration and anger in many countries. The fear of not being heard and loss of social status and security caused some sections of deprived people to raise their voices. This reached new heights particularly in Western democratic societies, where many former blue-collar and middle-class people felt betrayed as they lost their jobs, a direct result of globalization. They felt neglected by the liberal elites, losing jobs to China, even as technology took over traditional means of production. Factories that previously needed thousands of workers could now produce more and better products with just a few hundred employees. In this situation, how does a nation deliver inclusion and redistribute wealth?

Today's polarization and political dynamics is outside the fold of enlightenment and humanistic values, and even rationality, in the US, UK, the EU, India and several other countries. A new wave of anti-democratic populism has been ignited and is sweeping the world. Polarities are sharp, and ideas to bridge the division are rare. Inequality between races, religions, income, class and education has played a significant role in contributing to society's polarization.

Inclusion and the Media

Social media and the Internet have become instruments to build echo chambers, steering people away from opposing views and unifying convictions while simultaneously disabling discourse and debate. The need to search for facts, and to distinguish truth and untruth, has been successfully distorted by social media through vagaries in information flow. Opinions, emotions and beliefs are sold as facts, and people prefer to believe them rather than ascertain the truth. China's rise and the associated narrative on social media to compete and dominate global markets have resulted in a US trade war. This has supported the populist view of tightening borders, promoting local production and bringing nationalism back to the mainstream.

The problem with social media is twofold: (1) The revenue and profit model based on number of clicks and number of users; and (2) Fake unauthenticated users who prefer to hide behind opaque walls, promoting misinformation and spreading lies to generate conflicts, fear and hate, confusion and contradictions, and engaging the people in such a way as to create more clicks, resulting in more revenues and profits for social media companies. It is possible to stop this by enforcing the authentication and identification of users and holding them responsible for their behaviour. However, this will reduce the number of users, the number of clicks, and revenues and profits for the social media giants. Are governments ready for this battle? If it is not fought, people will continue to misuse social media to maximize personal gain at the cost of democratic values and public interest.

While there are numerous exchanges on social media, poor communities suffering from economic depression do not understand the contradiction between GDP growth and the closing of shops and small businesses. They feel betrayed, isolated, rejected and excluded and irrelevant. Big banks are a part of the clique as they get billions in bailouts, making the people lose trust in the system. But how can we remedy this? This is populism, post-rational politics.

People know that democratic elections are expensive and backed by money power. In many countries, during elections, people are openly bought and sold. In the US, congressmen and women spend most of their time raising money to fight elections. To remain politically relevant, they are compelled to chase funds all the time. When do they get time to work for the people? In the US presidential elections, billions of dollars are spent on media and management. Expensive consultants are hired to decide on strategies and to choreograph events that package and portray their candidates, just as a product is marketed. In reality, people should know the leader's character and not be lured to cast their votes through false promises.

Even in a developing country like India, billions are spent on elections and the associated marketing machinery. Some of it goes in buying candidates, swapping political parties and filling private pockets. Political spending has become a well-oiled corrupt machine, with built-in demands that give payback with significant returns.

But the general public is aware of money power and associated corrupt practices. Today, technology can enable citizens to cast their vote securely through decentralized digital platforms using smartphones, avoiding the need for voting booths, volunteers, poll workers, official executives, time off from work, travelling to polling locations, waiting in long lines, etc. It would also make the voting experience convenient, free of tension and cost-effective. If used in conjunction with a ban on TV ads, it could save billions and reduce the influence of money power. But is there political will to reform elections? Can we address the tricky questions of electoral funding, money power, lobbies and other issues so that we can bring democracy back on track?

Recently, the American Academy of Arts and Sciences published a report by the Commission on the Practice of Democratic Citizenship, which proposed a set of recommendations to increase citizens' capacity to engage with their communities. It called attention to promising local initiatives worldwide that attempted to combat rising threats to democracy and self-government and rebuild trust in political institutions. It recommended strategies to achieve equality of voice and representation, empower voters and ensure government institutions' responsiveness. It recommended a dramatic expansion of civic bridging capacity and building a civic information architecture that would support a common purpose. It wished to inspire in citizens a culture of commitment to American constitutional democracy and one another. This is a tall order.

We need a fair amount of additional work to make democracy work for all—especially for people at the bottom of the economic pyramid, with a clear emphasis on inclusion. This requires new paradigms and new leadership with character, espousing a commitment to selfless public service. Unfortunately, people prefer leaders who emerge as winners in debating societies, or television personalities who may not mean what they say and may not say what they mean. Leaders today lack high moral standing, wisdom, character, understanding, empathy, a sense of sacrifice, and a clear vision to benefit all. Until people elect such leaders, it will be a challenge to deliver on inclusion. We also need to rediscover, reinvent and redesign democracy to respond to hyperconnectivity. The idea of electing a politician for a few years who will go to the national capital and represent a remote population seems outdated today. We need interactive, participative and distributed democracy, empowered with hyperconnectivity, to express public interest. We need real-time participation from domain experts on national issues, policies and regulations through a novel digital political platform.

Free speech within a nation is a powerful tool to ensure equality for all. Free speech is necessary for voicing a variety of opinions. Compare the idea of free speech in the United States or Europe with that of the Arab world. Or compare free speech in India with that in China. A fundamentally different level of censorship is practised in each of these parts of the world. In many areas, including the Middle East, conflict in ideas and sentiments form barriers to free speech. Views on religion and sexuality form the basis of differences in opinions, leading to the curbing of freedom of speech. However, the downside to this is that taking away free speech may also take away power or authority.

Timely and fair access to justice is also a vital component of an inclusive society. Unfortunately, justice for the poor is expensive and time-consuming. For example, in India, 32 million court cases are pending. Often, it takes several years to get justice. Invariably, hearings are postponed, and adjournments granted time and time again, resulting in more delays, expenses and frustrations. There are not enough courts or staff to meet the demand for timely justice. Technology is hardly used to clear the backlog and improve productivity and efficiency. Even in the US, poor people do not have adequate access to justice. Many African-American victims cannot come up with $500 for bail to stay away from prison. How do we assure fairness to excluded people in this situation? How and when do we modernize our courts and judiciary to deliver timely justice and ensure inclusion?

In some democracies, populist governments have destroyed their constitution and the rule of law, the very foundations of the republic, by capturing major independent institutions such as the Election Commission, the Supreme Court, the federal reserve forces, the army, police, tax authorities and media. All these institutions are abused to manipulate elections, divide communities, promote hate and polarize society, propagate lies, ridicule the opposition, file false court cases, and commit tax fraud. They can engineer investigations, humiliate people, generate fear and be vindictive. Besides, they fabricate narratives that have nothing to do with facts, logic or scientific data to fulfil their political agenda and misguide people. They also promise the impossible, deny others' accomplishments and use emotional oratory to turn people against each other. In this kind of environment, democracy gets hijacked and decent, law-abiding citizens' voices get silenced. Unfortunately, this behaviour is the opposite of the basic principle of a hyperconnected world. Hyperconnectivity offers openness, networking, decentralization, democratization and the empowerment of individuals. However, courageous people must use it positively to challenge populist leaders to preserve democracy.

Today, gender, race, religion, caste, income and education are misused to promote exclusion. In the future, technology such as artificial intelligence, face recognition, big data, machine learning, etc. will be used to profile and further exclude more people. At the same time, genetic engineering will make it easier for people to change their physical appearance, skin colour, eye colour and redefine their ethnicity. What then will be the basis of classification and exclusion? How do we empower individuals and communities in an increasingly complex environment, where democracies are weakening and inequalities are increasing? When hyperconnectivity and new technologies are used to break free of the structures of caste and class, we can then possibly aspire to build an inclusive society.

Need for Empathy

Understanding the implications and impact of inclusion and equality in every aspect of life should start right from the individual level. Change always begins with the individual and from within. Each of us has a moral responsibility to treat other human beings with respect, dignity, equality, love and care. No amount of policy, programmes, laws, government rules, regulations and intervention can match an individual initiative coming from the heart, mind and soul of a person. The idea of respecting an individual's identity and understanding their perspective should be an essential aspect of the human mindset in the culture of every part of the world. It is unfortunate that our egos and the lure of social and financial incentives mould our impulsive behaviour and provoke us to give impulsive responses. We tend to judge people from their outer appearance rather than their inner core.

I have seen business people, politicians and government officers treat their drivers, cooks, household workers, shopkeepers, cleaners and other employees with disrespect. I have also seen people exclude and mistreat the disabled, old and weak. I have learnt early that I must first feel good about myself to feel good about you. If I am comfortable, I make you feel comfortable. If I am at peace, I give you peace. If I am happy, I make you happy. If I am insecure, jealous, competitive and anxious, then I will make you uncomfortable. The key is to respect the other human being and begin with trust, a positive attitude and contagious enthusiasm. Everyone wants to be good. Everyone wants to be respected and loved. It is always proper to offer a helping hand to build inclusive relationships.

Once, a young African American and his friend visited my eighteenth-floor office in a tower located in an affluent suburb of Chicago. I saw him looking down at the massive Oakbrook shopping mall. I casually asked him: 'Have you been there?' He said, 'No, this is my first time here.' Later, I learnt that he had never been downtown as he had never left his neighbourhood on the south side of Chicago. My instant reaction was to invite him and his friend to my house for a drink. They were surprised but agreed to come over. At home, we spoke about his background and upbringing, and he told me that his life in Chicago was spent within the confines of a poor community. His friends dropped out of school after they had learnt enough maths to sell drugs. He was bright but fearful, working at odd jobs to make a living.

He could not understand why an unknown person would be friendly enough to invite him home, and asked what he could do for me. I told him he had done me a great favour by accepting my invitation. When leaving, he remained thoroughly confused. Perhaps no one had ever treated him with ordinary decency, love and respect, things that any young person deserves. It was a moving experience for both of us. In a way, he changed me, and I believe I changed him. We connected. This is what inclusion is all about. It did not cost anything. It was a spontaneous, intuitive, emotional and empowering human experience.

Ideas and efforts to build an inclusive society should be encouraged, taught and practised everywhere: at home, schools, colleges, communities, work, sports, entertainment, etc. These efforts should also be backed by appropriate policies, programmes and laws to expedite and ensure their implementation. The majority of communities worldwide must take moral responsibility to include minorities in the mainstream of the city's social, political and economic development. Inclusion has to be a global concern. National leaders should declare the decade from 2020 to 2030 the decade of inclusion. Unless 'Inclusion for all' is incorporated into every business, institution and government's organizational architecture, it will not get implemented.

Inclusion does not mean promoting inefficiency or incompetence. It needs a systematic and sustained approach to implement diversity and equality everywhere. To ensure this, we need senior executives in charge of inclusion and diversity in every institution, who report to the CEO, secretary or minister of inclusion and diversity in government, who, in turn, would finally report to the prime minister or president at a national level. For example, at present, inclusion is among the UN's Sustainable Development Goals. As always, it will remain aspirational and never get implemented. If we are serious about assuring inclusion in a hyperconnected world, we can, within a decade, build a truly inclusive world. But do we have the political will to do so? Are there enough prominent change agents in the world who are respected and committed and want to drive this global mission? Is inclusion a part of the new world order? If it is not, it will remain a part of the unfinished agenda.

Any redesign of the world must begin with a global commitment to implement inclusion in all countries to deliver peace and prosperity to all.

5

Human Needs

'The world has enough for everyone's need but not everyone's greed.'

—M.K. Gandhi

The second pillar in the redesign of the world deals with providing basic human needs to people at the bottom of the economic pyramid. The challenge is to enlarge the focus of human rights. If a hungry man is asked to choose between two square meals a day and the right to free speech, he will invariably choose to fill his stomach. To millions of poor, hungry, thirsty, sick, homeless and isolated persons, human needs matter much more than human rights—not that the latter are unimportant, but it is just human instinct to strive for survival. There are too many people in this world who require basic human needs urgently.

All human beings are deserving of human rights without discrimination—these include fundamental rights to life, liberty, expression, education, work, freedom from slavery and more. The UN adopted the Universal Declaration of Human Rights in 1948; it is an international code that calls on all peoples and nations to subscribe to it and aspire for the achievement of economic, social, cultural, civil and political rights. The UN started this initiative in

2006 with the Human Rights Commission, which was later made the Human Rights Council. Human freedom is a theme that cuts across all UN policies and programmes in critical areas of peace, security and development. However, these remain aspirational goals—many people still do not have access to freedom, justice, equality, education, work, etc. In many places, they are held as slaves. In a sense, the concept of human rights exists as a principle but is not readily available or implemented. It is often the same people deprived of human rights who also do not have access to basic human needs.

The objective of redesigning the world is to provide human needs and not just human rights. Fortunately, we now live in an era of surplus and abundance and not of shortages and scarcity. With advances in technology, supply chains, manufacturing automation and robotics, we can produce things in quantity. The key is to commit to producing and distributing items to meet the basic needs of poor people, and making sure that there are no hungry, thirsty and homeless people on our planet. Unfortunately, we are used to producing only for those who can afford to buy goods and services, not for those who need them. This must change.

Needs

People often decide their needs based on their ideologies and circumstances. People with environmental problems will seek to solve those first. People facing unemployment and poverty would like to change their priorities accordingly. It has now been proven that a focus on human needs and developing core competence can shape nations' fortunes. We can see this in the nations that went through drastic transformations after World War II—Japan, South Korea, Singapore, Taiwan, etc. Countries also experience freedom in diverse ways. In some countries, people have less space when authoritarian regimes govern them. The nature of needs in a communist culture would differ from that in a capitalist culture.

The differing cultures of the world have also influenced how norms are established to determine people's needs.

Similarly, the needs of people in urban areas are different from the needs of those in rural areas. The needs of people today differ from those of people who lived seventy-five years ago. Due to diversity in governance and ecosystems, we see a diverse approach to human needs. Yet, basic human needs are universal and need urgent attention everywhere.

Every year, during the Thanksgiving, Christmas and New Year holidays, I watch American consumers' shopping data. If American consumers buy more, then the whole world is happy because it enhances export numbers and ensures jobs for people in China, India, Bangladesh, Vietnam, South Korea, etc. Unfortunately, these shoppers are not necessarily the people who buy what they need. They buy what they want. The ones who need things to survive do not have the money to celebrate the holidays. We must reach out to them. Unfortunately, global production systems and supply chains are designed to produce and deliver products and services to people who can pay. This massive manufacturing machine to meet the ever-increasing human wants has been partly responsible for increasing inequality worldwide. The challenge is to innovate new business models and associated financial systems and provide basic needs to less privileged people while also meeting others' wants and aspirations.

There is a clear distinction between needs and wants. A person's needs are fundamental to survival, safety and security; on the other hand, wants are shaped by desires, affordability, circumstances, social mindset and the urge to show off. Needs arise out of a human being's biological and social structure. On the other hand, wants emerge from our desire to acquire more with our surplus capital. Today, extensive attractive technological gadgets are available to make our life more comfortable and enjoyable. While this is appreciable, ignoring millions of our people who cannot meet even their basic needs is not fair. We often leave them behind, while our own needs keep increasing due to new products and services, such as the Internet or smartphones.

This reminds me of a friend visiting his father in India after spending ten years in New York. He decided to take with him a nice, expensive white cotton shirt for his father as a gift. He said, 'Dad, I have a gift for you from America,' after reaching home. His dad looked at the shirt and said, 'Thanks, my son. It looks costly. But let me tell you that I already have three shirts; I am wearing one, the second one is in the wash, and the third is lying in my room. Why do I need a fourth shirt? What would I do with it? Maybe you should give it to your uncle. I know he can use a new shirt.' The father knew the difference between his needs and his wants.

Several global experts have studied human needs in the past. Different people have different ideas based on their own experiences and understanding and their location, culture, conditions and notions about their basic needs. These needs also keep changing with time, availability, options and geography. The psychologist Abraham Maslow suggested that human beings behave on the basis of fulfilling their hierarchy of needs. He indicated that the priority of needs begins from the physical requirement of survival. These needs include the environment, clean air, water and food. If these requirements are not fulfilled, the human body cannot survive. Needs also extend to safety, security, protection against violence and other abuses, as well as clothing, housing and health. When these two tiers of needs have been achieved, the hierarchy of needs will extend to affection, social belonging and self-actualization—which relate to social requirements such as the self, family and community. Basic human needs can be classified into three categories:

1. Environment, clean air, water and food;
2. Clothing, housing and health;
3. Self, family and community.

Basic Needs

Today, there are domain experts with substantial experience in producing and delivering diverse basic needs. We know a great deal about devising systems to ensure the same. But what the world really needs is for leaders to have the political will and commitment to ensure less privileged people are not denied the basic requirements in life. Unfortunately, most countries merely provide lip service, with their priorities, policies and programmes being focused mainly on geopolitical strategies, business, trade, technology, markets, military and matters related to growth. This takes attention and resources away from the problems of the poor, who have no collective voice in the political system. As a result, basic human needs are often ignored. Some people in power believe that the poor do not deserve support as they do not work. The same people also believe that spending public resources to provide basic needs to them will affect the national budget, and at the same time make people dependent on handouts. Often, if you are pro-poor, some believe you are too liberal. But the reality is that hundreds of millions on our planet do not have enough to eat. Hunger hurts. Unfortunately, such people are trapped in that situation and need help. To appreciate these issues, it is essential to review some of our planet's basic human needs. To help solve these problems, you do not have to be liberal or conservative, urban or rural, or believe in democracy or dictatorship; you just have to be human.

Air, Water and Food

The first set of basic needs relates to the environment, air, water and food. The environmental problems that affect people on this planet include air pollution, water pollution, acid rain, global warming, deforestation, loss of biodiversity, industrial waste, piling up of plastic, increasing forest fires, unexpected cyclones, droughts, floods and devastating hurricanes—all of these are linked to rapid industrialization, increased use of chemicals, and uncontrolled urbanization, which have resulted in an unprecedented disturbance in the planet. Most of the top fifty polluted cities in the world are in China and India. How did that happen? Is it because of the dense population, coal burning, steel mills or hazardous industries? No doubt developed countries have benefited the most from industrialization in the last fifty years. The US had heavy pollution not too long ago. I have seen Chicago's steel mills polluting the air for decades, resulting in brown and black clouds hanging over the sky all the time. I went to Pittsburgh in 1967, and my white shirt had turned grey by the evening. Even though air pollution is an issue that has been substantially addressed in the US, the same cannot be said about many other countries. People on the planet need fresh air and a clean environment to lead a healthy life.

Similarly, the list of water-related problems in this world is very long. According to the United Nations, 2.2 billion people lack access to safe drinking water, and 4.2 billion people lack secure sanitation services. People on the planet draw 4000 cubic kilometres of water each year, equivalent to all the fresh water in Lake Michigan. Of this, about 70 per cent goes towards agriculture to grow food, which is why I have seen people in villages worshipping wells, ponds and rivers. Now, most wells the world over are dry, groundwater is depleted, ponds are polluted and rivers are dirty. Women spend 200 million hours a day hauling water to their homes, some of them walking 5 to 10 kilometres a day to fetch about 40 pounds of water. Meanwhile, 90 per cent of all natural disasters are water related.

In 1987, I was heading the National Technology Mission in India, which had an objective of providing drinking water to 1,00,000 villages. It was a monumental task to provide, daily, 30 litres of water per person and 40 litres per head for cattle. We needed to access satellite imagery for water sourcing to set up plants to remove excess iron and excess fluoride from the water, establish desalination units and develop a nationwide network of water-testing laboratories, deep water wells, hand pumps and their associated technology and training. We also focused on rainwater harvesting—a great tradition in India that has now been forgotten. All the traditional rainwater harvesting structures designed hundreds of years ago and constructed near old temples are now being used mainly for dumping garbage. Unfortunately, water management is something that people and governments ignore, making the poor suffer in the process. The rich have solved their drinking water problems by creating a vast business, producing 500 billion plastic water bottles each year, creating an enormous global garbage dump. Water is a complex global issue, a depleting global resource that substantially impacts the economy, environment, food and health, requiring urgent international attention. If this trend in water shortage continues, it could be the next global battleground.

According to the UN, world hunger has been on the rise since 2015. An estimated 820 million people in the world suffered because of hunger in 2018. This number is going to increase substantially because of the COVID-19 pandemic. At the same time, weight gain and obesity continue to grow the world over. For the last seventy-five years, we have talked about eliminating hunger, and there have been numerous reports on the same from the UN, World Bank and many other institutions. Despite the significant progress we have made in almost every field, hunger has still not been eliminated from this world. Why? Is it that complicated? The answer is that we have not taken this issue seriously enough. Even though many people worldwide have been working hard to solve the problem of hunger, we still have a long way to go. It is believed that in 2030 we will have over 800 million hungry people.

In the 1950s and 1960s, many believed that India would not be able to feed its population, which was 500 million then. But thanks to the efforts of Indian and global agriculture scientists who spearheaded the Green Revolution and other related accomplishments, India today can feed its 1.3 billion people and produce surplus foodgrains. However, it still has 200 million hungry people who do not get adequate nutrition because of the lack of infrastructure and logistics required for storage, distribution and delivery. The situation in Africa is even worse.

In 2020, the UN World Food Programme (WFP) was awarded the Nobel Peace Prize for its efforts towards combating hunger. The Nobel committee mentioned that providing food security could improve peace and security in Africa, Asia and South America. It hoped that the award would draw more attention to the hunger problem. According to a *Wall Street Journal* report, the WFP is under threat in the face of slogans like 'America First'.

Washington has been the largest donor to WFP, contributing 43 per cent of the total budget of $6.35 billion. Germany provided $964 million and China $4 million. The WFP's executive director reminds us that 'food security, peace and stability go together.' But how do you make significant inroads in resolving the issue of world hunger with such a low level of financial commitment from leading nations?

Clothing, Housing and Health

The second set of basic needs relates to clothing, housing and health, and safety and security. People need clothing for their basic dignity and to protect themselves from exposure to the elements. According to fashion industry reports, we produce 150 billion garments each year. For a world population of about 7.5 billion people, this amounts to twenty garments per person per year. Strangely, out of this total, 45 billion garments are never sold. The average American buys seventy apparel items per year. That is one new piece of clothing every four to five days. The fashion industry creates 92 million tonnes of textile waste every year, of which

13 million tonnes are sent annually to landfills. It takes 2700 litres of water to make just one T-shirt, 7000 litres of water to produce one pair of jeans. An average person would take 2.5 years to drink that much water. The industry produces 2 billion pairs of jeans every year.

The textile industry has grown by 400 per cent in the last decade and continues to pollute our rivers, erode our soil, use excessive water and reduce our forest cover. Fashion is considered the second dirtiest industry in the world, and overproduction has a significant impact on the environment. The more we produce, the more waste is accumulated. The global economy misses out on $460 billion each year because people throw away clothes they could continue to wear. At the same time, hundreds of millions do not have enough clothing to simply cover themselves. The 2018 Apparel Industry Report mentions that the demand for clothing is growing, but fashion promotions often distort our sense of value. This industry is a classic example of what we can achieve if we focus on conservation instead of consumption. It is clear that if the fashion industry is appropriately managed, we can find enough resources to eliminate global hunger by this measure alone.

The UN Settlements Programme (UN-Habitat) estimates that 600 million urban residents and 1 billion people in rural areas of the developing world live in overcrowded housing with low water quality, lack of sanitation and non-existent garbage collection systems. The lack of housing is apparent in slums in all significant metropolitan areas such as Manila, Mumbai, Bogota, Buenos Aires, Rio de Janeiro, Hanoi, Lagos and many more. Bloomberg CityLab estimates that 850 million people, more than the entire population of the US and the EU combined, live in informal settlements.

Every day, in developing countries, over 2,00,000 new people move from rural areas into cities, looking for opportunities and livelihood. By 2030, it is estimated that almost 60 per cent of the 8 billion people on the planet will be living in cities, and we will need 250–300 million additional homes. This amounts to 25–30 million new homes every year. This is a huge business opportunity to generate jobs and provide security and comfort to people in need. Housing is the industry that requires minimum investment to create new jobs. Domain experts know how to meet requirements related to housing needs. They recommend affordable housing technology with incentives, tax breaks, relaxed zoning conditions, high-tech safety, funding via low-interest bonds, revitalization of neighbourhoods and special programmes to expedite implementation.

COVID-19 has sharpened the focus on global health and the crises related to it, making it a matter of immediate concern. Even though we have made substantial progress in medical technology through instrumentation and techniques in medicine and related fields, the cost of health services has skyrocketed. Health challenges have increased globally due to various reasons: poor diet, lack of exercise, smoking, drugs, infectious diseases, obesity, hypertension, diabetes, heart disease, mental illness, global warming, pollution, poverty, hunger, etc. People in poverty and those who live in rural areas have little or no access to medicine and health services. Hyperconnectivity offers new possibilities and hope in this regard, but governments worldwide have paid little attention to improving access to affordable health. Health is a substantial industry driven by broad business interests, but it is also a basic human need that must be part of every government's national plan.

Self, Family and Community

The third set of basic needs relates to the self, family and community. Once people's basic needs such as clean air, water, food, clothes, housing and health are taken care of, the focus shifts outwards: to the need to be part of a family and a community. To begin a productive life, people need to take account: Who are they? Where are their roots? Where do they come from? What do they want to do? For what purpose are they here? How can they be productive and happy? Finding answers to these fundamental questions needs the support of others. We all desire appreciation, recognition, respect and love. Many poor people feel that they do not get enough of this type of support early in life, which prevents them from being productive in the community. They are then ignored, abused, isolated and discriminated against by others.

Along with some support to build a strong sense of self, people also need family and friends to interact and socialize with. Family is an essential institution for people to feel stable, safe and secure. I am part of a large family of five sisters and three brothers, and I appreciate the benefit of growing up in an environment where I learnt to care and share early on in life. Family is the core of a happy childhood; it helps build a strong foundation for lifelong stability and security.

Unfortunately, family and community institutions have been weakening in the last several decades. Families are falling apart, and communities are closing their doors. The culture of selfishness has isolated and alienated people. I feel like individualism has been carried too far. In the process, we have lost the ability to respect, give, share and sacrifice. In today's competitive world, people compete to climb the ladder at any cost and often miss out on the joy of living and helping others. They are too busy chasing money and material at the expense of character and values, and feeling frustrated, agitated and irritated in this process. I strongly feel that basic needs are not just about hard assets but also about soft skills related to human values.

How do we resolve these issues? How do we ensure that our people have clean air to breathe, safe water to drink and enough food to eat? How do we save our people from droughts, floods, hurricanes, cyclones and hunger? The challenge is not handling the after-effects of hunger or calamities but anticipating such eventualities and preventing suffering from percolating to the poor. How do we make sure everyone has clothes to wear, a roof over their heads, and good health to live confidently? They also need dignity, respect, and the love and support of their family and community to be productive and happy. For me, this is a part of our minimum basic needs.

Income for the Poor

We have all the expertise to begin addressing the challenges being faced all over the world. There are many capable global, national and local institutions, including qualified voluntary organizations and individuals dedicated to studying and working on these challenges worldwide. We know the nature of these problems well, and are also aware of the solutions. However, we have never had the necessary political will to dedicate resources towards implementing solutions that can provide basic human needs for all. We have believed that development on its own will percolate down to the people at the bottom and that the poor will consequently benefit. This has not happened; in fact, inequality has increased.

I firmly believe that top-down methods do not work well for the people at large. We need a bottom-up approach towards development with wisdom, with the participation of local people and indigenous talent. We have tried some innovative experiments on a pilot basis in some countries, but with varied success. The key is to scale up these solutions for more extensive benefits without worrying too much about the financial implications. The real benefits will come from human development, which is hard to quantify and measure. The two critical, innovative ideas that come to my mind relate to the National Rural Employment Guarantee Scheme in India and the widely discussed Minimum Income Guarantee Scheme.

The Indian government passed the National Rural Employment Guarantee Act (NREGA) in 2005 (later rechristened as the Mahatma Gandhi National Rural Employment Guarantee, MGNREGA) as an innovative social measure to assure each needy person of their 'right to work', and guaranteeing a minimum of

100 days of employment in a year. The benefits of this scheme are available to about 100 million poor people living in rural areas. The plan provides a minimum wage level to enable poor labourers to enhance their quality of life. It also includes in its scope the creation of various permanent assets in rural areas, such as water wells, ponds, canals, roads, etc. The idea is to use the untapped and underutilized rural workforce to build these community assets and, at the same time, provide income to the rural poor to improve their lives. While guaranteeing employment, it has helped reduce urban migration, create durable rural assets, increase spending power, drive consumer growth and improve land and water resources utilization. It has even played a role in enhancing social inclusion for those living in rural India.

The minimum income guarantee scheme is a social welfare programme that guarantees citizens or families a sufficient income to live on. This idea has been around for centuries. However, it has been inactive in public debate again for the last few years. The intention behind it is to cover the cost of living and extend financial security to families in need. It provides a minimum living wage to cover job losses and keep people out of the trap of poverty. The scheme, also known as Basic Universal Income in some countries, is being rolled out elsewhere as experimental pilot programmes.

During the last national election in India in 2019, Rahul Gandhi, the president of the Indian National Congress, introduced an idea of providing the bottom 20 per cent strata of households an amount of Rs 72,000 annually as a part of a similar minimum income guarantee scheme known as Nyay (Justice). This was aimed at 50 million families in India at an estimated cost of around $50 billion. It is believed that such a scheme could significantly reduce poverty.

The key is to innovate, experiment and assure people who are struggling at the bottom of the economic pyramid that their basic human needs will be taken care of by society and the government as part of a national and global development programme. To me, it makes no sense to spend $2 trillion a year on military machinery to fight wars and not spend even one-fourth of this amount to assure millions of human beings the necessary wherewithal to rise above poverty. We are now in the Information Age with advanced capabilities and the benefit of hyperconnectivity. Can we not pledge to provide these basic human needs to people so we can promote peace and prosperity?

6

New Economy

'The true test of civilization, culture and dignity is character.'

—M.K. Gandhi

The third pillar in redesigning the world is a new economy. The challenge is to take capitalism to the next level with a focus on inclusion and sustainability. Capitalism was at the core of the world's design after World War II to help rebuild Europe, Japan and other parts of the world which had been ruined by prolonged global conflicts resulting in unimaginable destruction, devastation and death. Ultimately, the war was settled after the US detonated two nuclear bombs over the Japanese cities of Nagasaki and Hiroshima. As part of the global reconstruction after the war, world economies had to grow, jobs had to be created, cities had to be built, consumption had to be boosted, and new businesses and entrepreneurs had to be encouraged.

America had great experience and confidence in capitalism as a philosophy to reboot the world economy. Over the last seventy-five years, capitalism has done very well. It has helped Europe, Japan, the Asian Tigers and many other countries grow. It enabled American technology to emerge from the shadow of a defence-oriented economy, and led to the generation of new products and services to meet consumer requirements and aspirations. Compared to the centrally planned economy of the Soviet Union, capitalism was showing the way at the time. When the Soviet Union ceased to exist in 1991, the victory of democracy and capitalism was evident and celebrated the world over.

Two decades after that, China demonstrated that a command economy with well-planned and equally well-executed policies could grow even faster than that of a capitalist country. The China model was predominantly based on sourcing cheap labour from rural areas, sweatshops, discipline, hard work, with the condition of technology transfer and other controls extracted from other developed countries. With this regulation and careful oversight, China could meet the increasing demand from American consumers who wished to obtain cheaper products abroad. Global manufacturing rapidly moved to China, and blue-collar jobs largely vanished elsewhere.

Many believed that China excelled at using the developed world's laws to help get justice while denying the same to the rest of the world through its courts and institutions. Some also believed that China was stealing intellectual property to replicate and replace technology and products to compete in the international market at low prices. Meanwhile, in Western countries, wealth was concentrated in the hands of a few super-rich and tech-savvy entrepreneurs. Greed and corruption increased, and the desire to become rich quickly spread across the globe. Rising inequality and the loss of manufacturing raised many concerns and started a fresh discourse on the need for a new economy.

Economics is a necessary construct that explains human wealth and well-being. When making decisions, policymakers, business leaders and others often depend heavily upon economic assessments and models. Many think tanks and other organizations spend countless working hours carrying out widespread capital-heavy surveys to feed data into these models and theories that ultimately act as a guiding force for global and local markets.

However, the industrial era's economic ideas are no longer appropriate in this hyperconnected world and the context of twenty-first-century economies. The financial crisis of 2008 and the economic crisis of Greece in 2014 demonstrated the questionability of many of these long-standing theories and put theoretical models and assumptions to the test. The inability of a scientific discipline to accurately predict an economy's future, and hence that of a society, let alone influence it, has been a cause of great worry. It forces us to take a fresh, innovative look at economics and devise a system that is suited to the needs and dynamics of the modern world.

COVID-19 has essentially brought the global economy to a halt. Everything everywhere is now under the scanner and open to question. In the past, capitalism had promoted and facilitated globalization, privatization and liberalization, and helped create mega-corporations as per a model of top-down development, complex global supply chains, and with a sharp focus on profits for the corporations. It also gave birth to more mega-corporations, mainly in Asia, and created a large number of billionaires worldwide, leading to a further concentration of wealth and power in the hands of a few. The pandemic has now given an opportunity to pay serious attention to localization, decentralization, multiple supply chains, local human resources, in-country production, and health and food security. These issues will have a huge impact and could ultimately lead to the new economy we aspire for.

Gross Domestic Product

To understand the need for a new economy, we must begin with the controversial use of over-simplistic and inadequate tools such as GDP to measure economic growth and well-being. When the GDP methodology was initially developed in the US and UK in the 1930s and 1940s, the world was in the midst of a significant social and economic upheaval from the global wars and the Great Depression. President Roosevelt's government used economic statistics with theories related to GDP to justify policies and budgets to bring the US out of the Depression. When it became more likely that the US would become involved in World War II, there was a concern about whether this would jeopardize US citizens' living standards—they were just beginning to recover from the Depression. GDP estimates were used to show that the economy could provide sufficient supplies for engaging in World War II while maintaining an adequate supply of consumer goods and services.

Later, several other measurement standards, such as the foreign exchange reserve, balance of payments, trade deficit, exchange rates, etc., were introduced to evaluate economic health. These are all transactional measurements and do not address the real assets locked up in mines, minerals, land, forests, human resources, gold, jewellery, housing and much more. How do you judge a nation that is rich in assets but transactionally poor, or vice versa?

Since its introduction, economists have warned that GDP is a specialized tool. Treating it as an indicator of general well-being would be inaccurate and dangerous. However, over the last seventy years, economic growth measured by GDP has become the sine qua non. Per capita GDP, or per capita income, is frequently used to compare the quality of life in different countries. Governments often resort to calculating GDP as an indicator to demonstrate their economic and fiscal policies' success.

Today, GDP, and economic growth in general, is regularly referred to by leading economists, politicians, top-level decision makers and the media as though it represents overall progress. A recently released World Bank report by the Commission on Growth and Development states that nothing apart from consistent long-term high rates of GDP growth (specifically, a doubling of GDP each decade) can solve world poverty. This is like measuring a building's energy use and affirming that when more electricity is used, the building residents' quality of life is better.

GDP measures only monetary transactions related to the production of goods and services. It is based on an incomplete picture of the system within which the human economy operates. We know that the economy draws strength from natural, social and human capital. In turn, the quantity and quality of such wealth are affected by net investment from the economy. By measuring only market economy activity, GDP ignores changes in the natural, social and human components of capital on which the community relies for its continued existence and well-being. As a result, GDP not only fails to measure critical aspects of the quality of life but, in many ways, it may encourage activities that are counter to long-term community well-being.

Of particular concern is the fact that GDP measurement encourages the depletion of natural resources at a faster rate than their renewal. Another problem is that current economic activity is degrading ecosystems, thereby reducing the services that, until now, had been provided virtually free to humans. It may be argued that GDP encourages the depletion of forests because, in terms of GDP, lumber is valued more than the ecosystem services that the forest would have provided had it been left untouched. These services, including the presence of a biodiversity habitat, reduced flooding from severe storms, filtration to improve water quality in rivers and lakes, and the sequestration of carbon dioxide and manufacture of oxygen, are not considered part of the market economy and, as a result, are not taken into consideration in the computation of GDP. As Herman Daly, former senior economist at the World Bank, once commented, 'The current national accounting system treats the earth as a business in liquidation.'

Conventional Economics

Conventional economic thinking has classified social and environmental measures as wealth consumption, not wealth creation. This has been reflected in the fact that such efforts have primarily been remedial. Thus, health policies and health services have been more concerned with curing sickness after the event than positively improving the public health infrastructure and systems and enabling people to be healthier. As the Brundtland Commission put it, 'environmental management practices have focused largely upon after-the-fact repair of damage such as reforestation, re-claiming desert lands, re-building urban environments, restoring natural habitats, and rehabilitating wildlands'.

The twenty-first-century economic order will have to reject these conventional perceptions and policy orientations. The idea that economic policies are wealth-creating and social policies wealth-consuming, along with the argument that economic policies should, therefore, be given priority over social systems, is simply not realistic. The world is not like that. This is quite obvious in urban priority areas and other disadvantaged localities, and even in industrialized countries. In that context, the need for improved work opportunities, better housing, value-added health and social environment, quality education, upgraded leisure facilities, higher incomes, and, above all, an enhancement in the capacity and confidence of local people to do more for themselves, clearly has to be approached as a single constellation of needs—not a collection of distinct and separate requirements to be met in different and independent ways, some economic and some social.

Another concern raised about GDP as an indicator of progress is the 'threshold effect'. As GDP increases, the overall quality of life often increases, but only up to a point. Beyond this point, GDP increases are offset by the costs associated with growing income inequality, loss of leisure time and natural capital depletion. An increasingly large and robust body of research confirms that, beyond a certain threshold, further increases in material well-being have the negative side effects of lowering community cohesion, healthy relationships, knowledge, wisdom, a sense of purpose, connection with nature and other dimensions of human happiness. A strikingly consistent global trend suggests that as material affluence increases, these critical components of psychic income often decline amidst rising rates of alcoholism, suicide, depression, poor health, crime, divorce and other social pathologies.

In other words, traditional measurement tools such as GDP have repeatedly proven their inadequacy because they consistently ignore conditions of climate change; environmental crises; scarcity of financial and natural resources; the need to protect common assets spread across species and generations; the challenges posed by burgeoning technology, globalization, large multinational enterprises, etc.; an ageing-yet-still-expanding population with rising expectations and frustrations; and all this with growing complexity, uncertainty and concern for sustainability.

Several ways of measuring national-level progress have been proposed, developed and employed to address the growing realization that GDP is a measure of economic quantity, not economic quality or welfare, let alone social or environmental well-being. Some of these alternatives are the Index of Sustainable Economic Welfare/Genuine Progress Indicator, Green GDP, Genuine Savings (by the World Bank), Ecological Footprint, Human Development Index, Living Planet Report, Happy Planet Index, etc.

However, we are far from radically relooking at and creating a discipline that would respond effectively to the complex characteristics of the twenty-first century. We need to understand the world differently and take cognizance of various factors that have only recently come to light. Our current world dynamics contain many catalysts that have not yet been completely identified, measured and realized, let alone incorporated in our study of economics.

Internet Economy

An important example is the Internet. The Internet economy has specifically challenged old economics in a way that has never happened before. It is changing the way we work, socialize, create and share information, even as it organizes the flow of people, ideas and things around the globe. It has facilitated the creation of markets characterized by large scale at zero marginal cost, increased customization and rapid innovation. Above all, it has led to the collection and use of real-time consumer and market data. The last fifteen years have witnessed the emergence of platforms for online searches, e-commerce, online media, crowd-sourcing public solutions, financial trading, social networking and other activities. Yet, the magnitude of this transformation is still not fully appreciated.

The Internet accounted for over 20 per cent of GDP growth in mature economies over several years. In that time, we have gone from a few thousand students accessing Facebook to about 3 billion users around the world, including many leading firms who regularly update their pages and share content. Hundreds of billions in terms of the platform's valuation reflect the size and diversity of the users it hosts, the value of the businesses and markets it enhances, and the innovative solutions it generates for communities across the world at almost zero cost. Today the top five companies in the US, measured by the market capital they have developed, are all digital companies: Apple, Microsoft, Google, Facebook and Amazon. These are trillion-dollar companies. How do we justify and comprehend the implication of this new wealth and power?

Current economics assumes that individuals and companies are motivated by profit and self-interest and cannot act in a collaborative and non-profit environment. However, open-source software and applications and ubiquitous social media have challenged this theory. People collaborate, share and create over these platforms, driven purely by the psychological benefits of being a part of a community and because of the enhanced self-satisfaction it generates. The magnitude of content and the diversity of the solutions that social media interactions generate is immense and cannot be ignored. It is crucial to incorporate this data into mainstream economics and its assumptions, and deliberate upon a rational method that can be arrived at regarding its valuation and rights that accrue from this knowledge bank.

The volume and quality of real-time data generated by the Internet question the very need for an assumption-based discipline. Big data and data analytics have enabled corporations and economies to take responsive and predictive rather than pre-determined decisions. The need to access and analyse 'big data' and use the more massive data sets generated from every customer and interaction, from wired objects and every social network, cannot be underestimated. The sheer quantum of this data is staggering; enterprises globally store more than 10 exabytes of new data every month. This trend has the potential to not only drive competitiveness in the private sector but to transform government operations and governance fundamentally. Governments need to take cognizance of this data's availability and construct economic models with different world applications accordingly.

How do we create data-driven economics? How can economists help develop new governance mechanisms that leverage big data and analytics? There are also issues from this form of the Internet economy that we need to address: these questions are in the realm of determining profit-sharing, assigning proprietary rights for solutions that may be transnational both in their origin as well as implementation, complex disputes regarding data privacy, protection against online fraud, identity theft, cybersecurity, etc. However, the first step is still identifying and taking cognizance of these issues and their magnitude and considering the possibility of their utilization to address the global problems that may appear intractable at the moment.

While large enterprises and national economies have undoubtedly reaped significant benefits from this technological revolution, individual consumers and small start-up entrepreneurs have been some of the greatest beneficiaries of the Internet's empowering influence. The kind of scale that big ideas have been able to reach, with minimal capital investment, has disrupted some of the very fundamental economic assumptions we have worked with so far. The Internet has enabled fundamental business transformations that span the entire value chain in virtually all sectors and types of markets, not just the online ones.

These shifts include wholesale changes in how products are bought and sold and how products and services are designed, produced and distributed. Even a small business with a big idea today can operate with a dynamically managed supply chain that spans geographies and works with a virtual global workforce. It has the potential to disrupt many sectors and industries within a short period. WhatsApp, in itself, presents a strong example; it has shaken the telecom industry within a few short years. Examples like these are many and have given us starting points to understand how a small step in a networked Internet economy can disrupt sectors, thereby providing an impetus and an understanding of our traditional economic models in this new light.

The virtual and instantaneous nature provided by the Internet to mobile transactions and payments globally also raises questions on whether we need multiple currencies. If not for all sectors of the economy, can we consider examining the possibility of a common global currency, at least for virtual transactions? This is a significant question that new economics needs to address. Can the world survive with just five currencies—US dollar, EU euro, Japanese yen, Chinese renminbi and Indian rupee? Why only dollar-based global markets? Why not a call based on a basket of currencies? These are complex questions that need to be addressed in a world where one can buy a product in Chicago that is made in China, designed in France, to be shipped to a customer in Brazil and paid for in yen. It can also ensure that the merchant gets paid in dollars, the manufacturer in renminbis and the designer in euros, and all this instantly.

If the Internet were one of the sectors considered for the computation of a global GDP and agriculture, industry and services, it would significantly impact GDP structure. The Internet fosters competition, encourages innovation, develops human capital, creates jobs and builds a shared infrastructure. Yet, governments, policymakers and economists have not leveraged the Internet's potential for complex econometrics. It is time we look at this matter seriously.

Hyperconnectivity is bound to have a massive impact on current economic thinking, mainly due to four reasons:

(1) New products, services, markets, business models, distribution, delivery, etc., created by the Internet and related technologies.
(2) A new and innovative number-crunching power offered by big data, analytics, machine learning, IoT, blockchain, hyper modelling, etc. to incorporate and manage finer details.
(3) Demonetization of financial services, transactions, transport, education, health, entertainment, office space, etc. and its impact on employment and leisure.
(4) A new distributed and decentralized organizational architecture based on cooperation, collaboration, co-creation and global networking of ideas, individuals and innovations.

The main impact of hyperconnectivity on the economy will come from the decentralization of production and services, setting up of small factories with automation and robots, encouraging local production with local skills, scaling up through the networking of multiple supply chains, involving the local and global talent pool working from home and selling their products through online shopping and mobile banking, while at the same time improving their lives with mobile education, mobile health, etc. Agriculture technologies are set to enhance yields substantially—the food chain will be modernized; biotech, genetics and stem cell technologies will improve longevity; new energy technologies will provide cheap distributed DC energy; transportation will be demonetized; and new materials will improve quality and durability.

New Economy of National Resources

Although the Internet may have been an under-represented economic analysis factor, it has not been entirely invisible to economists' eyes. Slowly, it has started finding its place in financial models through the work of students and contemporary economists, though these studies are not yet widely accepted. However, there remain invisibles that are yet to be identified by economists and are still a long way from being incorporated. A strong example in this category is the rich national heritage of countries that have not been quantitatively ascertained in their balance sheets.

For the inclusion of such assets in the balance sheets of a nation, their book value needs to be determined and the importance of human resources emphasized, including their artistic, historical and cultural features. If we have to preserve our world's cultural diversity in an era where there is too much importance laid on a nation's economic homogeneity, a rational and scientific valuation of such heritage, historical assets and cultural treasures becomes essential. From another perspective, even if we look at taxpayers as investors who are expected to be rational decision makers and act as economic agents, then the assets (public or historical) maintained by the government become properties of public investment. Hence, information on their valuation needs to be transparently disclosed.

Some organizations and people have expressed the view that with the introduction of recognizing such hitherto intangible assets, there could be demanding workloads in arriving at valuations and estimations, the cost of which would outweigh the benefits. They did not see any particular benefits associated with such valuation that could not be achieved by any other means. However, while examining the proposition from a higher perspective, above that of logistical constraints, it is my view that this is a worthwhile activity in the context of global economies. It is not only an inclusive step for accommodating such measurements within the formal structure of computation of national wealth, but it will also act as a counter-balancing force against the biased weightage currently given to operational revenue-generating activities of countries.

The GDP is a gross measurement tool designed when there were no modern computing tools to appreciate big data and analytics. With advances in high-speed computing, extensive storage capabilities, big data, machine learning, automation, robotics, modelling, etc., it is possible to include assets and other valuables to measure a nation's economic health without depending solely on transactional data. Besides, all GDP data is based only on formal sectors and through reported information. It does not consider the informal sector, which, in most countries, is a much larger part of the economy. For example, in most emerging market samples, like in India, the informal sector, including artisans, artists, traders, small shops, daily wagers, farmworkers, etc., perhaps contributes much more to the economy than the formal sector. The underground economy, which does not declare transaction data and does not pay tax, is equally large in many other countries. How do you depend on traditional and conservative global standards and international measurements in this kind of situation?

While asset valuation in economic accounting is something nations need to look at, transnational dynamics are arising from globalization that compels us to take a relook at our economics. Most of all, it has placed an unprecedented emphasis on human capital and natural resource preservation, both of which are yet to find focused attention in the discipline of economics.

Geopolitical competition is reshaping the global economy and unravelling international power relationships and governance. As tensions between great powers rage, global businesses that once saw themselves as masters of the universe now feel like pawns in a game over which they have little control. Governments use standard-setting and legal and policy reforms to advance national interests and promote national champions, even by changing the game rules for crucial sectors and industries, both regionally and globally.

For example, there are competing approaches and standards for applying anti-monopoly tools to advance national interests in the name of market competition. In many instances, the stratagem of 'levelling the playing field' is used to justify protecting strategically critical economic outcomes.

The competition between states in the geoeconomic era will increasingly be driven by a quest for technology and markets rather than national resources. This is a significant development. During colonial times, competition revolved around direct control over land and sea, both for extracting resources and promoting long-distance trade with colonies on preferential terms. As settlements became independent, an ideological rather than economic contest took its place. Once the Cold War ended, oil emerged as the big driver of competition, creating strange new alliances and drawing the United States into the Middle East's security. Today, as the world economy suffers from the after-effects of the financial crisis, many previously stable economies are reeling under the pressure of slow or no growth. Indeed, the nature of strategic competition is changing again due to two significant factors.

First, oil resources are becoming cheaper due to the discovery and exploitation of shale gas and the oil revolution, and other technological advancements that reduce dependence on traditional suppliers. Second, in emerging markets, economic and demographic growth and human capital development make them an essential source of global aggregate demand and relatively cheap but qualified labour.

Modern multinational corporations' interests underpin the shift from the strategic competition for access to resources to the competition for inroads into new markets. Due to the breakthroughs in information and communication technologies and more efficient transportation and related logistics, these corporations have become genuinely global; they can invest and allocate goods and services, and even undertake individual production tasks across continents. This has shifted the strategic space of competition for natural resources.

The need for this access is twofold. Those who want to win in the new world should invest in skills. Those who want to provide human capital accumulation incentives should ensure access to a large (preferably global) market. Thus, driving this new trend is, on the one hand, accessing markets to make production more competitive by possible outsourcing to cheaper skill centres, and on the other, having large middle-class markets to whom these products are sold.

The winners of this new strategic competition are primarily countries with increasing per capita incomes and large and growing populations—mainly China and India. The highly skilled citizens of the developed world will also stand to gain as they become more productive in managing larger corporations and creating new technologies for broader markets. Countries and corporations that are adept at building inroads into new markets through their control over social, economic and communication networks will stand to benefit from these growing markets.

Simultaneously, the producers of natural resources are likely to see their power being eclipsed; hence, oil-rich countries such as Saudi Arabia, Russia and Iran stand to lose. And so do the medium-skilled workers in the Organization for Economic Co-operation and Development (OECD) countries. They now face competition from the cheaper but qualified labour force in the emerging markets. Countries unable to provide security and stability for economic enterprise and foreign investments will also be marginalized with this new globalization wave. During the 2011 conflict in Libya, China had to evacuate thousands of its workers from the country. Low-skilled workers in developed countries are still protected from this competition as their jobs are not yet outsourceable. However, automation and technical progress may be a threat to them.

If we are able to leverage or hedge against these dynamics for the benefit of the entire world, we must also learn to incorporate them into the mainstream appreciation of disciplines such as politics and economics.

Traditional economics has always been about comparative and relative advantages and resources, competition and market rivalry rather than collaboration, common wealth and community markets. However, globalization and our resultant networked world have also thrown light on the need to have greater understanding and recognition of the shared resources and wealth that we possess as human beings.

Common Wealth

Common wealth—which is to say wealth that rightfully belongs to all of us together—comes in tangible and intangible forms. Real gifts include nature and our atmosphere and ecosystems, while intangible human creations include such assets as our financial system. It also consists of the value added by complex systems within our economy—the 'emergent' amount that exceeds the cost of a system's parts. Consider what would happen if the Internet, our power system or our monetary system crashed—the individual components of these systems would have little value on their own. It's the whole that creates value more than all its parts. We need to make the invisible common wealth visible.

The market ought to regard common wealth as the wealth held in a trust for future generations and all humanity equally. The twenty-first-century economic order must systematically conserve rather than being systematically wasteful and polluting. Conventional economic thinking treats material economic activities as if each is a separate linear process, starting with the extraction of resources (from an infinite pool of resources of the natural world, which is often seen as being outside the economic system altogether), continuing with the use of the resources in the production of goods, followed by the consumption of those goods, and finally ending with the disposal of waste (into an infinite sink in the natural world, again seen as outside the economic system). The result is that today's financial system operates as if it were a machine, designed to take resources out of the Earth, convert them into waste and then return them to the Earth as waste. By its very nature, it is systematically wasteful and polluting.

Need for New Economic Models

The twenty-first-century economic order must, by contrast, see the whole of economic activity as a single continuing cyclical process, comprising countless interrelated cyclical subprocesses, with the waste from each providing resources for the rest. It must design the economic system as an organic part of the natural world, not as a machine external to it—a reintegration which will also mean a rejection of the deluded assumption that the natural world is a limitless pool. The new financial system must thus be one of systematic conservation.

The twenty-first-century economy must be designed and managed as a multi-level one-world economic system, with autonomous but interdependent parts at all levels.

Economic policymaking today is still based on old assumptions. On the one hand, national governments insist on controlling the spending of local government authorities as a part of national economic management. On the other, international economic relations are based on the idea of sovereign nations negotiating among themselves. Currencies are still issued nationally, not locally or internationally; money is denominated and controlled at the national level, not local or international.

The gap between conventional economic theory and practice on the one hand and economic realities on the other is already growing too contentious to ignore. The need for effective monetary policy at the local level is highlighted by cities' and rural districts' economic problems in many parts of the world. Meanwhile, recurring international ecological and economic issues, the increasing need for global economic coordination, the growing domination of the world economy by transnational corporations, and the emergence of a one-world financial system based on computer communication between London, Tokyo, New York and other centres emphasize the need for effective economic policymaking at the global level. To continue to focus on national economic policymaking—whether from a Keynesian, monetarist, socialist or any other standpoint—would simply be to ignore twenty-first-century realities.

It is necessary to re-examine and redefine many economic concepts. These will include wealth creation and capital accumulation, efficiency and productivity, dependence, interdependence, self-reliance, risk and security, needs, wants and scarcity. What will be the meaning of wealth creation and capital accumulation, along with greater efficiency and productivity for people and organizations, when each would be operating at various levels of an enabling and conserving one-world economy? And how will they best be measured?

Today, in most management and economic theories, the link to the broader ecosystem—nature herself—is missing, causing enormous, negative consequences. Today capitalism and the financial system are growing at an unhealthy rate for the overall system's survival. Consider them like the uncontrolled growth of cells which leads to cancer.

Capitalism has developed into a monstrous, web-spinning, self-organized system, encompassing the entire globe. The financial crisis of 2008 left even financial experts in despair. They were primarily fuelled through excessive liberalization and privatization, which benefited the 1 per cent on top and took away from the other 99 per cent. Besides, our current economic system is premised on the idea of single-minded growth, ignoring the finite boundaries of the biosphere and the laws of physics. Our financial and economic system can only function if it serves humanity and our planet as a whole. Today, society and the planet are serving the needs of financial and economic growth in an unsustainable manner, to such an extent that it is threatening our survival as a species. Today, it is not about the politics of liberal vs conservative or right wing vs left wing. These debates are outdated and fall short once we realize and understand our current problem's root cause.

One of the myths of today is aiming for infinite exponential economic growth on a planet with finite boundaries. We need to understand the significance of universal patterns that have shaped the cosmos and our Earth over millions of years and created a healthy, stable and sustainable environment with a delicate balance. How can we learn from creation, from the lessons that nature teaches us, to heal and redesign our capitalist system? The basic idea is to shift away from our linear growth-based economy towards a new sustainable economy.

We must first understand that nature does not stop at national borders; it is a complex, adaptive system spanning the whole world and connecting everybody. The jungles in Brazil are far away from Chicago, but they are, to a large extent, responsible for the air we breathe. Even if we live in a globalized world, we act and live locally most of the time. Second, we have to change how we perceive wealth. Wealth is more than just money in a bank account. There are other forms of wealth, such as human, cultural, environmental, spiritual, material and social capital. What does prosperity mean if we take a more holistic perspective? Before spending a lifetime chasing money and material, we should try to produce and sustain these other forms of diverse wealth.

Recent modern research in biology, neuroscience and other disciplines suggests that cooperation is far more widespread and fundamental than previously thought. Competition is only one part of the game. In a new sustainable economy, we need empowered participation. An independent system's health only emerges if there is a contributory benefit in one way or another on the health of the whole. Therefore, the idea is not merely one of self-interest; it is about the quality of each participant's integration with the larger whole. Today, we need to shift away from negotiating only for our own personal or national needs and to move towards co-creating well-being and systemic health in the broader context we are embedded in. Ultimately, this larger context is our Earth. Undoubtedly, the whole is always constructed from different pieces of the puzzle. Natural habitats take thousands of years to grow and to find a balance. More and more, we see how indigenous communities and traditions have been uprooted for profit. However, the false claim is made that it is part of a more extensive process benefiting globalization. Sustainable economics assumes a different perspective when, as a principle, we—all individual communities and places—integrate into the whole.

The key is to integrate localization and globalization effectively, encompassing the private and public sectors, small and large enterprises, organized and unorganized labour, products and services, multiple supply chains and networking of resources, via centralized and decentralized implementation, to optimize human capital to assure an improved environment and inclusion, basic needs, education, health and prosperity for all.

Human communities are mosaics of traditions, values, beliefs, peoples, cultures and local environments, and they are affected by the long-term impact of geography, history and the environment. Only if these unique qualities are understood and integrated into a global economy will we achieve healthy and resilient communities worldwide. Old farming techniques used different kinds of plants positioned next to each other for growth and mutual support, thus enabling fertile outcomes. Without diversity, natural and human-made systems are similar to monocultural farming—they become more vulnerable and lose abundance and profusion.

Nature herself is abundant in her diversity and beauty. And while we have specific limited resources, if we take the idea of a new economy seriously, we will realize that there is enough for everybody from a systemic perspective. What do we need to be vibrant and happy and live a meaningful life? Certain goods and products are necessary, but what has been empirically proven to be more fulfilling than any material wealth on Earth are friends and family, and contribution to a meaningful cause. How do we start changing our current economic model into a new economy to help redesign the world?

Is it necessary for a nation or economy to continue to grow forever? Is growth an excellent objective to chase? Is it possible to have zero growth and still be happy and content? Can we reach a state where needs are met before wants? Is it acceptable to have slow growth for rich countries and high growth for emerging countries? Can we design economic theories to expedite inclusion, equity and equality?

These will be among the kinds of questions in our minds as we turn to replace old economic ideas with new ones. It will take a long time to move from current financial practices to the new economy. It will demand a broader global conversation, not among economists, but with the people at large. It will require understanding and agreement on a unique design of the world to develop the new economy. This cannot be done in isolation. It has to be an integral part of the other four pillars of the redesign: inclusion, basic needs, conservation and non-violence.

7

Conservation and Sustainability

'You must not lose faith in humanity. Humanity is like an ocean. If a few drops of the ocean are dirty the ocean does not get dirty.'

—M.K. Gandhi

The fourth pillar in the redesign of the world is related to conservation and sustainability. The challenge in today's times is to move away from consumption-based spending behaviour, which was promoted after World War II to expand economies globally. We now have to create new opportunities and a new economy for conservation and sustainability to improve the environment, ecosystem and natural resources, and to meet human needs. This also requires changing our mindset and behaviour from disposable to durable products and services.

The US has been the biggest consumer of resources in the world. With 330 million people, its people's standard of living has accounted for almost 50 per cent of global resources for many years. (This has changed recently because of rapid developments in China and India, countries with a population of 1.5 billion and 1.3 billion people, respectively, which have been following the American model of consumerism.) Post–World War II, Americans started spending money on goods and services which were not available during the war years. The economic boom of the 1950s and President Dwight D. Eisenhower's administration in the US supported what was called the 'good life'. The 'good life' was defined in economic terms, and the Americans have enjoyed it for a long time. Now many other countries want the American 'good life'.

Consumption

Consumerism has always been a symbol of social status in America. People compare their acquisitions and aspirations with that of their neighbours, and decide what to buy from advertisements they see on television and the Internet. The common man reveres brand names, and their procurement is seen as an achievement. People always carry a 'wish list' of desired things and look for them in e-shops and purchase them to achieve their 'higher goals and higher status'. There is no doubt that capitalism and consumption have improved the overall quality of life and comfort worldwide. However, the problem with consumption culture is it does not stop at the individual level. It is one of the reasons the planet is plagued by environmental issues. Global warming and climate change are by-products of the ever-increasing demand we have created by setting up mega factories in many parts of the world, which can churn out products that people are ready to buy. In the process, poor farmers sell their land to build factories, roads and shopping centres. Even though they have cash in hand, they lose their livelihood and lifestyle.

Today's consumption undermines environmental resources and breeds inequality. And the constant cycle of consumption, poverty, inequality and impact on the environment continues. The real issue is not consumption itself, but its patterns and effects, and the inequalities that come with it. Globally, 20 per cent of people in the highest-income countries account for 86 per cent of total private consumption, while the lowest 20 per cent constitute only a minuscule 1.3 per cent.

The full-blown commercialized consumption that most people in wealthy nations and the most affluent in emerging countries practise is a relatively recent phenomenon, which started in the second half of the twentieth century. In fact, in the US and European nations, consumption used to be based on necessities, and saving and being frugal was the norm for most people. Spending on 'luxuries' was typically frowned upon and seen as wasteful. Of course, the wealthy elite of those times would spend generously on themselves, as they had been doing for centuries, while supporting religious and other belief systems that promoted limited consumption, thus sustaining disparity and maintaining control over most people. So, restricting consumption was perhaps a political tool for dominance in those times. Another aspect of limited consumption in the past was the lack of technology, tools and awareness to enable the industry to exploit resources and expand manufacturing. For the consumer to spend, luxuries had to be converted to necessities, and this was the task of the big marketing corporations. The middle class had to be converted into a new market. The present age of consumerism is the outcome of the money spent by big companies on marketing and advertising.

Advertising has always been directed towards changing the way an image is created in the minds of people. The goal is to aggressively shape consumer behaviour and desires to generate demand and convince the people to buy. In 1880, only $30 million per year was spent on advertising in the United States; by 1910, new businesses, such as oil, food, electricity and rubber, were spending $600 million. Today, that figure has climbed to well over $250 billion per year in the United States and over $525 billion worldwide.

Consumers were also enticed by the launch of shopping malls and attractive decorations in multiple department stores, restaurants, theatres, shops, etc. where clothing, jewellery, cosmetics, furniture, consumer products and services are laid out to entice people to buy the beautiful things they see and to spend their leisure time in this manner. Various coupons, awards, gifts, incentives and payment schemes were introduced to invite and engage shoppers to enhance their shopping experiences and encourage them to buy more.

Advertisements and shopping malls have thus served various purposes. People are led to make frequent purchases to remain fashionable, thus increasing the rate of consumption and leading to conspicuous consumption. By companies producing and selling more things and services, capitalism has thrived. The more nations have grown, the more people have purchased, and the more they have contributed to the so-called progress and prosperity. The most critical measure of economic growth is, after all, the GNP, the total of goods and services produced by a given society in a given year. It is a measure of the success and growth of a consumer society. However, the production, processing and consumption of commodities require extraction and natural resources like water, minerals, wood, oil, ore and land. They also necessitate the presence of factories that create pollution and toxic by-products.

Junk food chains are under attack from major environmental groups in the United States and other developed countries because of their ecological and health impact. Intensive breeding of livestock and poultry for such restaurants leads to deforestation, land degradation, and contamination of water sources and other natural resources. For every pound of red meat, poultry, eggs and milk produced, farm fields lose about 5 pounds of irreplaceable topsoil. The water necessary for meat breeding comes to about 190 gallons per animal per day, or several times what a typical Indian family uses in a single day. Overall, animal farms use nearly 40 per cent of the world's total grain production. In the United States, almost 70 per cent of grain production is fed to livestock.

We have developed disposable products and disposable culture instead of durable products and durable culture in the process. Everything has become disposable almost everywhere, from paper napkins to plates, cups, mats, bags, etc., eventually resulting in garbage mountains. With disposable culture has come a large volume of low-quality throwaway products instead of the traditional philosophy of owning fewer high-quality possessions.

Unfortunately, our consumption patterns are so much a part of our lives that to change them would require a massive cultural overhaul, not to mention severe economic dislocation. As economists note, a drop in the demand for products brings economic recession or even depression, along with massive unemployment. However, the decline in demand for disposable products can increase the requirement for high-quality durable products and other essentials required by the poor. The key is to change our mindset about manufacturing from 'disposable to durable', from 'consumption to conservation' and from 'wants to needs' and still create new jobs to keep the economy growing.

Conservation

Conservation is a movement to protect and preserve our environment. All its characteristics, including biodiversity, habitat, species, wildlife, forests, waters, mines, minerals and other natural resources, have to keep a natural balance, with interdependence and interactions between all forms of life and vegetation on the planet. Only then can we all lead a healthy life. This helps preserve resources for future generations to utilize, benefit and enjoy. Conservation is also the mindset where we, as individuals, make rational choices based on our understanding of the economy, environment, utility, convenience and other factors. We have been inclined to acquire things like clothing, accessories, jewellery, cell phones, furniture, vehicles, etc., unaware of where these things come from, what goes into making them, and what happens to them when we throw them away. Once we understand the entire cycle of consumption and its implications for the environment and natural resources, we will realize that there is a need to shift our perspective on conservation: we need to manage our natural resources, like water, trees, mines, minerals, plants and animals, and improve our environment.

During the COVID-19 lockdown, I had the time to analyse the things that I had mindlessly acquired over the previous fifty-five years without paying much attention to my needs. The eye-opener was my collection of suits, shirts, socks, pants, pens and ties. Did I need 700 ties and fifty pens? Now, very few people wear ties, and hardly anyone uses a pen. Unfortunately, every time I went to speak at an event, I was given a tie or a pen that I used to store on my shelves without ever looking at it again. What a waste of resources! But the tradition of giving gifts, invented by marketing minds, is such that you cannot escape it. We meet friends and family on many occasions, and they express their love by buying us something. This type of behaviour and associated consumption has to be controlled as it has vast implications for our environment. If we have 100 T-shirts and fifty pairs of jeans in the house, consider the quantity of water wasted on producing these clothes. Some of us in advanced countries have crossed the limits of consumption. It is time to understand the implication of this on the planet and start thinking of conservation.

I have decided to live a simpler life now, paying attention to cutting down possessions, reducing requirements, eating fresh vegetables, fruits and home-cooked meals, not driving around unnecessarily, staying at home and learning to live with less. In other words, use less and do more. Earlier, I would go to Miami or New York for forty-five-minute lunch meetings. Now I have regular lunch meetings on Zoom to discuss business issues. It is productive, efficient, focused and avoids travel, while conserving time, money and energy. Since I now work from home, I do not need so many suits, shoes, socks and shirts. I do not need to fill my gas tank every week, nor do I need to go every week to the laundry with six shirts and two suits. I can see the immediate impact of my desire to live a simpler life on the environment and water.

Seven types of conservation come to mind: environmental, water, animal, industrial, energy, household and human. A great deal is written on the subject, but the overall awareness in the consumer's mind is still missing. For example, in India, there is a common custom of offering a glass of water to a visitor. Usually, a full glass is provided, even if it is not asked for, from which a sip is taken, and the rest thrown away. Can you imagine billions of glasses of good drinking water wasted every day in a country where there is such a water shortage? How do we change this custom and give water only to a person who asks for it, and that too only a small quantity? Similarly, people always leave the lights on in their house or at offices. Cities are lit up at night with office lights on all the time. Why? Now we have sensors that turn off lights when they are not in use. But can we learn to conserve energy at home and offices on our own? Do we understand what effect the generation of power has on our planet and plant and animal life? In the end, conservation is a state of mind that can be moulded with a simple understanding of environmental implications.

Sustainable consumption is the use of products and services in a way that minimizes the impact on the environment while also ensuring that essential human needs are met, not only for the present but also reserved for future generations. When sustainable consumption is practised and resources used wisely, waste products and pollution are minimized. Our main aim should be to achieve more with less. In other words, we can find ways to meet our needs and wants without depleting our planet's finite natural resources.

The more pragmatic question is how the world can move to conservation and sustainability without losing jobs. If people are consuming fewer goods and services, does this imply that there will be fewer jobs in the manufacturing, sale and provision of those goods and services? The general belief is that the global economy will collapse if we do not consume enough. However, there will be new jobs created under the new economy of conservation so that we can continue to produce clean energy, clean water, clean air and higher-quality products and services. It is no longer about the economy of scale but about the economy of substance, choice and preferences. New jobs will also have to be created from producing goods and services for human needs, rather than human wants.

The standard solution to these problems is a fundamental restructuring of the economy. As we move forward, we see the growing trend of localization. The last several decades have been towards globalization, centralization, specialization and mass production. The economic argument for centralization is one of efficiency so that fewer people can produce more goods. However, this in itself has contributed to unemployment. The mass efficiency we see moving from small- to large-scale industry has resulted in less labour demand. Machines handling mass production are drastically reducing the number of jobs left for humans. Suppose we shift our attention from globalization to localization. In that case, we will create jobs closer to the consumers, employ local talent, build local infrastructures, create products to meet local social and cultural needs, and avoid unnecessary transport and logistics. Besides, we can network local businesses to scale for efficiency. This model can benefit from hyperconnectivity to increase collaboration, cooperation and co-creation to mobilize resources and logistics.

Local ownership and entrepreneurship bring out the uniqueness of local capabilities, resources, needs, markets and relationships. It also brings the community together to understand and appreciate each other and enhance safety, security, integration, and community harmony. I firmly believe that localization of production with commitment to small-scale businesses will decentralize, democratize and demonetize many services, deliver peace and prosperity and reduce violence. At the same time, it will revive local communities as independent cultural centres. It will also support local artists, musicians, culture and cuisine to bring life to local communities. By taking production away from them to remote areas, we have disconnected them from livelihood and starved them of the resources needed to live.

Today, people in developed and developing countries are prosperous beyond the dreams of their grandparents. The houses of typical families are larger than before, sprawling across expanding suburbs. These houses are filled with all kinds of consumer products, such as multiple TVs, stereos, books, art, rugs, computers, mobile phones, racks of unused clothes, washing machines, fridges, dishwashers, dryers, vacuum cleaners, kitchen gadgets, etc. These products often overflow into garages or hired storage rooms to create spaces full of accumulated 'stuff'. Houses are often centrally heated and air-conditioned, with spare rooms and multiple cars parked outside. Average wages are well above subsistence levels, and many people have extra income to spend on comforts and luxuries such as meat, alcohol, entertainment, holidays, etc.

These consumer lifestyles are indicative of unprecedented material wealth, which is good for human progress and comfort. But this is a form of socio-economic development that has been and continues to be extremely energy-intensive. It takes vast amounts of energy to construct our homes and high-rise buildings, to grow and transport our food, to produce and fuel the 1 billion vehicles that move people and products around the world, to light our homes and power our appliances, to have countless commodities that provide us with our technologically sophisticated goods, services and entertainment, etc. In short, it takes vast amounts of energy to support high-consumption lifestyles. It is essential to understand the impact of this on our planet. Simplicity and minimization is a virtue we all must learn to practise. I believe it will lead to fine taste, higher values, refined aesthetics and new markets.

This reminds me of a friend of mine in my neighbourhood who bought a big house with a large amount of land. Every weekend, for a few hours, he would be busy mowing the lawns.

One day I saw him seated, drinking beer while driving an electric lawnmower. He said he was getting tired of mowing the lawn and needed to relax while doing it. In eight weeks, he had gained weight and complained that he was not getting enough exercise. Now he needed to get a new treadmill machine to burn off the extra calories. This led him to set up an exercise room with modern equipment. It appeared that with the regular lawnmower, he was getting all the exercise he needed, and thus could avoid expenses on new exercise equipment. However, he wanted to move up the value chain in the neighbourhood. This is the competitive and complex world some of us live in. If we eat right and walk regularly, we can avoid the need for fancy exercise equipment, to name just one thing. The choice is ours to make.

In today's uncertain times, where the effects of climate change on water resources are alarming, and the world is facing exponential population growth, water challenges cannot be neglected. Human use and pollution of freshwater resources have reached a level where water sustainability is threatened. The resulting water scarcity and quality degradation will limit food production, reduce ecosystem functions and hinder economic growth. Pressures on water resources have increased dramatically over the past few decades due to rapid demographic growth, urbanization, higher consumption levels and climate change.

The demand for water has increased in almost every country around the world. Agriculture, industry and households are the main sectors that consume water, with agriculture being the most significant consumer. It requires 70 per cent of the total global fresh water pumped out from rivers, lakes and aquifers. An increase in water demand is expected in all three sectors. By 2030, half the world population will be living in severely water-stressed areas. This increased stress on water resources puts hundreds of millions of people at risk of hunger, disease, energy shortage and poverty. Climate change and its uncertain effects on water supplies also pressure different kinds of users and stakeholders. Furthermore, water issues are intrinsically linked to other sustainable development issues such as poverty, hunger, health, education, gender inequality, ecosystems integrity, climate change and natural disasters.

The need for proper use of minerals grows in importance as the world becomes more industrialized and urbanized. A technological society's complete dependence on mineral fuels, on machines made from refined metals, and on the vast number of everyday items made from various minerals contrasts sharply with the life that existed in the Stone Age. The requirements of Stone Age people for minerals were simple: a stone that could be sharpened or a rock that could be thrown. People's conditions have become more complex, with each discovery being a response to recognized needs. Each new research effort seems to create new demand for traditional materials and lesser-known and generally scarcer materials.

At the end of World War I, only fifty of the ninety-two naturally occurring elements were being used, and only twenty of them in any significant amounts. At present, scientists are finding potential use for nearly all the elements. About seventy of them are commercially available, and about thirty-four are used in sizeable quantities. In addition to basic materials, about fifty significant kinds of rocks and minerals are processed and marketed. Mineral resources are meaningful to our economy.

Many conservationists limit their efforts to only finding the least wasteful method of extracting a particular mineral deposit. This is indeed important, for mineral assets are not renewable in the same sense as food crops are—a new crop of minerals cannot be grown each year. Our mineral wealth's efficient and practical exploitation is encouraged, led by various economic and legislative measures. Another aspect of conservation that has received growing emphasis is the desire of many people to enjoy the natural heritage without interference from man's activities. Extractive mining has not always been accomplished in ways that preserve natural beauty. Competition between the need for minerals and the demand for beauty results in improved mining practices, reclamation of areas where minerals have become exhausted or mined-out, and improved conservation measures.

Because of our real need for mineral raw materials and the best possible environment for our growing population, maximum attention to both these requirements is necessary. The conflict between the need for urban areas and the need for minerals is a slightly different but closely related aspect of conservation. The key is to monetize mines and minerals without severe damage to the environment, and adequately compensate people living in such mining areas. They are usually relocated, and their land benefits go to companies with industrial or commercial concerns, living in urban areas or abroad.

The expanding population is creating a greater demand for minerals and, at the same time, spreading over a much greater area which thus becomes unavailable for conventional extractive mining. Ideally, minerals should be extracted before urbanization extends to those particular areas with exploitable resources where such logical development has not been possible. The newer extractive method, even in thickly populated areas, involves only a limited amount of mining exploitation. The conflict of interest between the extractive mineral industry and the conservation of our natural heritage and the growth of urban regions draw attention to the need for proper preservation. Wise entrepreneurs are those who use our resources to satisfy many purposes together. The multiple use of resources becomes possible only when we know what our resources are. We must plan their use in conjunction with environmental needs, which, in turn, have to be balanced with the developmental needs of the local population.

Sustainability

Sustainable food systems enable the production of sufficient nutritious food while conserving the food system's resources and lowering its environmental impact. Such systems are based on the idea that all activities related to food production, processing, transporting, storing, marketing and consuming are interconnected and interactive. Although the current consumption patterns have contributed to making the world food system unsustainable, it is also true that sustainable diets can help. Promoting such diets creates an essential bridge between agricultural, environmental and health policies. Sustainable diets aim to reduce the impact of food production on resources and the environment by encouraging the consumption of foods that require comparatively lesser quantities of resources than others. They also have enhanced nutritional value and hence lead to better health of the people.

Globally, it is estimated that around 40 per cent of food is wasted in advanced countries after it comes to the table, and in developing countries, about 40 per cent is lost before it comes to the table. The amount of food wasted or lost is estimated to be around 1.3 billion tonnes and costs $2.6 trillion annually. This is more than enough to feed all the estimated 800 million hungry people in the world. In developed countries, much of the food wastage occurs at the consumer level at the end of the retail chain. In the developing world, losses occur mainly in production and at the post-harvest stage due to the inadequacies of processing, storage and distribution.

There are many options for reducing food loss at the front end of the food supply chain. These include assisting small-scale farmers in organizing centralized storage, efficient transportation, cooling and other facilities to reduce losses at the production and post-harvest stages. It also involves providing food producers training to help them abide by food safety standards so that less food needs to be thrown away. Likewise, there are many alternatives at the back end of the chain—increasing public awareness about the importance of not wasting food is one of them.

Although a lot of food is wasted during production, food processing or at the retail stage, a much higher ratio is wasted due to overconsumption. This overconsumption is due to the nature of social vanity and waste, which is a direct result of advertising and our need as a society to consume as much, as fast and as quickly as possible. This creates greed. For instance, a person may want to buy a car, and s/he will not feel happy until it is purchased. It is a similar process for food shopping, though emotional connections are far more ingrained with food; we have a biological reaction to it, arising from taste, nostalgia, etc. The advertising campaigns of many companies hone in on this nostalgic quality of products. We see a food product on the shelf and we want it, even though we already have enough. We buy it, even though we are not hungry. We want it because of the attractive packaging or the advertisements we have seen on TV. Consumerist culture has had the same effect on our food shopping as it has had on our general purchasing and consumption; it has become a never-ending vicious cycle.

Food is a complex system that relates to local soil, weather, gene pool, seeds, tastes, labour, livelihood and a lot more.

Most of the world population depends on small local farmers for food. These farmers work hard for livelihood, income and a better future for their children. They are not business people. Big corporations have now started dominating food business with advanced technology to improve efficiency, productivity, markets and profits. This is a threat to the freedom, entrepreneurship and livelihood of millions all over the world. Corporatization of the food business could destroy small farmers, move wealth from rural to urban areas, and reduce the prospects of rural growth and prosperity. These issues are fundamental to conservation and sustainability in food systems. These are also fundamental to the power struggle between big and small businesses.

One of the essential elements is conscious consumerism when it comes to habitat conservation and wildlife protection. This means that conservation is not only about what we actively do—it is also what we choose not to do or buy that makes the difference. The future of our world's forests, a haven for many endangered species, is heavily impacted by consumerism. For instance, many products readily available to us are sourced from illegal logging. Similarly, body parts of endangered species are still found in some traditional Asian medicines or are sold as souvenirs, but we should not purchase them and create demand for such products.

Since plastic bags have invaded our lives, almost all garbage and food waste are disposed of in them. These bags spill out on to the road from municipality dustbins. Because they are usually tied in a knot at the mouth, cows cannot reach the food leftovers inside and end up eating the whole bag. Because of the cow's complex digestive system, these bags never get expelled and, over time, accumulate inside the rumen, which is the first stomach of the cow. There, these bags get entangled and become as hard as cement.

There are thousands of temples, villages and towns along India's rivers where untreated sewage and garbage flow into the water. Hundreds of kilometres away, waste and plastic are deposited at places where wildlife feeds and drinks. Many animals thus die a painful and unobserved death. Greenpeace says that at least 267 different species are known to have suffered from entanglement or ingestion of marine debris, including seabirds, turtles, seals, sea lions, whales and fish. Some of these species are found in the North Pacific Gyre.

It is true that cutting down forests or converting natural forests into monocultures of pine or eucalyptus for industrial raw material generates revenues and growth. But this growth is based on robbing the forests of biodiversity and their capacity to conserve soil and water. This growth comes by depriving forest communities of their food sources, fodder, fuel, fibre, medicine and security from floods and drought.

Plastics that are disposed of eventually converge in the ocean where currents meet. As a result, vast islands of plastic are created. The Great Pacific Garbage Patch is located in the central North Pacific Ocean and is more extensive than Texas. Deep inside the ocean, the massive bulk of plastic stands very much like a natural mountain, with peaks and flatlands. The Great Pacific Garbage

Patch, in turn, symbolizes the magnitude of unconscious waste that the modern world is producing. People are unaware of such issues because they do not affect their day-to-day lives.

Over a few decades, humans have managed to dump tonnes upon tonnes of garbage into the ocean. One of the most devastating effects of this pollution is that plastic takes thousands of years to decay. As a result, fish and wildlife are becoming toxic. The toxins from such plastics have entered the food chain, threatening human health. In the most polluted places in the ocean, plastic's mass exceeds plankton six times over. This is a significant piece of undeniable evidence that highlights the problem of polluted oceans. It is upsetting that more efforts for cleaning up the oceans are not taken seriously. Such issues are often placed in trade-off situations, with individuals left to choose between the environment and their own needs, wants and desires.

We should emphasize the positive side of green purchase decisions in marketing and make the production and consumption of low carbon products aspirational. In other words, consumers must have the necessary knowledge so they know what they benefit from when putting their money on greener, though more expensive, product alternatives.

Earth and its climate have a natural rate of stabilization. Ever since man achieved civilization, he has been leaving behind on Earth a continuous and growing footprint created because of his activities. Earth is experiencing the effects of human presence in the form of substantial changes in the balance of soil deposits, water flows, subsoil confinements and the composition of flora and fauna. In modern times, society's capitalistic ways have created a demand for activities that have left large carbon footprints with immense and adverse ecological impact. Energy exploitation, hydrocarbon extraction, burning with consequential thermal and carbonic emissions, mineral exhumation, chemical processing and production, agricultural soil exploitation, economic externalities and wastage are some of the new-age problems the climatic system of the planet has had to absorb. Many countries, with different cultures, lifestyles and development rates, are the arenas where such conflicts arise. Nations are not ready to take collective responsibility for this continuing catastrophe; further, the general disagreement among nations on carbon footprints is of primary concern. The lack of awareness that consumers, producers, wealth and politics are interrelated leads to this grave situation, even in countries like America.

Conservation and sustainability go hand in hand. If we learn to conserve, we can learn to sustain our natural resources by cutting fewer trees, using less water, burning less energy and using fewer minerals. The real challenge is about changing our mindset and behaviour and reducing negative implications on our economy and employment. I do not believe that we need to make more, spend more and buy more to create more jobs. Some of tomorrow's jobs do not exist today, and they could even emerge from the economy of conservation and sustainability. Today, we produce large volumes of low-quality goods, and perhaps tomorrow, with an emphasis on conservation, we will have smaller works of high-quality goods. In this hyperconnected world, we are rapidly moving from the economy of scale to the economy of scope and economy of preferences. In a sense, it is all about 'disposable' versus 'durable' and sustainable culture. Indeed, this shift has to be made to preserve our planet and protect our people.

8

Non-violence

'Non-violence is not a weapon of the weak. It is a weapon of the strongest and bravest.'

—M.K. Gandhi

The fifth pillar in the redesign of the world is non-violence. The challenge is to transform people's mindset and behaviour and turn them away from violence towards non-violence. Similarly, the government's policies, programmes and military spending for wars should be transformed into action to generate peace and human development.

From the beginning, humans have been inherently hardwired for violence because of the constant fear of survival arising out of living in the wild with animals. Today's human beings have evolved over the millennia by using their intelligence and understanding and exploring science and technology. Over the centuries, they have created social, political and economic systems to organize their lives and enjoy modern comforts. However, the primary mindset of violence and fear has not yet changed from when humans lived in caves. The tendency towards violence is not genetically transferred, but it can undoubtedly be culturally conditioned.

When early humans, living in caves, started to assemble into larger groups, it eventually gave rise to villages and towns. In these dwellings, there were individual clans that controlled the territory and resources. Violence, fights and killings settled conflicts among families. As civilization progressed, minor conflicts started to reduce and larger states were formed. The states eventually began warring with other countries and competing for resources or territorial expansion. Specialized weapons and military systems were developed to wage these wars, with the goal of competing with others and inflicting more significant damage through violence to maintain and retain control and superiority. In the process, territories were invaded, people captured, houses burnt, slavery practised, colonies established and millions of people killed. The resources, properties and powers of the losing side were invariably captured. In some way or the other, this primitive tribal mentality and related practices continue to command and control resources through espionage, intimidation, trade, technology and wars. It is unfortunate that today, in the advanced countries of the world, more money is spent to support military-industrial complexes and to kill people than on public health systems.

Military Mindset

The total worldwide military spending is estimated to be around $2000 billion. The five largest spenders—the United States, China, India, Russia and Saudi Arabia—account for over 60 per cent of the spending, with the US accounting for almost 40 per cent. China and India are the second and the third largest military spenders. To put this in perspective, it is essential to note that we will need no more than $250 billion per year to eliminate hunger from this planet. It means that reducing military expenditure by merely 12.5 per cent can eliminate hunger from the planet forever.

Similarly, reducing 10 per cent of military spending per year for five years can provide $1 trillion to build housing for about

200 million low-income families worldwide. During peacetime, military expenditures are entirely out of proportion compared with the planet's and the people's real needs. The fear of war with other countries, the desire to protect national borders, control global resources and defend markets make modern nations keep expanding their military prowess and continue funding military-industrial complexes that divert essential funding requirements for human development.

Military-industrial complexes are major global institutional infrastructures that employ millions of people in research, design, development, manufacturing, deployment and services. They are at the top of the global economic food chain. They are also responsible for value creation in all major countries, feeding on fear and the 'fortress' mentality. This way of thinking is nurtured by political bosses, big businesses and military magnates who ensure that funds are provided each year for rapid growth.

The positive side of the military industry enjoying global respect, rewards, dignity and power and contributing a great deal to development—mainly because of US defence research—has led to the commercialization of many technologies which, happily, can also be used to benefit the people at large. It cannot be condemned entirely or opposed because it has done some good and carries the pride of nationalism, border protection, security, safety and sovereignty. Yet, it is an industry that feeds violence and wars, and keeps advanced countries in the forefront. In some countries, there are national parades that proudly display military power and nuclear warheads. There are exhibitions and fairs to market fighter planes and firearms. Weapons are sold to less developed countries, even though they cannot even feed their people. Unfortunately, many countries pay billions to buy military hardware for war while being unable to provide clean water, adequate food or appropriate housing for their citizens. In some Asian and African countries, warlords are encouraged to equip themselves with the most modern equipment to fight while employing many hungry and helpless youths in the army. This industry is designed to maintain peace, but it ends up fuelling terror and violence.

Violence

Violence is seen not just amongst nations. It is at home, in the family, neighbourhood, communities, villages and cities. It is everywhere: violence against children, women, older people, family members, fellow workers, neighbours, etc., can be witnessed in every society. Violence comes in many forms—verbal abuse, property damage, threats, beating, captivity, kidnapping, slavery, forced/bonded labour, rape, human trafficking, injuries, killings, bombing, etc. Acts of violence are resorted to by individuals as a way to meet the uncomfortable realities of life. They could be reactions to their childhood experiences, upbringing, living environment, hunger, social development, uncontrolled anger, ego, greed and jealousy, hate and other negative emotions.

From my experiences, I have learnt that some people have fragile self-esteem, and they get hurt very easily. Some are too sensitive about humiliation, honour, ego, insult, respect and personal status, resulting in anger and arguments. At times, these situations escalate to violence. They cannot manage anger or resolve differences through dialogue. In a sense, this form of violence springs from an inner imbalance that takes varied forms of destructive activity, resulting in violence, including verbal abuse, fights, attacks, murder, terrorism, battles and wars.

The world is a collective of individuals, wherein each individual is an actor, playing out his or her part within global consciousness. An individual can promote a peaceful environment or destroy it. Violence becomes evident when an individual, deprived of feelings of belonging, becomes distracted and inimical and begins to hurt other people. Suicide bombings and shoot-outs by such disturbed individuals becomes the cause of unrest in the community. Everyday conflicts in the family or at work have been proven to drive people to some form of violence. In the US, easy availability and ownership of guns have added to violence in society.

The varying ideologies, beliefs, religions and differences can give rise to hatred, misinformation and misunderstanding between people and communities and nations. Self-proclaimed superiority, including the rejection of others, continues to polarize our world. In the last seventy-five years, we have avoided World War III, but we continue to enter into conflicts in Korea, Vietnam, Afghanistan, Iraq, Libya, Kuwait, Syria, Lebanon, Bosnia, Nigeria, Somalia and Sudan, to name a few. Most of these wars could have been avoided with effective diplomacy and honest dialogue. However, at times, wars are designed and created to sell arms; conversely, arms are manufactured and pledged to fight battles. In the past, people and nations have been driven to violence and to wars to capture and control markets, wealth and resources, and promote ideologies. This made sense in an economy based on scarcity. Now we live in an era of surplus where there is more than enough for everyone. Does it still make sense to wage wars to control resources?

Just after my marriage in 1966, the US government drafted me for the Vietnam war. All Americans below the age of twenty-six were required to report to the local facilities. I was against the very idea of war but had no option. I did not see the American government's logic in fighting an ideological war against communism on the other side of the globe. It made no sense to take up arms against the poor Vietnamese and convince them about democracy's merits. I went to my boss at work and told him my views. Some friends even suggested that I could decline to join the US army for religious reasons. But I could not do that.

For several months, I was anxious about being drafted. Every day, I saw on television scenes of bloody battles in Vietnam, where thousands of brave young Americans and Vietnamese were dying, only for the avowed purpose of upholding national pride and prestige. As it turned out, since I was also studying for my PhD, I could get what was known as 'occupational deferment' and not go to Vietnam. This is what I finally did.

The war lasted for many years after that. At the end, when America was forced to leave Vietnam, the images of people boarding helicopters from the roof of the US embassy to get back home made me think again about the purpose of that war. I am sure political and military leaders had their logic. However, many who had sacrificed their young children were relieved that it was over.

In the appendix to this book, I have referred to the discussions I had with General Giap at the time when I was heading C-DOT. He was a veteran soldier who had fought both the French and the Americans in Vietnam, and had come to Delhi to discuss communication technologies on the advice of the Vietnam president. During my interactions with him, I thought that this was the man America had been fighting against during the Vietnam war. I found him to be a gentleman full of curiosity and concern for poor people in his country. Sitting across the table from someone like him, it was difficult for me to believe that the US and Vietnam could not settle disputes through dialogue.

It made me think about the complexity of communication while warring groups negotiate for peace before ultimately going to war. It is difficult to believe that we cannot avoid war between nations through honest and open dialogue in this civilized world with support from other well-meaning countries. Terror groups are altogether a different matter. Their unjustifiable anger comes mainly from disorientation, indoctrination, inequality and injustice. They, too, need understanding, listening and honest dialogue to avoid violence. I strongly feel that if you desire peace, no one can stop you. It is important to note that people want peace and not wars. In wars, people die, their properties are destroyed, they are forced to migrate, their young children get injured and killed, their lives get disturbed, and they leave deep scars on societies. World leaders and military generals must think much more about the people's pain before waging war to achieve their objectives.

Similarly, I had an opportunity to spend an hour with Mikhail Gorbachev when he was the president of the Soviet Union in 1989 at the home of the then prime minister of India, Rajiv Gandhi, in Delhi. During our long interaction on technology and development, I could not see him as an enemy of America. How could a man like Gorbachev, at the helm of a vast country with twelve time zones, not think of collaborating with the leading nations to build a better world for everyone? At times, I felt that we tend to define our enemy based on our past experiences instead of future opportunities, hopes, aspirations and possibilities. I saw immense possibilities in my interactions with Gorbachev. Two years after our exchange, several new countries with democratic aspirations were born without violence or war.

This reminded me of a conversation I had with a government minister in the Soviet Union in Moscow in 1988. During dinner, the minister said to me: 'We are very impressed with India because, without guns, you have been able to hold together a very vast and diverse country with multiple languages, culture, religion, and ethnicity. The day we turn our guns around, the Soviet Union may fall apart.' I did not understand the depth of his comments until 1991, when the Soviet Union broke up into several countries.

The key is to initiate peace early enough and prevent violence between people and nations. The seeds of violence planted in people's minds must be weeded out to avoid the emotions that cause suffering and destruction and innocent people's deaths. The idea is to adopt a path that will prevent violence from germinating. Having a peace process is essential to resolve conflicts through understanding, acceptance, communication, collaboration, cooperation and adjustments. We must first begin non-violence with an attitude of open minds, empathy, inclusion and unity towards all impending conflicts.

Non-violence

Non-violence is in the teachings of the Tirthankaras of Jainism, formulated around the seventh century BCE. Their philosophy is not to cause or even desire to cause any harm or injury to any living thing. This idea is not limited to human beings, but also extends to plants and animals. This belief in non-violence (ahimsa) is practised in speech and actions and thoughts. A practitioner of this way of life feels compassionate and tolerant towards oneself and every other energy form. Ahimsa is the core belief of Jainism; all the different facets of life are dependent on this philosophy of non-injury towards the self and all others. The teachings of Mahavira, the twenty-fourth and last Jain Tirthankara, are considered the first recorded documents of the philosophy of non-violence. Jainism believed that the entire cosmos is filled with life in every inch; one cannot live, but with the possibility of hurting others. Thus, the ideal way is to live in such a manner as to cause no harm or injury. It is a remarkable idea where no living creature, from a tiny insect to a large predator, is harmed or killed. This way of life made it possible for the Tirthankaras to cultivate a similar attitude in their environment and with fellow humans. This principle has been emphasized in the Buddha's teachings and can also be traced to ancient India's yogic literature.

The idea of non-violence is not only about not causing injury to any living being, but also about respect, dignity, love, compassion and empathy; this emerges from the wisdom that we are all interconnected and interrelated. Non-violence is also related to forgiveness, reconciliation and concern for the weak and underprivileged. We all depend on each other; what affects one ultimately affects all of us. We all share the only planet we have.

In the last century, among many advocates of non-violence, three global leaders in particular have promoted and practised it: Mahatma Gandhi in India, Martin Luther King in America, and Nelson Mandela in South Africa.

In the early twentieth century, a young Mohandas Karamchand Gandhi, an Indian barrister, travelled the path of non-violence with determination. While living in South Africa, he confronted discrimination and injustice. Later, he returned to India to fight for freedom against British colonial rule. He incorporated the ideal of non-violence and non-cooperation as instruments to inspire millions and help dislodge the most powerful empire from its stronghold in India. This confident, simple, straightforward and committed Gandhi, a firm believer in non-violence, mobilized the entire nation to join him and fight the British, while at the same time rejecting violence. He and his people were humiliated, harassed, beaten and jailed, but they never took the path of hate, anger or violence. They remained calm, collected and careful under challenging conditions and continued to follow the path of non-violence as they fought for freedom, human rights, justice and independence without weapons. The weapon of non-violence was rooted in moral authority and character, with a clear vision of what was right for India's people.

Gandhi aimed at propagating non-violence in all spheres of life and towards all people. His passion for ahimsa was total, and it remained the core value of his life. Gandhi emphasized that there was no point in resorting to violence to solve a conflict; he was convinced in his heart that a permanent solution could never be arrived at through a violent struggle. He continued to wield his moral authority and non-violent methods against the powerful forces of the British Empire, and was ultimately able to lead India towards independence. Finally, after over 200 years of domination and colonization, the British left India.

Gandhi believed that violence could result in temporary peace or victory, but it would be short-lived. He emphasized the need for a change in mindset and spirit and gave little importance to physical matters. He always stressed that the change must begin within each one of us. This will start a domino effect to change a violent environment to a non-violent one, and ultimately change the oppressor's heart. He said that when we act violently, we harm ourselves and others, becoming our own enemy. If we intend to achieve peace, we must first remove the negativity and prejudices towards others and find our peace within.

Dr Martin Luther King, a great African-American leader, was introduced to non-violence in college. Later, he learnt about Gandhi's emphasis on non-violence, truth, trust and love as a social transformation method. He experienced the power of non-violence at the Montgomery bus boycott in 1955. King finally decided to abandon the use of armed bodyguards against his associates' advice, who were concerned about the threat to King's life. It made him feel free and liberated. When his home was bombed, he responded with compassion and not anger and rage. His trip to India in 1959 helped him connect with Gandhi's life and legacy. He believed that the choice was no longer between violence and non-violence but between non-violence and non-existence. One of the fundamental tenets of Dr King's philosophy of non-violence, as described in his book *Stride Toward Freedom*, is that non-violence is a way of life for the courageous; it seeks to win friendship and understanding; it also seeks to defeat the idea of injustice and not to defeat people; it offers love instead of hate. Unfortunately, Dr King, a champion of non-violence and the tallest civil rights leader in the USA, was killed by an assassin's bullet in 1968.

His dream remains unfinished. Racial discrimination in the US has not made the desired progress, as illustrated by the events that led to the Black Lives Matter campaign. With a population of 300 million, the US has the largest number of people in prison, and more and more jails are being built. To deal with this, the police have been militarized with high-tech equipment. Is that the answer? The city of Chicago, where I have lived for over fifty-five years, is one of the crime capitals of the US, with countless cases of homicide, rape, robbery, theft, arson, drugs, gang shootings and murders. There are over 500 murders here every year. Gang violence is widespread in all major cities in the US, with most of the violence taking place in specific neighbourhoods.

Despite many serious efforts by the Chicago city administration, police and community organizations, not enough has been accomplished in the last fifty years. The answer lies in spending resources on advocacy and practising non-violence, and not on policing violence. A new innovative mindset and a novel approach is required to deal with young gangs, encouraging community participation, promoting anger management and conflict resolution, and generating leadership. If I had an option, I would take 100 gang leaders from Chicago on a six-month global tour to visit select countries and expose them to other cultures and customs—this would surely open up their mental horizons.

Nelson Mandela, the anti-apartheid icon who spent twenty-eight years in prison for struggling against White rule in South Africa, followed Gandhi's non-violent approach. When he took over as the president of South Africa after the first free elections in the country's history, he set up the Truth and Reconciliation Commission to have former oppressors confront their sins. He did not take revenge by going after former White rulers, but extended them a helping hand of friendship to move forward. His ability to forgive was seen as a Gandhian gesture. To forgive is an integral part of the process of non-violence.

It is the nature of wild animals to resort to revenge and violence. Humans have evolved from hunting animals for food and living in dark caves to advancing in a more developed world, certainly not to practise violence, but to accept a human gift, the philosophy of non-violence against other human beings and nature. A violent world can never really develop any further. How can we provide people with equal rights while exploiting the weak and hurting them with violence? How can we live and prosper in peace if we indulge in conflict all the time? Yes, we have a capacity for violent destruction, but why should we waste our energy when we have so many opportunities to construct peace through the practice of non-violence?

The human mind needs a unique understanding of training and collective efforts to redesign our psychological mechanisms and adopt a non-violent mentality that is calm, relaxed and considerate. A violent mind seeks methods to destroy and breed hatred, whereas a non-violent one has exponential potential for peace, creativity and development. If we dispose of the old prejudices of hatred instilled in us by history and society, we certainly shall create peace. When we accept the diversity in nature, we expand our horizons, increase tolerance, embrace inclusion, and enhance the concept of equality and justice. We are then able to move away from a self-centred narrow zone to a higher collective power. We can then walk the path to prosperity for all. The ideal of non-violence does not harm or exploit anyone but benefits all.

To inflict violence requires some effort and will, but non-violence demands astonishing bravery and requires immense courage. To be non-violent is not a weakness or an excuse to shy away from the dangers of the world. When there is a danger to human dignity and honour, a non-violent person must not remain silent or succumb to exploitation. Non-violence is not for the weak.

Non-violence begins with us, then finds a place in our immediate family and our community until it reaches the city, and finally transcends to the nation and the world. Non-violence at an individual level is an urgent priority. Today's polarization between rich and poor, right and left, nationalists and globalists, urban and rural, educated and uneducated, etc., need not be so far apart from each other that it generates friction, tension, and, at times, violence. The number of people at risk from hunger and poverty, inadequate housing and healthcare, unemployment, lack of education and skill training, etc. is rising. At this time, it is critical to build an institutional framework to promote non-violence.

To build a non-violent world, the idea of local consciousness is necessary; it is a means of building respect for all life varieties and the environment. The feeling of hostility and alienness has to give way to a more humane world. If we can develop a sense of belonging in all human beings, a shared understanding will evolve as a uniting factor based on a joint universality. As long as the world remains divided based on religion, caste, race, gender and class, violent acts will occur and not be seen as immoral and unethical. All humans' divisive feelings are to be replaced with universal respect and honour towards each other.

The new world order is possible only with non-violence in our hearts. This is the lesson taught by non-violent leaders like Mahatma Gandhi, Martin Luther King Jr and Nelson Mandela, and many other unsung heroes. This shift in our thinking can be imbibed from a significant share of the world's population, which has already participated in non-violent struggles to gain freedom from colonial and dictatorial forms of oppression. Unfortunately, many people who have benefited from non-violent struggles have taken to violence to advance their personal power and prestige and create fractured communities. We need global leaders like Gandhi, Dr King, and Mandela to bring non-violence on to the international agenda.

The philosophy of non-violence can indeed transform the future of humanity. It can help de-fund military-industrial complexes and, over time, divert the required financial and other resources towards human development. However, education and awareness about non-violence must systematically begin at home, in schools, in communities, at work, in the government, and various other institutions. It must be taught even in places where people are traditionally trained to fight wars but not to practise non-violence. We need a global institute of non-violence at the same level as the UN. We also need a minister of non-violence in every national government, like the minister of defence. The real question is why we need to fight wars in a hyperconnected world, where the economy is one of surplus. The future of humanity lies in non-violence.

9

Innovation

'Science can flourish only in an atmosphere of free speech.'

—Albert Einstein

Innovation, driven by people, culture, diversity, ecosystem and opportunities is the starting point of the redesign of the world. In this hyperconnected world, we have a unique and timely opportunity to transform human civilization's future through innovations to improve our quality of life and strive to achieve equity, peace and prosperity for the people at large. However, innovation involves thinking differently, creatively and insightfully—it can impact multiple fronts and deliver a new social and economic contract. Innovation requires us to ask difficult, complex and fundamental questions like what is the meaning of nationalism, borders, passport, visa, immigration, labour, income, wages, wealth, work, freedom, trust, religion, organization, control, leadership, management, education, environment, etc. The old ideas and present paradigms do not make sense in a hyperconnected world. The new paradigms are about openness, inclusion, democracy, dialogues, networks and endless new possibilities. Innovation and hyperconnectivity are about going forward and not looking backwards. It is about a brave new world without any boundaries for humanity to explore new frontiers.

Innovation is also about transforming the status quo to create a new reality and approach to dealing with the planet and its people. Unfortunately, when we think of innovation, we assume that it is only about the high technology related to computer hardware and software, Silicon Valley, communications using satellites, or emerging technologies such as robotics, 3D printers, quantum computing, biotech, nanotech, entrepreneurship and so on. In reality, innovation is a broader platform with far-reaching implications on everything we do. It is not just about what happens in laboratories; it is also about processes, programmes, management, governance, economy, health, education and the way we work.

To innovate for the world's redesign, people must believe in the third vision of the world, which emphasizes openness and inclusion. Innovations begin to happen when what we believe in, what we think, what we say, what we commit, what we plan, what we practise and what we do are all in harmony. Innovations also happen when barriers between organizations, institutions, communities and individuals are broken; when we listen, take risks, tolerate failures and support an egalitarian work culture, while also enhancing collaboration between people and institutions across multiple disciplines and multiple cultures. People innovate only when they are trying to solve a problem.

There are well-known product and process innovations in business that improve costs, productivity, efficiency and markets. However, social, political, economic and organizational innovations that have enormous implications on society are not well recognized. For example, the concept of democracy and judiciary, the operation of money, the UN, the World Bank's formation, etc., are all taken for granted. Despite the passage of time, these inventions continue to evolve, requiring a great deal of conversation, consensus building, experimentation and fine-tuning.

It is essential to keep in mind that building a nation is very different from building a company. Building a business needs a clear focus and a command and control architecture, primarily to optimize shareholder value. On the other hand, building a nation requires a constant balancing of various interest groups to collaborate and cooperate with different organizational dynamics and often conflicting values, priorities and aspirations. Nation-building is forever a work in progress and continuously demands innovation.

To help implement a redesign of the world, it is essential to understand that all significant innovations are multidisciplinary—they require a great deal of collaboration. They are taking place faster than ever before at present, which means more communication, collaboration, cooperation and co-creation is being demanded from many stakeholders globally than ever before. Innovations also happen at the periphery and not at the core. This is why the five richest digital companies in the US (Apple, Amazon, Microsoft, Google and Facebook) were not born out of IBM's one-time computer giant.

It is commonly believed that the core always resists change and focuses on continuing to do what it thinks it does well. We need a catalyst to break this status quo and initiate change. This implies that the innovations required to implement a redesign of the world may not come from the US, China, the EU, UN, the World Bank or other global institutions. Some of these countries and institutions will even resist the proposed changes because of the fear that they would disrupt existing equations and affect the power balance. In reality, innovating for a redesign of the world requires many independent change agents from all over the world—they will have to collaborate and develop a consensus to help bring about a generational change.

Three important scientific forces have changed humanity's destiny in the past: the force of gravity discovered by Newton; the electromagnetic force by Maxwell, Faraday and Tesla; and nuclear force, represented by the formula $E=mc^2$ by Einstein. Now, the fourth force, that of hyperconnectivity, is changing humanity's destiny once again. The key is to understand and appreciate the power of hyperconnectivity to innovate a new world order.

Innovations in the Hyperconnected World

Hyperconnectivity, the Internet and the Web bring a whole new dimension to innovations and offer unprecedented opportunities related to democratization, decentralization and demonetization. These, in turn, also result in political, social and economic transformation. Hyperconnectivity allows new models of collaborations, new relationships and new potential to deliver growth, peace and prosperity. It further promotes openness, access, transparency, accountability and networking, which has enormous implications for individuals, institutions and infrastructures. Unfortunately, we have used hyperconnectivity to digitize our existing personal, business and government processes and systems until now, with the intention of only improving efficiency to better guard our capitalist system and the financial interests of the super-rich. We have to do a lot more.

In the name of this fourth industrial revolution, business leaders are still promoting the same model of capitalism, consumption, globalization, privatization and liberalization. It has worked for a few, but unfortunately, it has not delivered to most people dignity, respect, livelihood, basic needs and security. Besides, the present development model has created a considerable problem of income inequality and colossal environmental degradation. If we are to innovate and implement a redesign of the world and achieve inclusion, equality, justice and sustainability, while at the same time fulfilling basic human needs, then we need a change of heart to appreciate the new world order. We need to consciously decide to experiment with new innovative models of development for the economy and social and political systems. We need a hyperconnectivity revolution to flatten our society, and not another industrial or information revolution to build hierarchies. With hyperconnectivity, we need to search for new ways to empower people to resolve local and global challenges.

We need innovations in distributed governance and decentralized decision-making, and mobilization of local resources, talent and production. We need small businesses, local entrepreneurs and networks to scale. We also need to focus on the informal sector and unorganized labour. We need many other innovative ideas to create local opportunities for local livelihoods. The present centralized production model with a top-down approach makes and retains wealth only at the top in urban areas, and never percolates down to the people in rural areas, resulting in inequality. Decentralized model will ensure a better distribution of income, opportunities, participation and resources. Innovations in government will require a new approach to e-governance and service delivery based on electronic IDs, smartphones, common database, standards, integrated digital payments, networking, etc. to break the current vertical departmental silos with independent systems created in the last three decades. Hyperconnectivity offers unique potential to transform local, state, national and global governance all together.

The pre-hyperconnectivity world may have seemed limited in its approach to problem-solving, compared to the potential afforded by big data and analytics, artificial intelligence and machine learning, robotics, IoT, drones, sensors and other new technologies. The key lies in using these tools to help people in the unorganized sector, and others at the bottom of the pyramid, and not exploit them and their natural resources in the name of the new industrial revolution.

If we are to benefit from hyperconnectivity, we also need innovation in our democracy, governments, institutions and financial systems; we need to innovate in industry, manufacturing, supply chain and the economy. This is a tall order. As I have said earlier, at times, I feel as if we inhabit a world spread over three centuries. We retain a nineteenth-century mindset of exploiting people, preserving power and controlling wealth; we work as per twentieth-century processes with mistrust, complexity, perks and privilege, patronage, protection and particular preferences; and we have twenty-first-century needs which are essential to urgently lift billions of people to a decent standard of living. To take real advantage of the power of hyperconnectivity, we need a totally new mindset, new processes and new innovations.

Technology Innovations

Technology is the most significant social leveller, second only to death. It is often seen as exotic, fancy, urban, elitist, complicated and sexy instead of as a tool for problem-solving. Indeed, it cannot be denied that technology has resolved many problems. It has improved longevity, reduced infant mortality, enhanced communications, transport and agriculture productivity. But it has not solved the issues of poverty, hunger, environmental blunders, climate change and energy security. Technology is an entry point to bring about a generational shift; it is not an end point. We know that some systems abuse technology, while some make effective use of it. Technology is also a double-edged sword, bringing diversity, complexity, comfort, beauty, opportunities, employment and prosperity, while also having a dark side when it is misused. Technology is a reflection of the divine, just like nature—as elemental, and at times as unpredictable. Technology is an extension and acceleration of evolutionary life, a selfish system with its urges and desires.

The US has been the unquestionable leader in science and technology in the last seventy years. With their life-changing impacts, almost all fundamental innovations, such as transistors, laser, integrated circuits, microprocessors, software, fibre optics, DNA, genetics, etc., have emerged from the US, which spends heavily on basic science and proudly owns some excellent national laboratories, universities and a global talent pool to explore frontier science. I have been involved in one such initiative at the board level at the Fermi Lab in Chicago, where billions of dollars are being spent on learning and detecting neutrinos. It may take ten years to gather the results of this science, which will expand our knowledge of neutrinos. When it happens, it is sure to open doors to new discoveries.

Our world has greatly benefited from investments made by the US in science and technology. The truths revealed in fundamental science ultimately affects our planet and people profoundly. We know that there is no future without science and scientists. Science has the power to revolutionize societies, benefiting longevity, health, agriculture, environment, education and urbanization in an extraordinary way and democratizing its dividends.

US technology has its roots in defence, which is based on a high cost structure. The world is fascinated with the US model of development, primarily based on consumption. However, at this stage, in most developing countries, the US model is not sustainable, scalable, workable or even desirable. The world needs a new technology model that is development-based and can be implemented with an emphasis on affordability, simplicity, inclusion and sustainability. This is the real challenge. We need innovations that benefit the entire planet and all the people, especially those at the bottom of the economic pyramid. For this, there must be a clear focus on the five new pillars for redesigning the world: inclusion, human needs, new economy, conservation and non-violence.

New Innovation Initiatives

Innovations to ease climate change will be one of the biggest challenges of the next few decades. All major countries are making public commitments to eliminate greenhouse gases and become carbon-neutral. They promise that they will remove all the carbon dioxide they have placed in the atmosphere. It is a tall order when 85 per cent of the world's energy is still generated from polluting fossil fuels. It means we will have to invest substantial resources in discovering new ways to create clean energy, considering alternate energy sources, energy savings, novel battery technologies like lithium or metal-based solid-state batteries, hydrogen-based engines and turbines, distributed architecture, microgrids, biofuels, wind energy, ocean energy and much more.

Similarly, innovations to improve the quality of life of people will also be among the biggest challenges. Because of social media, I foresee an increase in divisive politics, hate, lies, greed, conflicts, anger, violence, terror, tension, intolerance, competitiveness, egos and envy. But why must this be so? As we become more prosperous, comfortable, knowledgeable and wealthy, we ought to be more loving, caring and concerned about the broader public good.

I always wonder why two people from the same family, who grew up under similar circumstances, turn out so different from each other—one might become a professor, while the other goes to prison. But at the same time, I find so much good in people that I wonder why the goodness does not multiply. Millions on this planet work selflessly to help the sick, the elderly, children, the poor, minorities and the physically challenged. They also help animals, plant trees, protect the environment and provide security. Billions are spent on innovating and ensuring quality products. Can we invest more in nurturing people who can assure peace and prosperity on the planet? Can we transform our education system to focus less on employment and more on building character, values and ethics? Can we use social media to do this? Can we spread more truth than lies? Can we promote love and respect for each other rather than competitiveness and profits? The presence of good people on the planet will dictate the quality of life in the twenty-first century.

Some exciting innovations are being investigated to help our planet. These relate to clean energy sources, carbon capture, ways to expand green coverage, plant-based plastic, and drinking water at low costs. They also relate to innovative new areas such as developing bald chickens to minimize waste feathers from hundreds of millions of chickens killed for food every year; increasing the yield per acre by ten times to enhance global food supply; vertical and desert farming; genetically modified food; engineered fake meat, etc. We have emerging technologies exploring nuclear fusion, energy-efficient waste management, water sourcing, water purification, improved mining methods, intelligent sensors, smart cities, smart microgrids and much more. To me, the most exciting scientific study today is one that is exploring the possibility of bringing extinct species back from the dead. This could bring thousands of animals, birds, insects, plants, flowers and fruits back to life for future generations to experience and enjoy and make our planet more diverse and prosperous. Can we, in the next ten years, bring dinosaurs back with gene-editing technology?

Another exciting scientific endeavour is refining compounds that carry instructions for assembling the protein that helps the fireflies light up. When scientists delivered this compound into the cells of a mouse, guess what happened? The mouse started to glow. In the next ten years, will it be possible to have a tree that glows at night? What does it mean for lighting up roads and public places? Will this be the new energy source that makes all the difference?

Similarly, what does it mean to grow ten or a hundred times more food on the same farm while using less water? Will this demonetize food? What will that mean for work and livelihoods? Will we need to spend our lives working for food and survival, or can we explore the planet in our free time?

Lots of progress is being made in health science to improve longevity, reduce pain, enhance life quality, replace body parts, treat cancer, ease the ageing process, lower infant mortality, produce vaccines and more. Technology offers hope for nutritious new fruits, vegetables and grains, improved building materials, modular housing, durable, long-lasting textiles, smart self-cleaning clothing, intelligent materials, light transport, better light sources, intelligent adhesives, smart glass, advanced sensors, etc. We hear about portable test devices, more applications, better entertainment, quality education and games on smartphones, and high-speed communication. We also know about creating rich content for learning, training and skills, and enhancing the ability to educate, enjoy and explore destinations and diversity. Many new possibilities are being investigated by science and scientists for a better future for us.

There are some serious ethical issues and concerns about genetically engineering life and producing children with certain desired features, functionality, colour, sizes and shapes. Should we be playing God? Can we engineer a new form of life by combining, say, a goat and a dog? While these issues are globally debated, science will continue to break barriers and explore new frontiers. We now have many strategic tools in science and technology, such as quantum computing, DNA and gene modelling, stem cell growth, modelling, analytics, new materials, self-healing devices, etc. All of these are coming together for the first time to open new doors with a multidisciplinary approach—this will undoubtedly help expedite innovations. Recently, a friend of mine talked to me about developing a genetically modified material to form a new lining in the stomach to make protein from whatever we eat. What a great idea! These kinds of thoughts were inconceivable once upon a time.

Around 2000, India launched the National Innovation Council to promote innovation on a nationwide scale. It consisted of thirteen prominent people from diverse backgrounds. The idea was to focus on innovation at various levels in the government, industries, businesses, laboratories and universities, and help innovate for small-scale industries and people at the bottom of the economic pyramid. We used innovation as a platform in a country of 1.3 billion to reach out to various domain experts and institutions and encouraged them to think differently. We built the National Knowledge Network at a cost of $4 billion, which connected 1100 nodes with optical fibre—this linked all universities, research institutions and libraries and encouraged them to collaborate at a national level. We launched another optical fibre network at an additional cost of $6 billion to connect 2,50,000 local governments, enabling us to bring digital technologies to villages and remote areas. We created state-level innovation councils to take innovation to various states in India. We emphasized innovation in industrial clusters working in bamboo, pharma, furniture and brassware. Five hundred thousand people were working on brassware in one city alone. The idea was to sensitize people to think differently and innovate while doing their jobs efficiently and creating new opportunities. To promote a redesign of the world, we would need a similar global initiative on innovation.

I recommend creating a Global Innovation Council at the UN level to help innovate and implement the world's redesign with autonomy and independence. It would have various working groups on the pillars of inclusion, basic human needs, new economy, conservation and sustainability, and non-violence. I also recommend similar initiatives at the national level to empower local talent, meet local needs and design programmes to suit local conditions, which can be championed by local domain experts. To change mindsets is not that simple—it requires a Herculean effort at various government levels, including institutions and private sectors, where we can all focus on innovations to redesign our world. There are mainly three areas where hyperconnectivity innovations will have an immediate visible impact: health, education and work.

Innovations in Health

COVID-19 has put the spotlight on the global public health system. The world has paused as doctors and healthcare workers scramble to save lives. It has been seen that present health systems are not equipped to respond to a pandemic. There has been a great deal of debate and discussion on the nature and efficiency of health systems in many countries in the process. In general, it is agreed that health security is a global challenge and needs reforms at various levels to improve access and outcomes. In countries like the US, the health system is remarkable, but with striking disparities. It is expensive and not available to everyone. In Europe, Canada and many other countries, the government supports universal health coverage, and that too at a reasonable cost. However, long delays prevent people from utilizing its benefits when they need it the most. In most countries, health systems need innovations to take advantage of hyperconnectivity and new possibilities.

Medicine has advanced considerably in the last few decades because of new instrumentation, biotechnology, drug discovery and growing research in genetics, stem cells and DNA. At the same time, health costs have increased substantially. The cost of bringing a new drug to the market is prohibitively high, even for big corporations. The cost of end-of-life treatment is equally exorbitant. In general, modern medicine focuses more on treating the illness rather than preventing it. Developments in the health system are related to expensive hospital infrastructure, new drugs, new technology and increasing medical tests. Innovations are required to provide universal health at a low cost to millions of poor people worldwide. The health system needs a holistic approach beyond the development of medicines—with hyperconnectivity, it must include individuals, families and the community. In my view, it is impossible to provide universal health coverage unless we look at new ways of empowering individuals to take responsibility for their health. The focus has to be on food, nutrition, body weight management, developing good habits, anger management, exercise, yoga, low-cost traditional health practices, herbal medicines, etc. This will be possible by bringing together hyperconnectivity and the existing health infrastructure.

Health systems worldwide consist of two key players—the patient and the doctor. They are supported by eight or more persons or networks, including nurses, clinicians, test labs, hospitals, pharmacies, drug companies, insurance and payment systems. The key is to empower both patients and doctors with hyperconnectivity to control health information systems and management to meet their needs. Unfortunately, the system's power has been passed on to institutions with financial interests; health has become a massive industry with many vested interests and multiple profit centres.

The US spends more on health systems than any other country on the planet, that is, almost 20 per cent of GDP, amounting to close to $4 trillion, with a per capita expenditure of $12,000 per year.

This reminds me of how my mother, in a small tribal village in a poor part of India, delivered eight children at home, at zero cost, without a doctor, nurse, pharmacy or even a phone. All eight children turned out to be mentally and physically healthy, doing well in studies and settling in America. She must have done something right. Unfortunately, we have forgotten our roots. Most of our traditional health practices are now ignored, though our ancestors once followed them. They were based on ancient wisdom, herbal medicinal plants, body massage and other natural remedies. Growing up, I do not remember going to a doctor at all. My mother would use herbal plants and oils at home to treat minor injuries, infections, boils, fever, illness, etc. She would even give a small drop of morphine to a crying baby to make it fall asleep. My first visit to a dentist was when I turned fifty.

The key lessons were to breathe fresh air, wash hands, eat right (we were vegetarians), walk regularly, never drink or smoke, control weight and be happy with family while also remaining busy with work. These lessons have stayed with me all my life.

In 1990, I realized that India was home to about 8000 herbal medicinal plants, unique to our Indian climate. Remembering my mother, I realized the importance of this national heritage and decided to partner with a domain expert—we launched a non-profit foundation to document India's herbal medicinal plants. The mission was to prepare a digital database and preserve the genetic pool. Unfortunately, no one in the country was interested in our mission, mainly because it was not related to Western medicine. It was not attractive enough to get public attention and political mileage. Finally, we got a grant from the Danish government. Thirty years on, we have documented most Indian herbal plants, created a genetic pool, and built a hospital based on traditional medicine. We established a full-fledged university to study transdisciplinary medicine in Bangalore, India. We manage 115 herbal gardens with over 500 acres to grow herbal medicine and provide jobs in rural areas. In the process, we have proven that some basic traditional health practices effectively prevent problems. The key is to know what works with conventional medicine to minimize costs and what needs treatment through modern medicine. This quest motivated us to launch a transdisciplinary university to integrate traditional and modern health science.

Every country and every culture—whether it's India, China, Mexico, Russia, Japan, Korea, Africa, the Middle East or Europe— has its traditional health knowledge, with unique capabilities that need to be explored to meet local needs at a low cost. The challenge is to innovate with an open mind and clear objectives and provide universal health services at the lowest price.

I had benefited from the traditional health system as a child growing up in India and from modern medicine later in the US when I had a quadruple bypass, cancer treatment, hernia, cataract and other procedures. I admire the dedication of health workers all over the world. They are our real heroes, as has been seen during the COVID-19 pandemic. Based on my experiences with both systems, I believe that we need to explore the following innovative ideas to improve global health systems in a hyperconnected world.

- Provide every person with their personal health records, accessible on their phones, along with ownership and access to essential local health services and health providers;
- Educate people regularly on the phone and motivate them to eat right, take walks, exercise, control weight, control sugar, teach good health habits, manage conflicts, meditate, keep discipline, socialize, engage, interact, network, etc.;
- Use well-accepted traditional and modern health practices wherever possible to treat minor ailments at home, such as colds, coughs, cuts, bruises, fever, injuries, allergies, etc.;

- Empower doctors with real-time access to patients and their related information on smartphones and encourage telemedicine;
- Build national health portals in local languages and promote health awareness and education;
- Strengthen local and community health systems with telemedicine facilities and assure instant access to the best available talent;
- Decentralize and simplify health systems and related payment processes with emphasis on localization;
- Encourage independent doctors to be entrepreneurs and enhance doctor–patient relationships and responses so that we can help break the monopolies of big hospitals and insurance companies;
- Put the patient and public interest ahead of private business and pure profit interests;
- Lower the cost of new drugs, including discovery, trials, approvals, distribution, delivery, etc., as well as the cost of hospitalization. Also lower the cost of hospitalization to extend end of life;
- Promote patient- and doctor-centric health systems instead of big business from hospital chains and insurance and pharma companies.

Innovations in Education

Education can empower and redefine a person. For hundreds of millions of youths, knowledge enables discipline and development, curiosity and creativity, connectivity, and a path to break away from ignorance and poverty. Eventually, education provides the path to employment and prosperity. I know this well because, as a poor kid from a tribal village in India, I was fortunate to get a master's in physics in 1964 for just over $10 in fees. Where else in the world can you do that? Having studied physics in India and electrical engineering in the US, I acquired a new caste as an engineer. I helped uplift my entire family of five sisters and three brothers. This enabled them to get a college education, enlightenment and lifelong prosperity. This is the dream of many young students globally. However, higher education has become expensive and is inaccessible for millions of poor people in this world. Simultaneously, the demand for education has increased even as the nature of education has changed. The world over, education is crying for innovations to make it affordable, accessible, relevant, useful and meaningful. Education is also the key to understand and implement a redesign of the world.

The present education system, which was designed centuries ago, is rigid, disconnected, expensive and obsolete. The entire world has accepted that it should take eleven or twelve years in school, four years to get a bachelor's degree, and two years for a master's degree. Why? Who has decided that it must take four years to obtain a degree? For some reason, the entire world follows this model.

The present education system means a classroom, a duster, the blackboard, a teacher, some textbooks, lectures, homework, tests, examinations, grades, and finally, a certificate. This model has not changed for centuries and is still being followed globally to allow for the transfer of credits and the needed mobility. This model rewards institutions with real estate, fancy buildings, expensive staff, sports facilities, a small student–teacher ratio, large endowment funds and costly fee structures. Various independent organizations grade the so-called best education institutions to attract more students, restrict admissions and prescribe expensive fee structures. This model has produced several world–class schools, colleges and universities and has helped elite students to graduate and lead businesses, governments and economies worldwide. This model is neither scalable nor sustainable any more. It breeds inequality.

In the present system, the teacher plays a vital role in creating and delivering content through a broadcast mode so students can listen and take notes. Learning material is provided and homework assigned. Many students in the class follow this routine, which is more like a manufacturing process. If Henry Ford landed upon this earth again, the only place where he would find his manufacturing process working is in education. It may be said that large manufacturing factories are set up to churn out graduates in huge numbers like machines. Everyone is supposed to learn at the same pace. There is minimal emphasis on personalized learning. Everywhere else, manufacturing has advanced from economies of scale to scope, and now to preferences. In education, it continues to be about the economy of scale. This is about to change forever.

The present system also does not recognize or reward learning acquired from family and the environment. Growing up in a joint family, I learnt a great deal from my grandfather, uncles, parents, brothers and sisters. Learning was not only about what was taught in school but also about what was practised at home. My formal education started only in fifth grade. By then I had already learnt a great deal in the joint family environment which made me confident enough to enter school at age eight. Learning in the village about water, wood, food, festivals, sharing and caring, rituals, customs, conflicts, shops, manners, discipline, values, etc., was very useful.

Hyperconnectivity will have far-reaching implications on education with new learning models at home and in schools in the future. Hyperconnectivity with the Internet, high-speed computing and smart devices has the power to democratize learning, decentralize teaching and demonetize education. Intelligent machines and hyperconnectivity essentially provide a window to the world. With the Internet, a poor kid in an Indian village can visit any part of the world and see its wonders. What a fantastic opportunity to innovate in education!

A vast quantum of content is now available on the Web, created and curated by global experts for free delivery at any time and at any place. It no longer makes sense to go to a class to get content delivered by a teacher. Simultaneously, there is a disconnect between what is taught and what students need to be successful in a real-world situation. Many soft skills related to communication, comprehension, collaboration, teamwork, etc., are required in real life and can be learnt through the Internet. Students can learn about math, science, analytics or any other subject, along with the discipline and creativity required to progress, as well as ethics, character and morals. They can develop openness and accountability and help themselves and others to succeed.

Digital education is not just about video lectures on the Internet or lessons displayed on blackboards by teachers. It is about having appropriate platforms and the usefulness of their technology and tools, interactivity, curation, content and more. At the end of the day, education is all about motivation, time and content. If you are motivated and willing to spend the required time to learn, there is enough content on the Internet, created by global experts, on every possible subject. The challenge is curation and mentoring. Unfortunately, teachers are trained to teach and not to curate and to mentor youth. As a result, students cannot get much help to benefit from this new way of learning. Digital education requires flipped classrooms, where you do exactly the opposite of what you do today in schools and colleges. Instead of listening to teachers delivering lectures at the school, you can listen to them at home. But homework can be done in a classroom with others. All of this requires a new mindset and a new framework for students, teachers and school administration. Are we prepared for all this?

I had an opportunity to be on the advisory board of the open courseware initiative around 2005 at the Massachusetts Institute of Technology (MIT). In those pioneering days, open courseware was available on a trial basis when it was just an idea. This ground-breaking initiative was launched by the then president of MIT, Dr Charles Vest, to provide rich and world-class MIT course material online for free for millions of learners and educators worldwide. In the last twenty years, it has captured the imagination of students all over the world. Now, MIT courseware is being used by millions of visitors each year in all parts of the planet: it is estimated that its benefits flow to many: 42 per cent students, 43 per cent self-learners, 9 per cent educators and 6 per cent others. It includes over 2400 courses from all engineering disciplines with the benefits of an education portal, an instructor, podcast facilities and various other resources. These sites get 500 million visits a year and attract thousands of learners every day from all over the world, enabling, empowering and enriching students' minds. A poor student in Africa can study MIT engineering course material free of cost if they are motivated and willing to spend the required time to learn. This is a classic example of the democratization of expensive engineering education.

Learning is a lifelong process. You cannot afford to stop learning after graduation. Education must continue as a part of various job profiles and keep changing all the time. The real challenge today is to make everyone a self-learner while in school. If we can do this, we can let them decide what to learn when to learn, and at what pace. We all have our own speed and individual capacity. What we need is a method of customized learning so that we can meet our professional and personal goals. Web learning allows us all the flexibility that we need.

Today, it costs over $2,00,000 to get an MBA from prestigious colleges like Harvard, Kellogg, Wharton, Stanford, London Business School, etc. How many students can afford this? It is possible now to get a business education from the Web through online courses conducted by global business gurus like Peter Drucker. Besides, TED talks, YouTube, special lectures, seminars, workshops, etc., can also provide substantial resources at a minimal cost. While they do not match a certificate from an Ivy League college, they do offer an attractive, low-cost alternative MBA education. Similarly, medical education is also costly and time-consuming. Is it essential in this information age to spend eight to twelve years to qualify as a doctor when you can learn the basics online?

Expensive education has created a substantial financial burden for aspiring youth in America. Student loans are considered to be the largest household debt after home mortgages, with about 45 million American students having substantial loans. The total amount of outstanding student loans reached an all-time high in 2019 at $1.5 trillion. A typical medical student will have to borrow over $3,00,000 to get through medical education and become a doctor. How does a poor student pay this off? Why is education so expensive in America? The privatization of education has created a whole new education industry to make money for many. Some of my friends on university boards are always busy raising money for their colleges. Even universities with billions of dollars in endowment funds need more money to sustain the high cost of quality education. Hyperconnectivity offers a unique opportunity to demonetize education, provided we are willing to innovate new learning and delivery models.

In the past, education was based on being able to remember things because instant access to information was not assured. Now that we do have instant access in this hyperconnected world, shouldn't education be redesigned to focus on learning more about problem-solving rather than just facts and figures? We need to change course content accordingly as it seems our traditional learning materials are obsolete because of what is currently available on the Internet. What does it mean to have a textbook now? How should we design books, tests and exams in this Internet age? Are we teaching students how to use the Internet to enhance their educational experience? Are we using the Internet to explore new ways of learning? Do we understand what is worth knowing and learning and what is not?

Education must respond to new technology and new tools to access, understand, organize and analyse real-time information. What is the impact on the education structure when big data and analytics become part of the syllabus, along with machine learning and artificial intelligence, voice recognition, image processing and other new technologies? How will all this change our old learning systems and what we teach? What happens if we offer a certificate, not at the point of exit from college, but while entering the job market? These are uncomfortable but very important questions that we are afraid to ask and address. The answers will find resistance from legacy systems and established interests, where the main argument would be about quality, human interactions, networking, etc. However, innovation in education cannot wait any longer.

Today, if I were to build a university for tomorrow, it certainly would not look like a typical Ivy League campus with an extensive physical infrastructure of classes, libraries, sports complexes, restaurants, dorms, laboratories, etc. It would predominantly be based on online education with a shared infrastructure created from community resources, where students can meet at coffee shops, shopping centres, hotel lobbies, etc., for interaction and socializing. Students could also get practical experience by doing internships at local businesses. The course material would be redesigned to meet multidisciplinary education, emphasizing the planet's challenges in a hyperconnected world. The real job would be to curate content that meets the student's needs with varied but customized interests. This will help decentralize and customize education in the future.

Innovations in education require a new mindset and political will that will not hesitate to redesign global education institutions and infrastructures—this is the only way to democratize, decentralize and demonetize learning.

Innovations and Work

Work is at the centre of all human activity. It can be based on personal needs, such as cleaning, reading, entertaining or providing a service such as cooking, taking care of kids and older parents, neighbours and the community. We need to work to earn money to manage personal and family needs related to food, clothing, shelter and health. The nature of our work has changed over time with innovations in technology, tools and techniques. During the early days of civilization, work was centred on food, family and shelter. Later, work involved discipline and order, and implied the distribution of tasks related to agriculture, textile, craft, marketing, etc. During the industrial age, work to earn money changed drastically due to new opportunities that improved manufacturing lines. The invention of steam engines and the growth of the auto industry changed employment and labour in factories and offices. It created new organizational systems with hierarchy, authority and command–and–control systems to enhance productivity, efficiency and standards. These systems enabled the management, owners and governments to keep workers engaged on the shop floor while profits and privileges were retained at the top. Once prosperity percolated downwards, labour started mobilizing themselves and demanded safety, security and other benefits. This resulted in the standard of forty hours of work per week, a safety net of health insurance, retirement benefits, pension programmes, etc., for factory and office workers, which are still prevalent even today.

New technology and new machines eliminated old jobs and created new ones, which could never have been imagined before. When automatic dialling on the telephone instrument was invented, all the US telecom operators who handled calls by plugging in cords went on strike. They argued that the new technology would eliminate their jobs. If we had listened to their argument, then many human beings would be working as telephone operators even today. The process of eliminating old jobs and creating new jobs has been going on forever.

The steam engine was invented 240 years ago. Just another 120 years later, the floodgates of new inventions were opened, with electricity, the telegraph, the telephone, photography, the radio, the car, plane, cinema, etc., which increased human comfort and changed lifestyles and living conditions altogether. Then, after another eighty-five years, the television was invented. The invention of the transistor in 1947 opened the floodgates again, eventually leading to the hyperconnectivity that has developed over the last seventy-five years. Now the pace of innovation has increased, mainly because of networking amongst a larger pool of talent and tools, enabling the cross-breeding of ideas and utilities. The pervasive nature of hyperconnectivity will ensure that the world of work will further change in a way we could never have imagined before—this will have far-reaching implications for every job on the planet.

COVID-19 has put many of us in self-quarantine at home for the last several months. In the process, we have learnt to work from home more effectively and efficiently. I feel I am busier than ever before on Zoom calls and get more done than I did in the office. Do I need an office? Many companies have decided to allow people to work from home. I find this is a significant new trend. Most office jobs related to management and executives and supervision of banking, insurance, accounting, legal matters, consulting and advisory services, etc., can be done from home equally well. Some jobs may require going to the office once in a while.

I feel that meetings on Zoom are more productive than in person. They avoid having to get up early to go to the airport, parking difficulties, long flights, taxi expenses, and often save about twelve hours in all—all this for a thirty-minute conversation. What we need is a mindset change. I have four cars, but I have not driven one in the last twelve months. Do I need four vehicles? All office workers use about 150 square feet of office space for eight hours a day. What a waste of resources! Once robots get entrenched on factory floors and loading docks, many manufacturing jobs will also move home.

Let us take the example of self-driven vehicles. When these are introduced in the next five to ten years, no one would prefer to own a car. Why would we want to own a car when we can have one delivered at our door in five minutes, just by ordering it on the phone? It would eliminate the need for a garage, car insurance, driver's licence, car plates, fuel and parking spot. All the public parking lots in the heart of the city or at airports, train stations, hotels and conference centres, schools and colleges or hospitals and public places would become empty. What will we do with all the vacant land? Ultimately, we will not even need millions of traffic lights because these vehicles will have built-in intelligence to know when and where to stop. Simultaneously, they will eliminate millions of drivers' jobs for trucks, limos, cars and other vehicles. What would these people do? Where would they find alternate jobs?

Today, we produce around 50 million cars a year. Most vehicles are parked 90 per cent of the time and are in use only for the remaining 10 per cent. Once self-driven vehicles are being used, why would we need to produce 50 million vehicles a year? Maybe only 5 million cars should be manufactured in a year. What will that do to manufacturing plants? It will reduce the requirement of steel and other raw materials. What will be the impact of producing only 5 million cars a year on urban traffic jams and busy roads? Just this one invention of a self-driven car will reduce millions of jobs, hundreds of factories, millions of parking lots, millions of traffic lights, eliminate urban traffic jams and reduce the need for steel and other raw materials. It means that future innovations will allow us to do a lot more for a lot less. It will free up people, resources, raw materials and space. It will also help us optimize our resources, reduce clutter, and give us more time to rest and relax.

In the future, we will begin to demonetize essential services related to food, water, transport, telecom and energy because of our ability to produce more for less. Telecom services are almost free. In the future, transportation will also be free; it could be a part of the city tax. Once an inexpensive, distributed DC energy source is available, energy will be demonetized. Meanwhile, education is about to be demonetized. If the population stabilizes at 10 or 11 billion people who continue to work from home, there will be enough housing available at a reasonable price to live comfortably. If flying cars are introduced, we will not have to build rural roads. I feel in the next twenty-five years, there will be adequate physical infrastructure. The challenge will be to build soft infrastructure to deal with human development and increase human potential.

If jobs are eliminated, and everything is demonetized, who will pay tax, and how will the economy work? This is where we need innovations. Perhaps robots will pay tax, and we will all get a minimum income to live comfortably. Maybe there will be new jobs that we cannot imagine now. There are no answers to these questions in traditional terms. We need a whole new form of thinking. We need a paradigm shift. How do we decide on a market for something that does not exist today? If we had told people in the year 1800 about hyperconnectivity, how would they have reacted? Maybe we can spend time discovering our diversity and travelling to experience life.

Today, we all work forty hours a week so that we can make a living. In the future, we will perhaps work for only ten hours a week, and this would be sufficient to earn and survive. Maybe we will need multiple skills to do various things and find suitable work for ten hours a week.

Hyperconnectivity and related innovations will empower people to take on more things to do through the democratization of knowledge and the decentralization of activities. In the process, it will free them from routine and manual jobs. On the one hand, more jobs will be performed by machines and robots, even as big data, analytics and machine learning will fine-tune processes to enhance productivity and optimize resources. On the other hand, people will be free from mundane jobs to do other exciting things. However, they would still need to work to make a living. This is going to be the fundamental challenge of the hyperconnected world. At this stage, we do not have all the answers.

10

A Manifesto to Redesign the World

'Be the change you wish to see in the world.'

—M.K. Gandhi

This manifesto outlines the new world's vision with a clear focus on the planet and its people. It is based on the unyielding recognition that we need to improve the environment to take care of our planet and improve everyone's quality of life. Each human being is created equal and has dignity and self-respect and the right to stand on a par with all others. The manifesto is based on optimizing environmental and human capital and not financial capital, trade or growth. It focuses on sustainability, inclusion and a hyperconnected world. This manifesto has the potential to transform our world and take humanity to the next level. It is an appeal to individuals and world leaders to work towards achieving the goals outlined here.

This is a global call to action.

Background

The world's last design was conceived after World War II, with five main pillars: democracy, human rights, capitalism, consumption and the military. All countries follow this rule-based system to run their affairs. This design has served us well for a long time in preserving peace, expediting growth and development, and lifting many from the clutches of poverty. But it has outlived its utility and cannot work in today's hyperconnected world.

Seven tipping points have profoundly changed the world in the past seventy-five years: decolonization, the rise of China, the fall of the Soviet Union, the terror of 9/11, the rise of technology, increasing inequality and the COVID-19 pandemic.

At present, there are two competing and contradictory visions when it comes to world affairs: the American vision and the Chinese vision. The American vision is 'open' and based on the continuation of the existing design of the world with a clear emphasis on democracy, freedom, capitalism, consumption, military and geopolitical equations. The US is focused on dominance in technology, finance, trade and markets as well as military matters so it can retain its position as a leading and unquestionable global superpower.

The Chinese vision is a 'closed' one, based on a strategy of taking the lead in global geopolitical matters, including markets, finance, trade and technology through the BRI. It intends to provide an alternative to the American style of governance.

These two competing visions of the world are predominantly designed to enhance each country's power, prestige, presence and national interest, and expand global markets for their respective products and services. They aim for global dominance through traditional command-and-control structures instead of international development through improved communication, cooperation, collaboration, co-creation and networking.

The Third Vision

Through this manifesto, we propose a third vision of the world, one that puts the earth and all living beings at its centre. This vision is based on nations building a network to increase understanding, enhance collaboration and build bridges to promote peace and prosperity for all.

All life on earth is interconnected, interdependent, interwoven and interrelated. What affects one affects all of us. The planet is in pain because of past environmental blunders and a future that looks bleak because of global warming. Meanwhile, people the world over are also in pain because the fruits of democracy, freedom, justice, capitalism and technology have not reached the billions at the bottom of the economic pyramid.

Ultimately, we must make two fundamental aspects the cornerstone of the new world's redesign: sustainability to resolve the planet's pain, and inclusion to soothe the situation of its people.

We have two roads lying ahead of us. One, we can continue with business as usual and accept that inequality, poverty and hunger will continue along with crony capitalism, corruption, exclusion, injustice, violence, terror and war and climate degradation.

Or, we can be brave and bold and build a global opinion, develop consensus, empower leaders and initiate a movement for a generational change that will help us all. This choice is ours to make.

The new proposed redesign of the world articulates our universal hopes and aspirations and sets the agenda for the future. Nations and world communities must strive to achieve the objectives laid out in this new design to bring about generational change. The five pillars for the world's redesign are as follows.

1. Inclusion: To strengthen and expand democracy to take us towards an inclusive world with equality and opportunities and dignity, respect and justice for all.

2. Human Needs: To enforce fundamental human rights while ensuring the availability of basic human needs related to food, clothing, shelter, health and education.

3. New Economy: To course-correct greedy capitalism and move towards a new economy, focusing on the environment and human capital; to redistribute wealth more equitably while developing small businesses, local capabilities and globalization.

4. Conservation and Sustainability: To move from mindless consumption to sensible conservation and sustainability, making products that are more durable and doing away with the one-time-use philosophy; to promote affordable, scalable and sustainable products and services.

5. Non-violence: To promote and practise non-violence at all levels and abjure violence entirely; to start the process of defunding the police and the military and using them more for peaceful purposes and providing security.

These pillars are fundamental to the creation of a new global platform; they are integral parts of the hyperconnected world's third vision to take humanity to new heights. This five-pronged approach is simple to understand and easy to communicate to all. It requires a change in mindset in individuals and communities as a whole, and particularly those in leadership positions in government, business, civil society and academics. It also provides a new direction to the economy and the idea of development, with a call to allocate more resources to improve the planet and the lives of all people on it.

Global Action Points

Following is a ten-point agenda of the main focus areas that will help us move towards the third vision of the world.

1. Hyperconnectivity is the most disruptive innovation of the century and should be effectively used to implement big changes to help redesign the world. It is transforming the self, family, friends, relationships, habits, values and work, as well as the nature of trade, markets, manufacturing, entertainment, education, health, institutions, infrastructures, the government and much more. Hyperconnectivity brings democratization of knowledge, decentralization of implementation, and the demonetization of services—it is the perfect tool to redesign the world.

Many of today's ways of working are nearly obsolete; what is needed is a new approach to work and problem-solving. For the first time in human history, we are all connected with smart devices, the Internet and applications. This must prompt us to think differently about policies, processes, programmes, services, benefits, governance and development because we are now globally connected. Hyperconnectivity must be used in a creative way for the speedy implementation of the five pillars of the world's redesign.

2. The **environment** urgently needs to be preserved and protected.

We need fresh air to breathe and clean water to drink; we need our green forests to flourish and our animals to thrive; the sky to remain blue and the oceans breeding more marine life; birds to fly free; and nature to take back control.

The environment has been on the global agenda for over two decades. However, there has been little action on the ground. We still burn coal, choke our cities, pollute our rivers, create mountains of garbage and give lip service to environmental issues. This must change quickly to assure sustainability and our long-term survival.

One of the first collective and coordinated global actions that the new world order has to undertake is to get climate change under control. Representatives of 196 countries have negotiated the Paris Agreement to keep the global average temperature below 2 °C above the pre-industrial level. The agreement's objective is to reduce carbon dioxide emissions and increase renewable energy and energy efficiency so that the planet can achieve the desired targets. It involves trillions of dollars of investments and opportunities the world over and is expected to create millions of new jobs.

This is a massive undertaking and will require leadership, technology, talent, innovation and enormous investment in new energy sources such as solar and wind, storage technologies related to new batteries, distribution grids for delivery, electric vehicles, and whole-scale conversion from polluting to clean energy.

3. Democracy is the bedrock of human freedom, development, justice, potential, aspiration, experience and empowerment. It needs to be strengthened to enhance people's representation and participation to enable them to choose their destiny. Democratic institutions must function with independence, autonomy, freedom and flexibility with an eye always on public interest. The world needs open governments which operate on the basis of transparency, accountability and responsibility on high moral grounds.

Government organizations which were designed decades ago with vertical silos, traditional hierarchical structures and control-oriented processes are good at maintaining the status quo and following rigid procedures instead of enabling innovative new initiatives. In many countries, people see the government as a club of politicians, big business and administration with no connection with or concerns about the masses' real needs.

These bureaucratic organizations need to change and take advantage of the hyperconnected world to listen to people's voices on the ground and collaborate with multiple organizations and agencies. For this, we need business and civil society's active and official participation in all major governance initiatives.

We must elect leaders with vision, character, capabilities and commitment towards unity, justice, democracy and human development. Anti-democratic forces that promote authoritarian attitudes and divisive politics must be rejected. We must promote truth and not lies, trust and not mistrust, love and not hate, diversity and not uniformity, inclusion and not exclusion, collaboration and not conflicts and non-violence and not violence. We must unite and not divide people. We must share, care and sacrifice for a better future for all. We must focus on public good and not personal gain.

Local democratic forces must encourage people to experience freedom, flexibility, autonomy and fulfilment. We also need people to drive democracy in their community because they have the knowledge and wisdom to increase local participation.

We must seek to minimize the influence of money power on democratic forces and government policy, programmes and preferences by controlling election funding and simplifying voting processes by using new technology and tools.

Decentralization of political power, a distributed form of decision-making and a bottom-up development that encourages active participation and wisdom from the local people are essential requirements in today's world. Institutional autonomy with freedom, flexibility, responsibility and accountability is an essential part of a functional democracy. It is critical to build and strengthen global, national and local institutions with domain experts for speedy and timely justice, enhanced security, universal health, universal education and food security.

4. We need a new **economic model**, one that moves beyond GDP to GEP (Gross Environment Development Product) and GHP (Gross Human Development Product)—going beyond shareholders' values to stakeholder values, commonwealth and trusteeship. We are living in an era of surplus and not scarcity. We can produce enough for everyone's needs, but, unfortunately, we are still busy making for the wants of just a few. We must change production priorities to meet basic human needs first. A small number of people control most of the world's wealth, while a large number of people live in poverty and slums. This must change.

We must bring more transparency and regulations to manage global financial and stock markets which at times operate like casinos run by big money power to manipulate local markets, currencies and natural resources. We need a bottom-up economy that encourages unorganized labour, small businesses, local talent, local markets and local art, music, food, customs and culture. Hyperconnectivity will help networks and small businesses to go global and create a new shared economy and multiple opportunities to sift income, wealth and jobs from urban to rural areas.

Globalization and fair trade must be given due importance to ensure products and people can move freely, without unnecessary barriers and boundaries. In deciding what to localize, nationalize or globalize, local individuals and issues must be at the centre of the decision-making process, not corporates and their concerns for profits and lower costs. The key is to understand and appreciate what to localize and what to globalize.

We need autonomy, flexibility and accountability at the local level, for which we should promote the local economy, education, talent, language, culture, food, businesses, production, health practices and capabilities. We must pay special attention to the unorganized sector and unorganized labour.

We must also pay more attention to the local genetic pool, soil, water, environment, festivals, etc., to encourage and celebrate local tradition.

5. We must believe in **science and technology** and scientific mindsets, logic and reasoning. As Einstein said, science can flourish only in an atmosphere of free speech. Without science and scientists, there is no future.

Technology has been the most significant social leveller, second only to death. In the last seventy years, science and technology have increased human comforts and extended longevity while at the same time substantially improving our access to energy, transport, communication, education, health and other sectors.

Technology must be an entry point to bring about generational change and expedite development, such as in rural and poverty-stricken areas. We must also invest substantially in science and technologies related to food and water to improve productivity, efficiency, quality and distribution. Similarly, we need innovations in health, education, environment, economy, elections, government, work, services, organizations and processes to implement the world's third vision with new business models, delivery and distribution.

We must use technology to minimize human suffering in emergency situations like pandemics, climate change and natural disasters.

Digital infrastructures, platforms and technology must be used to transform the fundamental nature of our institutions. A total redesign of age-old processes is required to deliver public services in an efficient, accurate, timely and seamless manner. This necessitates new approaches to identification, authentication, verification, security, privacy, networking and data management. It will also require new system architectures for e-governance with a focus on cloud computing, open-source software, smart devices, unique ID, security, privacy, common data centres, interoperability and standards.

6. It is believed that there is a crisis of **leadership** in the world. Many leaders today are narrow-minded, parochial, divisive, self-centred, power-hungry, authoritarian and ineffective. They are focused only on their constituencies for immediate gains with an eye on the next elections. They are busy raising funds and hardly have time to serve people; they spend time drafting new budgets and new laws containing thousands of pages to deal with day-to-day issues. When will they have time to think of global issues that affect everyone?

To redesign the world, we need political will at the highest level, and leaders with character, charisma and global presence. The last world design was conceived under the direction of US President Roosevelt. Is there a similar global leader on the horizon who can network nations, mobilize opinion and initiate a new narrative?

We need leadership with character, education and experience not only at the global level but also at national, local and institutional levels. We also need more women leaders with compassion and empathy to promote family values, peace, non-violence and equality.

Human development is key to the new world order. People have lost trust in each other and the institutions that govern them. We must encourage civility, discipline, humility, honesty, openness, collaboration and cooperation, and strive to minimize ego, anger, jealousy, conflicts and tension, drug issues, violence and terror. The focus should be on improving the self, the family and the community, and productive work to assure wellness and happiness. Many people are isolated, alienated, lonely or depressed. Communities have a significant role to play in human development, safety and security, and in connecting disconnected people.

7. The **media** is front and centre in this new design. It must be independent, responsive, responsible, fair, ethical and moral, and ensure that its focus is mainly on representing facts and not on the expression of biased opinions. It must not twist facts, suppress the truth or promote lies.

Social media giants require better policing and a change in business models to promote truth and guard democracy. Digital platforms, social media, print, radio, television, etc., can be used effectively to help take this manifesto forward.

8. Innovation is required at all levels in government, business and civil society to respond to the new realities of the hyperconnected world. We should encourage bio, nano, material, energy and cyber technologies to improve the environment, food, health, transport, infrastructures and comfort. We need new thinking to bring about generational change.

In particular, we should emphasize low-cost local innovations in developing countries to take technology to people in rural areas to enhance access to essential human needs and human services. Technology and innovations are often available, but the mindset to change and human capacity to adopt them is lacking. Innovations will drive and expedite the proposed redesign of the world. We need innovations in organizational architecture in government and institutions to benefit from hyperconnectivity. The old organizations with vertical silos are designed to meet the needs of the hierarchical and feudal mindsets focused on command and control. We need egalitarian architectures with flat organizations to network talent and resources for speedy implementation with openness and accountability. We do not need gatekeepers any more. We need dynamic change agents and catalysts to build bridges. A friend of mine recently pointed out that the present ministry of defence works more like the ministry of war and similarly the ministry of health works more like the ministry of sickness. It is time to change this. To implement the redesign of the world, we need a separate minister and ministry reporting to the president or prime minister on inclusion, basic needs, new economy, sustainability and non-violence.

Based on my experiences with India's technology missions, I believe that all organizations and institutions need mission-oriented approaches with egalitarian management, youthful team members, measurable milestones, civil society's participation, and new technology and tools. This will demand a change in bureaucratic culture that stifles rapid development in governments all over the world. Organizations are like people; they take birth, grow, mature, get old and must die to make room for the new generation.

9. The **reform of major international institutions** like the UN, World Bank, IMF, NATO, WHO and others will go a long way in addressing a number of global issues. These institutions have made significant contributions to keep peace alive, manage financial meltdowns, fuel growth, reduce poverty, develop nations, etc., but over time, stagnation has set in in their functioning. They could have done a lot more to help poor and emerging countries on the path to development. Unfortunately, lingering prejudices and procedures from the colonial era have exploited natural resources and minerals in poor countries to benefit the rich, with little to show in return for the local population. These institutions have traditional organizational architectures that need to be urgently modernized and replaced with small, task-oriented, self-designed flat organizations that will enable networking to deliver visible results.

Besides reforming present global institutions, we have to create, at the UN level, new global institutions to deliver on inclusion, basic needs, new economy, sustainability and non-violence. Unfortunately, in the last seventy-five years we have not paid attention to create new institutions to meet new global demands. For many years, I have been going to New York during UN General Assembly meetings to attend meetings of the Broad Band Commission. During this period, the entire city of New York is virtually under siege because leaders and dignitaries from all over the world visit the city, arriving on private jets loaded with a large staff and a line of limos just to give a thirty-minute talk. Does such wastage of time and resources make sense in our hyperconnected world?

For instance, cybersecurity is a new battleground that deserves global attention. It is time for the UN to set up an independent UN Cybersecurity Council and train a global cyber police force to help member states. I had proposed this idea with a detailed plan a decade ago to Ban Ki-moon, when he was the UN secretary-general. As expected, it did not receive any response. We know that the next generation of wars will be fought in cyberspace with digital attacks on governments, businesses, banks, stock markets, courts, elections and leaders. It will require agents who are specially trained in various new technologies and tools to guard national and global interests.

There is a need for several international courts to draft and follow new global business rules and regulations. Presently, the laws of the country where a business is located are applied and not the laws of a universal international system.

Similarly, we need one international court to file and follow international patents on the Internet to avoid multiple local patent laws with expensive and time-consuming processes. At the same time we need to make sure that patents are not used just to control markets and benefit only big companies but are used to expedite human development. The key is not to create new physical infrastructures but to focus on soft and virtual infrastructures to meet our global needs without interfering in national affairs.

We also need a global federal reserve system. At present, over 180 financial currencies are being used around the world, with the British pound being the oldest. Meanwhile, the currency most in demand today, the US dollar, was introduced in 1792. Most of the global business and trade settlement is conducted and transacted in US dollars. Do we need 180 currencies as a legacy of the past in this globalized world? Why can't we create a basket of seven currencies such as the US dollar, Chinese yuan, the euro, Indian rupee, South African rand, Russian rouble and Japanese yen? This will simplify the global financial system to promote international trade and global peace.

10. We need to start a **new global conversation.** At present, there are as many constitutions as there are countries on the planet—democratic, dictatorial, communist, monarchical, Islamic and others. Is there a way to begin a conversation on a global constitution and agree on a common minimum programme? Can we agree on the value of human life and the environment to reach a consensus regarding people's rights, duties and responsibilities?

Several prominent people and organizations are already working in this area and need to be supported. Can we consider establishing uniform guidelines regarding our common property such as earth, air, water, soil, forests, birds, animals, mines, and the environment? At the same time, can we agree on democracy, freedom, autonomy, flexibility and responsibility to live our life the way we prefer while maintaining our local values, wisdom, customs and culture?

A global government is an equally important concept for the future. To effectively manage and protect our planet and secure the future and well-being of our people, we need one global voice. The idea is not to govern local affairs and protect national borders but to improve communication and cooperation to enhance peace, human development, the environment and smooth movement of products and people.

The present G20 group could be re-energized and repurposed with appropriate new structures to provide a global governance model in the future. Again, the idea is not to build physical systems but to create soft structures to meet the hyperconnected world's needs.

We must begin a serious conversation on these two subjects: the global constitution and global government. It might take decades to agree on some issues, but it is essential to start the process now.

Change Agents: Making This Happen

Each of us has the power to look inside ourselves and search for the inner light that will lead to a brighter future. If we cannot change ourselves, we cannot change others. We need to promote the need to change in our families, friends, communities and countries. We need to encourage people with character and values: people who believe in democracy, freedom, justice and truth; people for whom the importance of trust, love, respect, dignity and decency are important; people who will work with fellow human beings towards assuring ourselves of a world where collaboration, co-creation, peace, humility, happiness and family are invaluable; people who see the larger picture and rise above petty politics and personal gains; people who are accomplished, confident, comfortable and want to share and care. Simultaneously, we must listen to other voices, with different opinions, to learn and expand our horizons.

We need to identify, encourage and empower many change agents worldwide with expertise in different domains to begin a new conversation on the redesign of the world. Our safety, security, peace and prosperity lie in us working together so that we can protect the planet and human civilization. This is an opportunity to break barriers and borders, reach out to diverse groups of people, irrespective of race, religion, nationality, faith, etc., from all over the world and find common ground. This is the time to unite all humanity with a shared passion for empowering people to exercise their right to freedom, well-being and pursuit of happiness. This is our historical moment, and we cannot afford to miss it.

We want the US, India, EU, Japan and South Africa and others who believe in the concept to lead the initiative to redesign the world. The US has been an unquestionable leader of the free world; it has promoted democracy, seeded new technologies, helped globalization, opened markets and maintained peace. For the redesign of the world to gain traction and succeed, the US and India could take the lead. Both countries have leading universities, institutions and think tanks with global talent, diversity, technology, tools and experience. These are indispensable attributes to drive this international agenda. But without proper leadership, it may remain out of reach.

We must all initiate a new global conversation to help find new solutions for human development. We need millions of young people in all parts of the world to use social media creatively to promote the redesign of the world. There are many brilliant people and various great institutions in this world, with unique domain expertise and a lifetime of good work, from whom all of us can benefit. They have spent time studying, learning and living with many of these issues. We will reach out to these institutions and accomplished experts and mobilize them to verify and refine ideas to lead the change.

Conclusion

This manifesto is illuminated with the third vision of the world. This vision transcends from the national to the global and from market and trade to environment and human development. The third vision is rooted in democracy and based on the model of universal freedom and inclusiveness. It gains strength from a new form of capitalism that is multipolar, open, transparent, collaborative, local and predominantly focused on what is good for the planet and the people. It is hoped that the reform of existing institutions and the creation of new ones, and the focus of a new global constitution, will ultimately lead the global government to network, communicate, collaborate and cooperate. This will be the foundation on which the aims and aspirations of the people of this world will be achieved.

As has been said before, the redesign of the world is not about liberal or conservative, left or right, capitalism or socialism, public or private, democracy, dictatorship or monarchy, open or closed, government or business, trade or finance, geopolitical or military, rich or poor, urban or rural, east or west, White, Brown, Black or Yellow. It is all about improving the present and securing the future of humanity.

In summary, a global call to action is to study the new manifesto, initiate new conversations, be a change agent and mobilize other change agents, energize social media and encourage domain experts. The purpose is to ultimately bring a group of democratic countries together to implement the world's redesign. It is a call to start a new movement to respond to the new reality emerging from the hyperconnected world.

To me, it is primarily about going back to fundamentals. Who are we, and what is our purpose on the planet? What does it mean to live? Is it about the individual, the family, the community, the nation, or about all the people on the planet? Is it about personal gains or public good? Is it about my tribe or me? Is it about being selfish, power-hungry and greedy? Is it all about chasing money and without morals? Is wealth more important than values and wisdom? Is it about consumption and competition? Is it about the vulgar display of wealth? Or is it about inclusion, equality, justice and love for a fellow human being? Is it about my generation or the next generation? Am I a custodian of the planet for my grandchildren?

What can make me healthy, happy, content, and fulfilled? What kind of a world do I want to leave behind? We all have a beginning and an end. In reality, we all came here with nothing and will go away with nothing. But the planet will be here for millions of years to come. This again reminds me of what the chief of Seattle's Duwamish tribe said: 'The Earth does not belong to man; man belongs to the earth.' To earn the privilege to live on this earth with respect, dignity, dedication and duty, we must follow the advice of the Potawatomi elders who, in the eighteenth century, encouraged their children to live by the seven golden rules: truth, trust, love, humility, bravery, wisdom and respect towards each other. To make this world better for my grandchildren and their generation and for the generations to come, I am convinced that now, seventy-five years after the last great war, it is time for us to redesign the world.

I dedicate this manifesto to the wisdom and good sense of the people on this fantastic planet.

'In a gentle way, you can shake the world.'
M.K. Gandhi

Appendix

Who Am I to Write This Book?*

'A hundred times every day I remind myself that my inner and outer life are based on the labours of other men, living and dead, and that I must exert myself in order to give in the same measure as I have received and am still receiving.'

—Albert Einstein

This book is about redesigning the world to meet the future challenges that will be faced by our planet and our people. The world was last designed seventy-five years ago, around the time I was born. I believe this design has outlived its utility. Now, hyperconnectivity and the COVID-19 pandemic has offered up a unique opportunity to redesign the world for the next seventy-five years, to take humanity to the next level. However, I need to tell you a bit about myself, so you know who I am, where I come from, and why my connectivity journey in the USA and India has led me to think and propose the world's redesign.

I have spent over fifty-five years working in telecom and information technology as an entrepreneur and innovator in America, and as a public servant and policymaker in India. I have

---

* A version of this chapter has been published in *Dreaming Big: My Journey to Connect India* by Sam Pitroda and David Chanoff.

kept a close watch on technology through these five decades with a particular focus on connectivity. I have had a ringside view of the impact of connectivity on human development. I also had a front-row seat in business and government, shuttling between two great democracies, the oldest and the largest globally. All of this has enabled me to participate in local and global priorities, programmes and possibilities.

In my lifetime, I have seen the British Raj, colonial India, Indian Independence, the death of Mahatma Gandhi, the death of John F. Kennedy, the Vietnam War, the moon landing, the Green Revolution, the march of Martin Luther King, the Civil Rights Movement, the rise of the Asian Tigers, the formation of the European Union (EU), the rise of China, the transformation in India, the break-up of the Soviet Union, the fall of the Berlin Wall, and the return of Mandela. I have also seen the horrific impact of poverty, hunger, environmental blunders, multiple recessions and greed in financial markets. The horror of Apartheid, the agonies of the poor, and the unashamed luxury of the rich have saddened me.

I have also seen from close quarters and participated in the exciting march of technology and the birth of a new world powered by vacuum tubes, transistors, computers, ICs, microchips and fibre optics. I have observed how electronic diaries, laptops, mobile wallets, microprocessors, digital memory, etc., became everyday appliances used by millions. Before my very eyes, the growth of telecom, software, satellites, the Internet and complex digital systems has taken place. I have also witnessed the evolution of new branches of knowledge such as AI, biotech, nanotech, DNA, genetics, genomes, alternative energy and so much more. My travels to about eighty countries across all continents enabled me to mingle with various people, eat different kinds of food, listen to foreign languages, and observe diverse cultures, races, religions and landscapes. All this has taught me a great lesson to respect and celebrate the diversity of all our people.

I have also had three near–death experiences: over the course of two quadruple heart bypass surgeries and cancer. These events, observations and experiences have moulded me and my thinking to understand, analyse and question the current world order, and propose a redesign of the world.

Where It Started

I was born in the time of the British Raj, playing in the streets of colonial India, and was only five years old when Independence liberated our country. When Godse assassinated Gandhi at a prayer meeting, I was a six-year-old.

In 1942, Titilagarh in Odisha, where I was born and where I lived, was a small tribal village in India's most inferior part: no electricity, or running water, no toilets, no telephones, no radio and naturally no TV. My father had been educated only till the fourth grade. We were three brothers and five sisters in the family. My family taught us to share and care early on in life.

In front of our house was a Muslim family; next door was a Jain family; another was Sikh; and behind us resided an Oriya tribal. We all lived in peace and harmony. As children, we played together and celebrated all our festivals in a spirit of unity and mutual respect. This life taught me to respect diversity and inclusion, as also the tribal way of life. I received most of my early education at home. Since we were Gujaratis, my parents had a great emotional connection with Gandhi and the Indian Independence movement. We were taught Gandhian values in our childhood as a way of life. In our small house, we had large pictures of Gandhi, Jawaharlal Nehru, Sardar Patel, Subhash Chandra Bose and Maulana Azad, continually reminding us to revere our national leaders and their sacrifices.

In 1950, along with my brother, I started formal education in a boarding school, a thousand miles away from my parents; I was eight and he was eleven. At an early age, we learnt to survive on our own. We acquired new skills, took risks, thought out of the box, and resolved our problems. We did not have any traditional baggage of social taboos; right and wrong were decided by ethics, values and honesty, not by prejudices and social pressures. We had no older people to appease, nor parental orders to follow. We knew our parents loved us and that they were there to support us in our educational endeavours. We set our guidelines, arranged our schedules, managed our financial situations, acquired our education and maintained social interactions. We were practically living the lives of entrepreneurs with autonomy, freedom and flexibility. We realized that responsibility has to be accepted and not just handed out to you by somebody else early in life.

Five years later, we left boarding school and moved to Baroda—a bigger city than our birthplace—where we lived on our own in a rented apartment. I went to an engineering school where I studied mechanical and electrical engineering and design; it had workshops where we had to build things with our own hands. Later, I went on to MS University in Baroda and acquired bachelor of science and master of science degrees in physics, focusing on electronics. One fine morning, as a young adult, I read in the newspaper that the American president, Kennedy, had announced that before the end of the decade of the sixties, the US would send a man to the moon. It sounded very romantic. In 1964, with the support of my father and elder brother, I decided to go to the US for a PhD in physics. I was just twenty-two years old. I had no money so I borrowed some to pay for travel and half of the first semester's tuition.

I took a boat from Bombay to Karachi and passed through Aden in Yemen; Alexandria and Cairo; and Naples and Genova in Italy. I took a train from Genova to London, my first-ever flight from London to New York, and a bus to Chicago. It was there that I learnt that it took five to seven years to get a PhD in physics. I decided to change my subject to electrical engineering. I received my master's degree in electrical engineering from the Illinois

Institute of Technology in Chicago within a year. Immediately,
I asked my girlfriend to join me from India in the US. We got
married in a simple Indian ceremony in the cold winter of Chicago
in 1966, in the company of friends, with no relatives present.

My Heroes, My Passion

Gandhi and Einstein had always been my heroes; they fascinated
me. Gandhi, marching to Dandi to protest against the salt tax,
fasting to bring about change and reconciliation, and transforming
the course of history by the strength of his immense moral force.
Einstein created an entirely new science, with no equipment, no
instruments and no computers. Visualizing things in his mind,
with only paper and pencil in hand, he could predict and measure
relationships between particles, waves, energy and velocity. He
changed the whole direction of science, and, with it, our world
and humanity. Gandhi became my role model for truth, simplicity,
love, sacrifice, character and ethics, while Einstein became my role
model for scientific thinking, imagination and innovation. The
Gandhian boarding school taught us discipline, tolerance, morals
and character. University education gave me tools for analysis, risk
management and scientific thinking.

After graduation, I got an opportunity to work on digital
switching in 1966 at GTE, a major US telecom operator. We had
a small team of five engineers dedicated to exploring new frontiers
for the next generation of telephone-switching technology. After I
joined GTE, the US government drafted me to go to Vietnam to
fight the war. With my commitment to non-violence, I could not
see myself on combat duty. I applied for occupational deferment and
got it. I continued with my part-time PhD studies. While at work
on state-of-the-art switching technology, I filed several essential US
patents to generate digital tones, hold digital conferences and switch
digital voices. After spending almost eight years at GTE, I decided
to be an entrepreneur and joined two local business people in

1974. We started the switching company Wescom to manufacture the next generation of PABX and automatic call distributors for businesses and airlines. Here I quickly learnt a great deal about technology and management.

As an entrepreneur at the age of thirty-two, with multidisciplinary activities, risk-taking and deal-making, I gained swift knowledge of legal systems, contracts, marketing, distribution, production, delivery and finance. Within five years, I became knowledgeable about management without ever going to a business school. I learnt a great deal by observing and listening to people around me. I realized that the ability to listen was critical to my personal growth in the business world. I also realized that I was living multiple lives: as an engineer, entrepreneur, inventor and businessman.

On the one hand, I was dealing with a competitive American business environment; on the other, I was living a family man's life in a very traditional Indian joint family, where three generations lived together under one roof. I had to balance my role on both sides. Because of the joint family system, raising children became personally a lot easier for me. There were several family members to look after them, so I had the time to pay full attention to my profession and earn. I often feel now that I did not get enough time with my children while they were growing up.

Wescom was sold in 1980 to Rockwell International for around $50 million in cash. At the age of thirty-eight, I had made enough money to attain the financial independence I needed to pursue my dreams. By now, I started to experience the benefits of pursuing the American dream and the freedom and flexibility associated with it.

Phones and Digital Switches for India

Shortly after we sold Wescom, I went to India. From a Delhi hotel, I tried to call my wife. The telephones in India just did not work. I realized that before going to America, I had never used a phone in India. I was too poor to have owned a phone, and those who did have phones were too rich to be my friends! In 1980, it used to take ten years to obtain a telephone connection in India. I realized that this was an excellent opportunity to make a meaningful contribution to the country. After some careful analysis, I decided to spend the next ten years of my life connecting India through telephones. Later, I engineered an opportunity to meet with the then prime minister, Indira Gandhi, who gave me one hour to make a presentation on telecom to her in the presence of her entire cabinet. My message was that telecom and information technology should change the face of India.

With a population of 700 million people, India had only about 2 million phones. Today, with a population of 1.3 billion, India has over a billion phones. Besides, India generates around $200 billion every year in the export of software and related services. Software export has been India's most critical success story.

My meeting with the prime minister resulted in the establishing of C-DOT (Center for Development of Telematics), committed to building indigenous capabilities for technology development and manufacturing in India while employing young Indian talent. The challenge was to design a family of digital switching systems in thirty-six months for $36 million. It was considered an impossible task, since leading foreign companies demanded $1 billion to develop a similar design. Our strategy was to create modular systems starting from small rural exchanges and connecting 6,50,000 villages in India, despite hostile conditions of high temperature and high humidity. The plan was to use the most advanced technology of microprocessors and C++ software in the 1980s with the key objective to improve access to telephones in India, instead of telephone density, a policy promoted in developed countries.

Fortunately, bright, young local engineers accepted the challenge and delivered on the dot. It was a huge undertaking to transform attitudes, administration, environment, work ethics, work norms, work environment, etc. Unfortunately, right after the government established C-DOT, Indira Gandhi was assassinated by her security guards in a brutal attack at her home. It was a great shock to the entire country. After her death, her only living son, Rajiv Gandhi, became head of the Indian National Congress party and won the national election with a massive majority. He was sworn in as the youngest Indian prime minister ever. By then, I had established a personal relationship with him. He was the real force behind C-DOT's formation, as part of his vision to modernize Indian infrastructure and institutions. For me, Prime Minister Rajiv Gandhi's political determination was the most critical factor in implementing India's telecom reforms. Together, we had a dream to modernize India and take the country into the twenty-first century using the ideals of self-respect, dignity, democracy, freedom and development, with a foundation of new technology and tools. Technology development was a massive task in a country preoccupied with religion, race, rituals, caste, customs, tradition, taboos and an entrenched bureaucracy. C-DOT's success led me to expand my initiatives. It helped me take technology to rural areas so people at the bottom of the economic pyramid could have an improved quality of life.

Along with the rural switches, we needed public telephones. For that, we designed Subscriber Trunk Dialling (STD) and Public Call Offices (PCOs), known as STD/PCOs. The unique yellow colour on STD booths visually stood out in the same way as the red British telephone booths. If you saw yellow, you knew there was a public phone there. The phone had a little meter attached that monitored the length of the call and billed it. The shopkeeper owned the phone, but it was the customer who dialled. At the end of the phone call, the shopkeeper collected the fee, keeping 20 per cent for himself and remitting 80 per cent to the phone company.

The STD/PCO phones were the property of the managers. The phones allowed them to make a living. They maintained the phones and made very sure that no one vandalized them. They often took them home at night and in the morning plugged them in at their tables in the booths. The idea was not just to make phones accessible but also to employ a large number of people. We set in place a policy that gave job preference to people with disabilities. Later, many women became phone managers as well. These STD/PCO phones poured out of our manufacturers, and various telecom operating companies installed our switches in village after village. Eventually, we placed more than 2 million of them throughout rural India. Everywhere you went, you could see a yellow public phone. In towns behind mountains and across the desert, yellow phones dotted the Indian landscape. Now almost anyone could make or receive a phone call. Village kids found they could earn a few pennies by running to fetch people to the booth if a call came in for them. If Sanjay wanted to reach his sister Ananda who lived in another province, he would call her neighbourhood phone, and an enterprising kid would run to find her. 'A call for Aria from Ishaan.'

In a short time, phones became the centre of social activities. People hung out where there were phones, waiting to make or receive calls, make business arrangements, or just chat with friends. Besides, the managers started selling small consumer items: tobacco, cigarettes, candies and a few sundries. It was a simple idea, but a fertile one.

People loved the phones. They created jobs, and did what I had envisaged from the beginning. They gave people access to the world beyond the confines of their distant and isolated homes. The phones gave them connectivity and brought them a step closer to modernity. The telephone was no longer a luxury but a necessity. A farmer could make a call to sell his produce; a mother could speak to her son who was a migrant worker in another state; a local shopkeeper could order his supplies. People started using public phones in various ways. As we installed an increasing number of rural automatic exchanges (RAXs), we also designed and manufactured our next switches, the 256–40K line exchanges.

The smaller switches were placed in villages and the larger ones in bigger towns, cities and metros.

Technology Was a Mission

In 1987, Prime Minister Rajiv Gandhi launched the National Technology Missions to give a new impetus to development. The missions underlined a conscious shift from directing people to empowering people. I was appointed adviser to the prime minister, with a minister's rank, to lead the technology missions. At this time, I decided to relinquish my US nationality and became an Indian citizen again. These missions addressed essential issues in the country, including drinking water in rural areas, immunization for children and pregnant mothers, literacy for adults, oilseeds to increase local production and reduce import of edible oil, telecom to provide wider accessibility and connectivity to the people, and dairy development to increase milk production and improve the cattle population. There were over 10 million people employed in these mission activities. The mission approach was required in the government to create a sense of urgency through missionary zeal, and the technological self-reliance and institutional infrastructure needed to deliver measurable milestones and results.

It was also required to provide a management focus with improved communication and better centre–state coordination, organized information and substantially increased participation. The delivery of these basic needs required a deep understanding of grassroot realities and a unique integrated approach in the use of modern technology and tools. We had to tap the talent of our youth, intellectuals, professionals and technocrats. It also required cooperation between various agencies, women's active participation, and a strong political commitment at the state and district levels. To succeed in these missions, we needed to rejuvenate our existing institutions and mobilize available national resources. We needed to simplify antiquated procedures, decentralize planning, eliminate duplication of efforts, and provide modern management for motivation. We had to ensure close monitoring and keep a careful watch on quality and continuity. We also needed to allow for social audit by people outside the system. We needed to bring traditional community participation back into our mainstream.

The mission approach to problem-solving required a missionary zeal. It also needed a new flat organizational architecture with leadership, teamwork and a clear eye on measurable milestones and tangible deliverables. The technology mission concept was an innovation in organizational architecture that enabled us to implement critical government programmes while bypassing the traditional ministerial bureaucracy. All mission directors were from their respective ministries and had the freedom and flexibility needed for speedy implementation from the office of the adviser to the prime minister. These missions attracted the UN's attention, and it set up a special UN team to study the new management approach to government. I went to Poland for a special meeting on technology missions, and the UN published a unique report. I firmly believe that all significant global challenges require global missions to solve problems within the specified time frame.

We essentially planted the seeds for literacy, drinking water, oilseeds, milk, telecom and the country's immunization needs. Literacy in India is now about 77 per cent. We eradicated polio only because Rajiv Gandhi pushed for immunization, and authorized us to manufacture vaccines in India. In 1985, India did not produce any vaccine. Today, India is the largest producer of vaccines in the world. India is also number one in milk production.

In those days, India was importing $1 billion worth of cooking oil. We reduced imports substantially by encouraging farmers to grow more sunflower, soya, mustard and other oilseeds. Eventually, we started exporting oil cakes. We established over 400 water testing labs in the water mission, set up plants to remove excess iron, used satellite imagery, and carried out nationwide geohydrological surveys. Our most important contribution was to create human capacity in telecom, information technology and software, which ultimately made India a global software powerhouse. Unfortunately, people have selective memories and rarely appreciate what it takes to build sustainable institutions and infrastructure.

Once we developed digital switching technology, the Department of Telecom deployed C-DOT switches to build a national network. The department was more interested in importing technology than encouraging local development. As a result, it was essential to take charge of the ministry. With the approval and support of Prime Minister Rajiv Gandhi, I became secretary of the department. I established a Telecom Commission to obtain the needed autonomy, freedom and flexibility to expand telecom and mobilize resources. The Telecom Commission had 5,50,000 employees, twenty-seven unions and national operations in every state. It was essentially a mammoth monopoly. My job was to redesign the telecom department in such a manner as to improve planning, productivity and performance, and also to begin privatization for future GSM mobile systems. It took almost two years of hard work to turn the department around.

As a part of the Rajiv Gandhi government, I was privileged to meet many global leaders and interact with them at official meetings, dinners and social events. The list included eminent personalities such as Mikhail Gorbachev, president of the Soviet Union; Helmut Kohl, chancellor of Germany; François Mitterrand, president of France; Prince Agha Khan; the prime minister of Italy; the president of Vietnam; and many others. State dinners at Rashtrapati Bhawan, the Indian president's residence, and at Hyderabad House were extraordinary events where I interacted with political leaders, leading global business people and intellectuals.

For example, one morning, I received a call from Prime Minister Rajiv Gandhi: he wanted me to meet with the president of Vietnam, who was then on a visit to Delhi. That same afternoon,

I spent an hour with him discussing telecom, technology missions and India's software industry. After carefully listening to me through a translator, he told me that he would be sending General Giap to spend some time with me in Delhi. While studying in America during the Vietnam War, I had often heard of General Giap: he was one of those rare generals who, in Vietnam, had fought against both the French and later against the Americans. He was the most prominent military commander during the Vietnam War, other than Ho Chi Minh, and was responsible for leadership and operations until the war ended. He died in October 2013 at the age of 102.

In Delhi, General Giap and I spent a full day at C-DOT, talking about our indigenous design and manufacturing efforts, the role of information technology, and the technology benefits for the people at the bottom of the economic pyramid. He listened carefully, took notes, asked questions and was keen to learn from the Indian experience. After his visit, C-DOT started exporting rural exchanges to Vietnam to improve their village communication.

Similarly, I hosted General Electric (GE) chairman Jack Welch during his first-ever official visit to India and convinced him to buy Indian software talent. He was generous enough to send a team of GE experts that ultimately resulted in our first $10 million order for software services. This marketing approach resulted in orders from IBM, Texas Instruments, Motorola and others to kick-start the Indian software export business. Rajiv Gandhi and I also convinced Gorbachev at the prime minister's house in Delhi to buy Indian consumer goods, computer hardware and software. We worked with the Soviet Union to establish a massive Indian science and technology exhibition in Moscow, Leningrad and Tashkent.

On the one hand, we promoted our technology, and on the other, we resisted offers from multinationals like Siemens, GEC and Ericsson to import equipment to build the Indian network. I opposed large loans from the World Bank for telecom equipment import. On one occasion, the president of the World Bank visited Delhi to have lunch with us and persuade us to reconsider. It was clear that we would avail of loans only to buy what we need, not for what the Bank wanted to sell.

In 1989, Rajiv Gandhi lost the elections, and the new government in power got after me with a sense of revenge, raising allegations, abuses, threats and false corruption charges. They knew well that I took only a 1-rupee salary (then just 10 cents in the US) per year for almost ten years. In the process, I had a heart attack and a quadruple bypass at a hospital in Delhi. Young C-DOT associates, the Indian public and the media came to my rescue and convinced the government to change the minister who was after me and set things right.

After My Heart Attack

After that, the government announced a new national election. I worked closely with Rajiv Gandhi as part of his team to help ensure victory. On 21 May 1991, at 10 p.m., I received a call from a friend informing me that Rajiv Gandhi had been assassinated by a suicide bomber during his campaign visit in southern India. I was shocked and shaken. All my dreams for India disappeared in a moment. The news broke my heart. I strongly felt that India would take a long time to recover from this loss. I had spent all the money I had had managing my family in India and the US. I was broke. I had two children ready to go to college. Finally, I decided to come back to the US to start earning again.

Unfortunately, before taking my assignment with Prime Minister Rajiv Gandhi, I had given up my US nationality in 1987. I came back to the US on a tourist visa, but I was not allowed to work. Fortunately, I owned a US patent issued in 1975 for the I-electronic diary. I realized that several multinational corporations (MNCs) were manufacturing and marketing my invention. I filed a case in the Cook County court against Casio, Toshiba, Sharp,

HP, Texas Instruments and RadioShack and settled for a hefty cash amount, which enabled me to restart my life.

It was strange that I had to use a tourist visa to come back to my own country. I have always felt that I belong to at least two countries—my birthplace, India, that gave me my roots, and my adopted nation, the US, which gave me my tools and my understanding of technology. I am equally committed to both countries. I do not have to choose sides. I can be in both countries at the same time. I admire the good and reject the bad in each of them. Both are democratic countries with freedom, flexibility, diversity and loving people. After a while, I applied for a green card in the US and focused on building an electronic manufacturing company in Wisconsin. However, that did not challenge me enough.

I wanted to do something for the telecom industry in emerging markets and use my Indian experience to benefit Asia, Africa and Latin America. That vision led me to Worldtel in London. In 1995, nearly four out of every five people in the world lacked the most basic telephone services. To help privatize telecom and get the needed investments in emerging markets, the International Telecom Union (ITU), a part of the UN organization, decided to launch Worldtel. This organization functioned as an investment bank/fund to develop and support privately funded telecom projects in nations where the need was most urgent. 'Worldtel's mission was to break the vicious circle that exists in developing countries,' the ITU launch announcement stated. Sound telecommunication capacity and capability were needed to stimulate economic growth. However, dysfunctional telecommunications deterred private investment. This was a Catch-22 situation that we hoped to cut through by Worldtel's initiative. I was named Worldtel's chairman in 1995.

I thought we had the potential to make a significant impact on communications in the Third World. The objective of Worldtel was to focus exclusively on telecommunications and information technology, and provide direct equity investment raised from private financial investors for implementing projects that would improve telecom infrastructure in developing countries. In the process, Worldtel improved operating skills and provided management support to help enhance productivity and efficiency. Worldtel investors were AIG, GE, Intel, NatWest and others.

I went to China for the first time after President Richard Nixon's visit in 1981, as part of a delegation of around twenty telecom experts. I spent two weeks meeting telecom experts in Beijing, Nanking and Shanghai. We also went to tourist attractions, including the Great Wall. In those days, all we could see were bicycles, Chairman Mao's uniform, empty roads and people staring at white foreigners. Telecom was mainly electromechanical and hardly available. After that, I worked with local government organizations to explore Tianjin's digital switching operations: however, this never materialized. Now China is, of course, a different country altogether.

While working at Worldtel, I founded a US company in 1998 to design and develop a mobile wallet. Those were the early days of the mobile wallet concept. I applied for close to fifty patents on this idea and set up design and business development teams in Chicago, Tokyo, Beijing, Singapore, Baroda, Pune and Vienna. Later in 2013, I sold the company to Mastercard. When I was working on the mobile wallet company, I found I had contracted cancer, requiring major surgery. Five years after that, I would need another quadruple bypass. I was concerned, but I survived the second open-heart surgery. Three near-death experiences—two quadruple heart bypasses and one from cancer—have moulded my views on what is essential in life and what is not.

Knowledge, Connectivity and Innovation

In 2004, national elections were held in India, and I decided to campaign for the Congress party. After our victory, Dr Manmohan

Singh was appointed the prime minister. He constituted the National Knowledge Commission to focus on matters relating to institutions of knowledge production, knowledge use and knowledge dissemination. The mandate of the commission was to sharpen India's 'knowledge edge'. The commission was also to focus on how India can promote excellence in the education system and meet the knowledge challenges of the twenty-first century. Its objectives were to encourage knowledge creation in science and technology laboratories; improve the management of institutions generating intellectual property; protect intellectual property rights and promote knowledge applications in agriculture and industry. It was to suggest ways in which the government's knowledge capabilities could be made more effective, and create a transparent and accountable government as a service provider to the citizen. I was appointed by the prime minister to chair the commission.

To integrate knowledge and connectivity, we built a National Knowledge network consisting of 1100 nodes to connect all 900 Indian universities and research and development laboratories for a potential 40 GB fibre-optic links. We also promoted optical fibre links to extend broadband facilities to 2,50,000 local government institutions in rural areas known as panchayats. E-governance was also implemented to improve productivity and efficiency in governance, including computerizing courts, police, prisons, hospitals, universities, schools, offices, departments, public services, finance, payments, commerce, etc.

After the National Knowledge Commission, I was appointed as the adviser to the prime minister with a cabinet minister's rank for innovations and public information infrastructure. We formed the National Innovation Council and declared 2010–20 as the decade of innovations in India. The objective was to promote innovations and creativity in all aspects of education, health, economy, business and governance. In the process, I worked on railway reforms, e-governance, high-speed networks, cybersecurity and public broadcast systems. We took up initiatives and recommended systems for national smart grids, digital payment, urbanization, transdisciplinary medicine, food banks, think tanks and various other national activities.

Once again, the Congress lost the election in 2014. I decided to stay in Chicago and focus on my family and spend my time building several high-tech businesses and running five non-profit foundations.

Today, at seventy-eight, I feel that I am a loner. I could never fit into any box, club or circle. I am not a businessman, politician, scientist, administrator, professor, intellectual or activist. I have always been an ordinary outsider, an intruder, a change agent and a catalyst who believed in creating systems to bypass outdated institutions and procedures to achieve the goal. I have never been a part of any central core. I have always been at the margins, and I have benefited by being there. I know that innovations happen at the edge and not at the core. In the process, I have built unique multidimensional innovative abilities to solve large complex problems. I have also created a network of connections and contacts with global leaders and global domain experts. I live in multiple realities, several countries and various cultures, all at the same time. I still have energy, and against all the odds, I can focus like a laser beam and get things done. I am a workaholic, impulsive and opinionated, a loner.

I believe in the power of hyperconnectivity, communication, technology, knowledge, information and innovations. I am indeed committed to the Gandhian values of truth, trust, simplicity, sacrifice and conviction, along with love, courage, perseverance, determination, discipline and clarity. Because of my upbringing in tribal areas, I am very concerned about the development of people at the bottom of the economic pyramid. I have learnt a great deal from the US, and it is the US that has empowered me to think big and dream big. I have benefited from encouraging young talent and its energy. I am a man in a hurry who knows that there is little time left and too many things to do.

As I have grown older, I realize that my roots lie in India's ancient wisdom, deeply embedded in family values and communities, and imbued with culture, democracy, duty, karma, simplicity and selfless sacrifice. The branches of my tree represent the nature of my American journey in technology, connectivity, information, energy, enthusiasm and entrepreneurship. I have learnt and benefited from many experts in America and India. My passions relate to new development models for generational change in education, health, economy, management, leadership, institutions and infrastructure. Gandhi is my true inspiration. Early on in life, I realized that building a nation is very different from building a company. Building a nation requires long-term commitment, patience, perseverance and character, all strengthened by values, morals, system-level thinking, analytics, hard work and leadership. Being a board member of the Institute of Design (ID) in Chicago for over a decade convinced me that design is critical to solving global challenges.

My story is a poignant account of my odyssey. It is in part about risks, rewards, courage, commitment, pain and pleasure. It emphasizes the need for political will and domain expertise at the highest level if we wish to achieve something transformational in a democratic federal system. It is also about flattening a social, political and economic system that is intricately hierarchical, feudal, complex and argumentative.

I have been poor—with only one dollar left after my marriage. I have been rich after selling US companies for millions of dollars. The lesson learnt is that we do not hurry to celebrate success and do not need to be afraid of failures. What goes up does come down, and what is down does go up; life is a roller-coaster ride. Enjoy the journey and the experiences.

My connectivity includes profound personal experiences with rich and poor, east and west, developed and developing societies, tradition, and technology, business and government, private and public, national and global, innovator and entrepreneur, profit and non-profit, bottom-up and top-down, simplicity and complexity and much more. This connectivity and my journey in telecom and the Internet have allowed me to create a redesign of the world from an innovative perspective, one that is global and human.

Acknowledgements

After my autobiography, *Dreaming Big*, was published by Penguin in 2015, I started to think about writing my next book, *Redesign the World*. I realized that the project was big, complex, challenging and ambitious. It required me to reanalyse my journey from India to the US, my work in information technology and connectivity, and the significant global events of the last seven decades to understand and evaluate the challenges faced by the people and the nations of the world. It is challenging to generalize our multifaceted and hyperconnected world because we all have strong views and opinions based on our upbringing, beliefs, interests, and experiences on what is right and wrong, fair and unfair, good and bad, etc. No matter what I say on global issues, it is open to many interpretations and criticism by one group or the other.

The idea of the book was not to promote personal preferences but to focus on the public good. From my conversations with many young people worldwide, I know that they are concerned about the current world order, environmental blunders, inequality, economy, unemployment and violence. They are searching for a new world order to assure lasting peace and prosperity for all. They are open, progressive, global, tech-savvy, and willing to experiment and change. As a result, I decided to write this book for the changemakers, more so than intellectuals, foreign policy veterans, academicians, business people and politicians.

The first question was, who am I to write a book on redesigning the world? Can I present my thoughts at the age of seventy-nine in a straightforward narrative for an average reader to initiate a new conversation? I am happy to say that many people have participated and contributed generously to help and support me on this adventure. I am thankful to every one of them, and some more, individually and collectively.

First, I would like to thank my wife, Anu, for supporting me to have an office at home in quarantine for a year to complete this book. Thanks to my son, Salil, daughter-in-law, Arpita, daughter, Rajal, son-in-law, Samir, and my grandchildren, Aria, Ishaan and Nylah, for the daily video calls to check, inform, entertain and inspire. I am fortunate to have friends in Chicago—some from my first year of college in India in 1958—who have always encouraged me to continue my adventures, crazy work schedules and shuttling between the US and India, including Dr Dinker Trivedi, Dr Piyush Vyas, Dr Divyesh Mehta, Dr Bhupen Trivedi, Dr Bharat Thakkar and Ashok Bhatt. I am thankful to them for regularly visiting me, checking on me, and keeping me healthy, happy and on course.

Several people deserve thanks for helping me in research, discussions, documentation, and editing, including Frank Schell, Javier Livas, Mitakshara Kumari, Niti Chopra, Mihir, Udbhav, Ari Sarkar, Ravi Thakran, Bob Sheard, Maulik Mehta, Rakesh Patel, Supriya Bhardwaj, Adrian Wagner, Leo Burke, Nigel Hamilton, Jay Naidoo and Lucie Page. I have been a part of a weekly Zoom call for the last nine months to distinguish senior innovators in India. These discussions on democracy, freedom, institutions and civil society have been beneficial. I am thankful to all the members of this group for their generous contribution. Special thanks to Mr Rahul Gandhi for several fruitful conversations on the American and Chinese visions of the world, and the third vision. Special thanks also to Mr C.K. Mathew and Mr Carl Malamud for their help in editing the draft.

My publisher Penguin Random House India has been exceptional. I convey my gratitude to them for their expertise and attention in expediting the publication of this book. I would like to thank Radhika Marwah for the overall project management, Shreya Chakravertty for editing and Akangksha Sarmah for the cover design. I would also like to thank Gaurav Shrinagesh, CEO of Penguin Random House India. Without exceptional teamwork and support from all concerned, this book would not have been possible in early 2021.

Now, I wait for the public's response, change agents, business, civil society, governments, leaders and media for their input and advice to initiate new conversations, new narratives and a call to action to redesign the world.

You may send your views/comments/observaations/ suggestions here – redesigntheworld21@gmail.com.

Made in the USA
Middletown, DE
13 June 2021